101 BEST
HILL WALKS
IN THE
SCOTTISH
HIGHLANDS
AND ISLANDS

Graeme Cornwallis

FORT

Fort Publishing Ltd

Contents

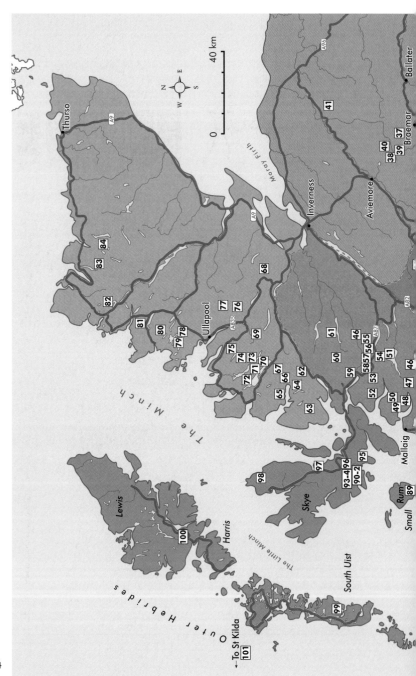

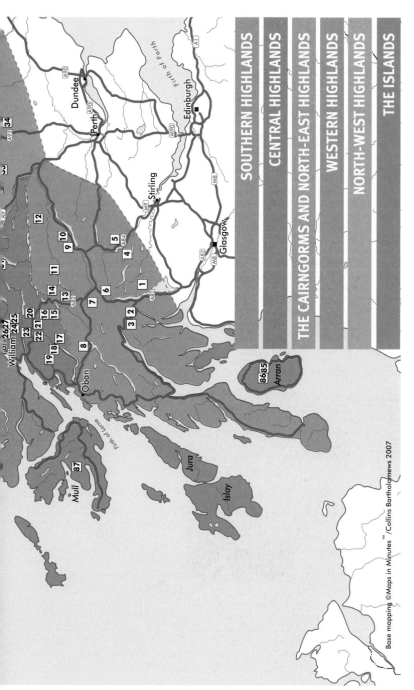

SOUTHERN HIGHLANDS

CENTRAL HIGHLANDS

THE CAIRNGORMS AND NORTH-EAST HIGHLANDS

WESTERN HIGHLANDS

NORTH-WEST HIGHLANDS

THE ISLANDS

Base mapping ©Maps in Minutes ™ /Collins Bartholomews 2007

5

Preface

When I am asked why I go hill walking, my diverse answers surprise some people. Amongst the most surprising is that hill walking offers highly rewarding experiences by stimulating the senses naturally and hence offers relief from the tedium of work and pre-packaged entertainment. More prosaically, being an energetic activity, the exercise can be a useful part of a healthy lifestyle. Learning how to adapt to rapidly changing circumstances and making strong bonds with walking companions is a character-building part of the experience, especially for young people. There is a feeling of challenge, with wild terrain and volatile weather conditions testing even the most experienced, pitting man or woman against nature and giving a sense of achievement when the route is completed. Hill walking can even be a spiritual experience to those receptive to such feelings. There are the added benefits of various intellectual pursuits, hobbies or sciences, from botany and bird-watching to history, photography and geology. On top of all this, I have had many great days out, enjoying fun and conversation with a variety of family members and friends over the years.

The Scottish hills are world-renowned for their beauty and are special in many respects. A general lack of tree cover and a good road network allows easy access, there is an absence of glaciers and hence few un-fordable rivers, and no dangerous insects or animals (apart from ticks and a rarely seen snake, the adder). Scotland is at the optimum latitude for a special soft light, prevalent at different times of day throughout the year and highly attractive to lovers of mountain and coastal scenery. Along the west coast and on the islands, the combination of sea and mountain landscapes is particularly impressive. Wild and changeable weather may be uninviting to some, but take time to wait for drier conditions; following the rain, the air is often clearer and colours are more vibrant. Fine mountain-walking areas elsewhere in the world may not have so much in their favour and hill walking in Scotland is possible throughout the year, unlike in some other countries where mountain access on foot is a summer-only activity.

Thanks to everyone who assisted with this book and especially to my late father, Frederick Cornwallis, who inspired me to explore many of the world's mountains, but also thanks to cartographer Linda Dawes, designer Mark Blackadder, typesetter Senga Fairgrieve, publisher James McCarroll and, finally, to Alistair Young for Gaelic translations.

This book is dedicated to the late John Heath, whose ideas were invaluable for the final selection of routes; sadly, he passed away while work was in progress.

Graeme Cornwallis
Glasgow
April 2009

Essential Information

Bagging Munros and Other Peaks

The Munros are Scottish hills whose summits are more than 3,000 feet (914m) above sea level. They are known around the world and large numbers of walkers take on the challenge of trying to climb (or bag) them all. There is even a Munro society for Munroists – people who have completed all 284 hills on the list. Most of the 219 Corbetts – peaks between 2,500 and 3,000 feet with a re-ascent of at least 500 feet on all sides – are quieter places than the busier Munros but there is still a substantial number of Corbetteers (people who have done all the Corbetts). There are many smaller hills that are as fine, if not finer, than their higher neighbours and these appear in other lists, including the Grahams and Marilyns. The finest walks in Scotland's Highlands and islands include hills from all of these lists and this diversity is reflected in the pages of this book.

Standards and Grading

The 101 best hill walks chosen for this book were selected by considering overall quality, resulting in a choice of routes with technical difficulty ranging from straightforward walking through to difficult rock scrambling. There is something for everyone, with walks varying from short excursions to gruelling multi-day trips. Four-wheel-drive tracks and footpaths are commonly utilised by the routes but some walks (or sections of walks) require crossing pathless areas, which vary from easy grassland to rough boulder fields. Rock scrambling is required for some routes, ranging from using hands for balance through easy and moderate to hard scrambling where some moves may be awkward and with considerable exposure. None of the routes described here require rock-climbing skills or equipment although experienced climbers may wish to tackle any harder variations described in the text. Inexperienced hill walkers should note that many accidents occur when descending but also when pride overrides common sense in bad weather (for example, pushing onwards to gain a summit when it would be wiser to turn back), or when people attempt routes that are beyond their ability.

When the hills are snow-covered, carrying an ice-axe is essential, even for the easier routes in the book. In severe winter conditions, some of the more difficult routes may require winter mountaineering skills, including the use of a rope, belay equipment and crampons. These routes are identified in the text and are given Scottish winter mountaineering grades, with Roman numerals I, II and III, grade I being the easiest. On rare occasions of extensive ice cover, normally easy hill walks may require the use of crampons.

Equipment and Safety

Before setting off on a hill walk, ensure that the planned route is within the capabilities of the weakest member of the party. Check the local weather forecast and avoid poor weather and strong winds if possible. Wear several layers of clothing since this provides better insulation and some layers can be removed if necessary. All members of the party should carry reliable watches, a whistle, a torch (with spare batteries), full waterproof clothing (jacket and trousers), spare warm clothes (including hat and gloves) and adequate food and drink including an emergency supply of quick-energy foods such as chocolate. A flask of hot tea, coffee or soup is also a good thing to carry. Wear boots with sufficient ankle support and good treads. At least one first-aid kit and one waterproof bivouac bag should be taken along. In snowy conditions, it is essential that each party member carries an ice axe in case hard snow or ice is encountered. While crampons are not, as a general rule, a necessity, they may be useful on occasion.

Hill fog, rain and high winds may occur at any time of year and hill walkers must be adequately prepared to avoid or deal with illness and injury. Turn back if the weather becomes intolerable; the hills will still be there on another day. In the event of an emergency, mobile telephone (cellphone) signals may be detected on some peaks but large areas in the Highlands and islands have no network coverage. Carrying a mobile telephone is no substitute for common sense and preparation; by comparison, carrying a detailed Ordnance Survey map and compass and having the ability to use them is essential. If you have a mobile phone, take it with you and ensure it is well wrapped up and fully charged before departure. Walking alone is not recommended and (for any size of party) details of the route, including expected time of return, must be left with someone at home.

For excellent, general advice on mountain safety, visit the websites of the Mountaineering Council of Scotland and the Mountain Rescue Council.

Route Summaries

Summary details are given for each route in this book. The location by name and Ordnance Survey grid reference is given for car-parking areas. Distance in kilometres is for the main route described in the text, from start to finish. The height gain in metres measures the amount of ascent required to complete the route. In most cases the amount of descent will be the same, although one route (the Five Sisters of Kintail) does not start and finish at the same place so the amount of descent is different. The quoted times give an approximate range for the entire route and moderately fit parties walking in good weather conditions should find the quoted ranges accurate. Slow parties taking long rest breaks, deep snow, hot conditions or bad weather will cause walking times to be much longer, while fit parties on a mission will complete walks in a shorter time. 'Terrain' describes significant ground surfaces that walkers will encounter during the walk. Standards vary from easy through moderate and difficult to very difficult, the word 'strenuous' indicating that a large amount of effort is required. Lastly, 'OS maps' indicates which Ordnance Survey topographic maps should be carried during the walk.

Maps and Access

The maps in this book are three-dimensional pictorial representations of the walking routes and should be used for planning purposes only. Slopes (gradients) are indicated by lines, which allow the human eye to interpret the map in three-dimensional form. Relate these maps and the text to the relevant Ordnance Survey sheets, at either 1:25,000 or 1:50,000 scale. Small sections of Ordnance Survey mapping are available from the Ordnance Survey website; use the grid reference given for the parking area to obtain 1:25,000 mapping for the walking route and zoom out to obtain 1:50,000 mapping.

Access to wild land in Scotland, including wild camping, became a statutory right with the Land Reform (Scotland) Act 2003. Hill walkers should be familiar with the associated Scottish Outdoor Access Code – see the Mountaineering Council of Scotland website for details. Deer stalking, particularly between early August and late October, is a sensitive issue in many places but it is no longer possible for land managers to prevent access. During stalking alternative routes, avoiding stalking activities, should be provided. Walkers should always make themselves aware of local stalking activities before setting foot on the hill and the rights of local people to engage in legitimate estate activities must be respected. Most land owned by the John Muir Trust, the National Trust for Scotland and Scottish Natural Heritage has no access restrictions at any time. For further details, obtain the current Hillphones leaflet from the Mountaineering Council of Scotland (this can be downloaded from the website) and consult the Scottish Outdoor Access Code.

Geology, Flora and Fauna

The complex geology of the Highlands and islands is the result of Scotland being subjected to hundreds of millions of years of movement and folding along continental margins. At one stage, when the country was attached to the eastern side of North America, vast beds of Torridonian sandstone were deposited on top of the Lewisian gneiss basement rocks. On a later collision with Europe, the huge Caledonian mountain range was created, with intense heat and folding deep underground creating the quartz-feldspar-granulite, quartzite and schists that are common from Loch Lomond all the way to the north coast. Large-scale faulting and thrusting led to significant features such as the Great Glen and Moine Thrust, which are still clearly discernible today. Intrusion of large granite masses and volcanic activity created the rocks of Ben Nevis, Glen Etive, the Cairngorms and Glen Coe. More recent volcanic activity (around sixty million years ago) led to granite and gabbro intrusions and basalt lava flows which can still be seen on Mull, Rum, Eigg and Skye, with dykes injected into older rocks throughout the area. While the geology affects conditions underfoot for walkers, it is also interesting to appreciate how current landforms have been created by the repeated glaciations of the last two million years. Corries and their lochans are amongst the results of the latter stages of cirque glaciation around ten thousand years ago.

Vegetation cover in the Highlands and islands varies depending on bedrock and (to a lesser extent) climate. The drier, eastern areas have more heather than central or western parts, where grasses are predominant. Native woodland is making a comeback but Scots pine, silver birch, rowan, beech and oak are still confined to relatively small areas. Large plantations of non-native, sitka – the trees are named after Sitka, Alaska – spruce and larch, with unnatural edges, are found in many glens, sometimes to the detriment of scenic beauty and direct access.

The impressive red deer are the most likely, truly wild animals to be seen on the hills. They often congregate in large herds and usually flee on detecting humans. Mountain hares change colour to white in winter and may be encountered, particularly in eastern parts of the country. Little rodents such as mice and voles often scurry through grass near walkers' feet and there are occasional lucky sightings of red squirrels in woodland. Wildcats, goats, badgers, snakes and lizards are relatively rare. The only poisonous snakes are adders; they have distinctive, diamond-shaped markings and should be avoided. Farm animals such as sheep and Highland cattle roam around relatively freely and may not be in obvious enclosures.

Birds are considerably more common than land animals, with a huge variety of species including grouse in heathery areas. Ptarmigan, which become white in winter, may be seen above around 750m. Golden eagles are icons of the Scottish Highlands but they're not particularly common, unlike buzzards which are often seen at low levels. White-tailed sea eagles were reintroduced to Rum in 1975 and may occasionally be observed throughout the Inner Hebrides, from Mull to Skye. Ravens may be heard croaking around mountain tops.

Biting insects are a hazard between June and September. Ticks are dangerous since they can pass debilitating diseases and must be safely removed as soon as possible, preferably using a type of hook available from veterinary surgeries. Midges are tiny biting mosquitoes and they may swarm in clouds particularly during calm dull weather or at sunrise or sunset. Clegs (horse flies or deer flies) are more active in sunny conditions and may spread diseases and parasites. Using a suitable insect repellent is advisable and, although it is not marketed as such, Avon's 'Skin So Soft' oil body spray is recommended. Nets that cover the entire head and offer refuge from the swarms are available from outdoor equipment shops.

Climate

Scotland has a temperate maritime climate with precipitation all-year round. Heaviest rainfall – with snow in the mountains when temperatures are low enough – occurs from September to January, while April, May and June are normally the driest months and June, July and August are the warmest. Areas east of the A9 Perth–Inverness road are considerably drier than wet areas to the west. Knoydart on the west coast is one of the wettest places in Europe with daily precipitation figures of 10cm

or more not unusual in winter. High winds are particularly dangerous for walkers; stormy conditions are frequent along the west coast and on mountain tops throughout the country. Moist air from the Atlantic Ocean creates dense and dreary cloud cover but rapid movement of weather fronts across the country often causes sudden weather changes, with low cloud and rain quickly giving way to broken cloud, sunshine and rain showers. Warm sectors of temperate depressions typically lead to low cloud bases and hill fog in the west, but cloud bases are often higher in the east.

Photography

Most hill walkers keep a record of their experiences by taking photographs and the beautiful Highland landscape is a perfect subject. The fickle nature of rapidly changing light and weather makes good mountain photography a more difficult task than most people imagine. Although some photographers capture segments of their walks on video, most people take still images. The technology for digital cameras is improving all the time and, for most purposes, a compact digital camera will suffice; another important factor is that large, single-lens reflex (SLR) digital cameras are relatively heavy and bulky. However, compact 35mm cameras or SLR 35mm cameras – with good-quality slide film – still take better pictures.

Most of the photographs in this book were taken by the author with an Olympus XA2 compact 35mm camera, a Konica-Minolta DiMAGE A200 digital camera or a Nikon D80 digital SLR. Slide film used with the Olympus XA2 was mostly Kodachrome 64 and Fuji Velvia 50.

All photographs in this book are available as A3-size or A2-size posters and these can be ordered from the author's website:

www. cornwallis-images.com

Scotland's Top Ten

The Cobbler
(Walk 2, Southern Highlands)

Only forty miles from Glasgow and part of the 'Arrochar Alps', the Cobbler's unique profile includes a spectacular summit tower that's among the finest of mountain tops in the country. New paths on the hill have significantly improved access.

Ben Lui
(Walk 7, Southern Highlands)

Majestic Ben Lui reigns supreme over its near neighbours with well-defined ridges and a great little summit providing some of the best views in the southern Highlands.

Bidean nam Bian
(Walk 22, Central Highlands)

The highest peak in Glen Coe features some of the wildest mountain scenery in Scotland, with soaring buttresses, steep scree slopes and an array of lesser peaks, all linked by fine ridges.

Ring of Steall
(Walk 24, Central Highlands)

Scotland's best ridge-walking can be found in the Mamores and the Ring of Steall is the grandest circuit of all, with some exciting scrambling on airy arêtes, great views and four Munros to add to the tally.

Lochnagar
(Walk 36, Cairngorms and North-east Highlands)

Lochnagar has the most formidable corrie in the Cairngorms and perhaps the most splendid in Scotland. The route along the upper edge of the huge cliffs leads to a fine summit tor, with an exhilarating scramble to the top.

Ladhar Bheinn
(Walk 50, Western Highlands)

Impressive, remote and wild, Knoydart's Ladhar Bheinn includes a magnificent corrie with narrow ridges and some thrilling scrambling. Often said to be the finest mountain in Scotland, it is a must-do for any serious walker.

The Saddle and Sgurr na Sgine
(Walk 53, Western Highlands)

The exceptional views across the peaks and ridges of the Saddle and Sgurr na Sgine make these mountains firm favourites with many walkers. If the Forcan Ridge seems too scary, an easier alternative route leads to the summit.

Beinn Alligin
(Walk 65, North-west Highlands)

The full circuit of Beinn Alligin, which requires a traverse of the Horns of Alligin, is one of the grandest routes on the Scottish mainland, with lots of airy scrambling, huge drops and astonishing views.

An Teallach
(Walk 75, North-west Highlands)

Another one of Scotland's finest mountains, An Teallach's huge buttresses, menacing cliffs, deep corries and exciting ridges should give walkers one of their best-ever Scottish mainland experiences.

Bla Bheinn
(Walk 95, The Islands)

An isolated part of Skye's Black Cuillin and another magnificent mountain with unbeatable views from the summit including wild mountains, vast corries, narrow rocky ridges, fearsome pinnacles, lochs, sea and islands stretching to the far horizon.

Map key

═══════	Road	⤬	Road or rail bridge
··············	Track	⫽	Footbridge
────────	Walk route	▦	Woodland
────────	Railway	⌇	Stream or river
P	Parking	■	Building

1

BEN LOMOND

Outstanding views of Loch Lomond and its islands

Parking: Loch Dhu, gr NN433038
Distance: 21km
Height Gain: 1060m
Time: 7–8 hours
Terrain: Track for 13km, pathless grass slopes then tourist path
Standard: Strenuous, moderate to difficult
OS Maps: Loch Lomond & Inverary (1:50,000 Landranger sheet 56), Loch Lomond North and The Trossachs, Callander, Aberfoyle & Lochearnhead (1:25,000 Explorer sheets 364 and 365)

Isolated Ben Lomond, on the edge of the Highlands and the southernmost Munro, provides outstanding views. The hill's name implies the summit was used as a warning beacon when the Britons ruled Strathclyde during the first millennium. Nowadays, Ben Lomond attracts large numbers of hikers via a tourist path from Rowardennan on Loch Lomondside, a straightforward route that hardly merits detailed description. For a quieter, albeit longer, option, try the rarely frequented and attractive eastern route via Gleann Dubh and Comer.

Leave cars in a small off-road area beside the Aberfoyle–Inversnaid road at gr NN433038. About 100m towards Aberfoyle, a sign reading 'Rowardennan' directs walkers along a gravel track, past Loch Dhu House then uphill into forestry of varying age. Follow signs for Comer at all junctions. Just before the second sign, a curious 2m-high tower on the left reveals the underground presence (within a 2.4m-wide tunnel) of the gravity-fed Loch Katrine aqueduct. The aqueduct has supplied Glasgow with up to 450 million litres of water daily since 1860!

The track crosses a wide pass and descends to Gleann Dhu; another sign directs right, towards Comer, where Mary Campbell, the wife of infamous outlaw Rob Roy MacGregor, hailed from. Continue to the banks of the dark Duchary Water and pass beneath high-voltage power lines. The forest ends by a

Ben Lomond (right) overlooks the islands of Loch Lomond

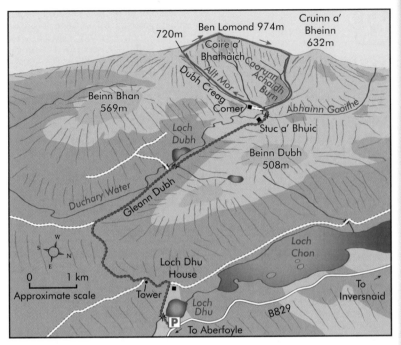

Ben Lomond 974m

Cruinn a' Bheinn 632m

720m

Coire a' Bhathaich

Caorunn Achaidh Burn

Allt Mor

Dubh Creag

Beinn Bhan 569m

Comer

Abhainn Gaoithe

Loch Dubh

Stuc a' Bhuic

Beinn Dubh 508m

Duchary Water

Gleann Dubh

Loch Chon

Loch Dhu House

Tower

Loch Dhu

To Inversnaid

B829

P

To Aberfoyle

0   1 km

Approximate scale

gate on the track. Beyond Stuc a' Bhuic cottage, keep left and cross the bridges over the Abhainn Gaoithe and the Caorunn Achaidh Burn. To avoid passing through the farmyard at Comer, leave the track 20m beyond the latter bridge, cross a small burn, pass through a gate in a deer fence, then head directly towards Ben Lomond to reach another gate about 200m north-west of the farm. Then cross towards the Allt Mor, which involves descent to a small burn en route.

Ascending Ben Lomond via the right-hand side of Allt Mor is pleasant, with a faint path through the grass. Scattered native woodland and the Dubh Creag cliff on the left both add interest. Steep slopes into the burn can be avoided by ascending on the right to gain easier ground above. At around 450m, a path crosses Allt Mor but stay to the right (north side) until reaching steeper ground, with little waterfalls and waterslides, then cross and ascend grassy slopes to a fence. Above the fence easier slopes become steeper again below a little col at 720m. Keep right on steep, grass slopes until the tourist path from Rowardennan is reached.

The tourist path leads directly to the summit but, for better views, ascend short turf

on the right and follow a fine ridge over the 959m subsidiary top. Ben Lomond's bald summit (974m, 4 hours) has a square-section triangulation pillar but no cairn or shelter. Superb views include the islands of Loch Lomond, the summit ridge, across to the Arrochar Alps, and out to the more distant Crianlarich hills and the Lawers group. On a clear day, Arran and the Paps of Jura are visible.

The descent to Comer via the steep north ridge looks scary but actually involves little scrambling (in winter, this section may require considerable care). Below 25m of steep rock steps, a good rocky path leads down to a level area at the base of the summit cone (768m), then heads off to the south-west for the Ptarmigan. Leave the path at the afore-mentioned level area then follow the broad and easy grassy north ridge to the col south of Cruinn a' Bheinn, turn right (east) and descend easily to the Caorunn Achaidh Burn. Use the gate in the deer fence at gr NN369045 and follow another fence through boggy areas and long grass to pick up an argocat track. There are several more gates before the gravel track back to the public road (6 km) is met at the bridge just north of Comer.

15

2

THE COBBLER

Exciting scrambling on the Cobbler's summit rock tower

Parking: Succoth, gr NN294049
Distance: 9km
Height Gain: 925m
Time: 4½–5½ hours
Terrain: Gravel paths, scrambling on southern approach and on summit tower can be avoided
Standard: Moderate
OS Maps: Loch Lomond & Inverary (1:50,000 Landranger sheet 56), Loch Lomond North (1:25,000 Explorer sheet 364)

The head of Loch Long is dominated by Ben Arthur, a spectacular, triple-topped peak more commonly known as the Cobbler, and named after the central peak's exposed rock tower. The hill presents a wonderful aspect from Arrochar when lit by morning sunlight. A complete traverse is no easy task for the section between the central and south peaks involves rock climbing. The route described here includes the north and central peaks only.

Leave vehicles in the car park between the A83 Tarbert–Campbeltown road and Loch Long, opposite the most westerly houses in Succoth (Arrochar) at gr NN295049. Cross the road and turn left onto the footpath to The Cobbler and its neighbour Beinn Narnain. The 1½m-wide gravel path ascends with lazy zigzags through recently-cut forestry to reach a gravel road. Follow the road left for 100m, then turn right opposite the masts and ascend a new path through young forest. It's mostly fairly easy going on long zigzags, with a few steeper sections, then the path traverses south-westwards to reach the edge of mature forest near the Allt a' Bhalachain (also called the Buttermilk Burn). The path then turns right and rises more steeply; the trees thin out and a great view of the three peaks becomes visible on reaching easier ground. A small dam in the burn on the

The Cobbler's central peak

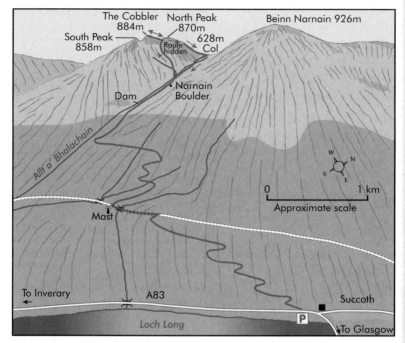

left diverts water into a pipeline to feed the Loch Sloy hydroelectric power station. Keep straight ahead, mostly a gradual ascent with some stone stairs and several burn crossings aided with large stepping stones.

The path passes the 5m-high mica-schist block called the Narnain Boulder and its smaller neighbour, which overhangs its base and provides basic shelter. There are great views of Beinn Narnain's cliffs and slabs high up on the right. Beyond a section of stone stairs, there is a junction where walkers can choose to keep right to the 628m col between Beinn Narnain and the Cobbler and ascend a steep path from there (this route is advised for descent), or take a more interesting route to the left.

From the junction, a path descends to the left, crosses the burn using stepping stones then rises past small cliffs and deteriorates steadily, becoming quite loose. This part may be quite icy in winter. Steep, rocky sections higher up require some easy scrambling but things level out near the foot of the north peak's cliffs. Clamber across boulders at the foot of the cliffs then pass below both an extraordinary needle-like rock formation and the impressive north peak overhang. A steep pull is followed by 15m

of stone stairs leading to the col between the north and central peaks, where there is a cairn. The direct ascent of the north peak (on the right) ascends an inclined slab, but paths traversing left around the peak's northern flank access easy routes on the other side. The north peak is a great viewpoint with spectacular drops all around – it's not to be missed.

From the north-central peak col, a path slants up the steep northern slopes of the central peak to reach a rounded dome next to the summit tower. To gain the summit (884m), scramble through blocks to reach the left-hand side of the tower, then pass through the first (northerly) hole to gain an exposed ledge on the other side. Scramble up the ledge, which narrows near the far end, and gain the summit platform from there. The views are magnificent, ranging from Ailsa Craig, Arran and Jura to Mull, Ben Cruachan, Beinn an Lochain, Ben Lomond and Loch Long.

Return to the north-central peak col then follow the path easily down to reach steeper ground with tight zigzags and stone stairs, ending at the 628m col with Beinn Narnain. Turn right down an easy gravel path to Coire a' Bhalachain, the Narnain Boulder and the way down to the car park.

3

BEINN AN LOCHAIN

A short, steep ridge on a well-defined peak

Parking: Easan Dubh, gr NN233088

Distance: 4km

Height Gain: 700m

Time: 3½–4 hours

Terrain: Footpath, often steep, possibly muddy, some very easy scrambling

Standard: Moderate to difficult

OS Maps: Loch Lomond & Inverary (1:50,000 Landranger sheet 56), Loch Lomond North (1:25,000 Explorer sheet 364)

This fine and relatively short walk leads along one of the most interesting ridges in the southern Highlands, taking hill walkers to the top of a well-defined and shapely hill on the northern fringes of the Arrochar Alps. Beinn an Lochain consists almost entirely of quartz mica-schist, a hard and contorted metamorphic rock that is frequently exposed as steep cliffs and crags.

Cars may be parked in one of the lay-bys on either side of the A83 Tarbert–Cambeltown road at Bealach an Easain Duibh (gr NN233088). From the northern end of the lay-by on the western side of the road, descend slightly towards the burn flowing northwards from Loch Restil, crossing the old road on the way. Cross the burn using the stepping stones just upstream from a concrete weir and the Easan Dubh waterfall, then head north-west on a fairly clear path across boggy ground; some parts may feel distinctly soft. The path trends right, past some large, broken boulders beneath the lowest crag on Beinn an Lochain's north-east ridge, then it ascends directly to gain the ridge just above the forestry plantation extending up the slope from Butterbridge in Glen Kinglas.

A clearly defined path goes straight up the ridge, initially broad enough to be considered a flank. This section is rough, steep and rocky, and may be unpleasantly muddy after rain. The path

Beinn an Lochain's steep north-east ridge (right)

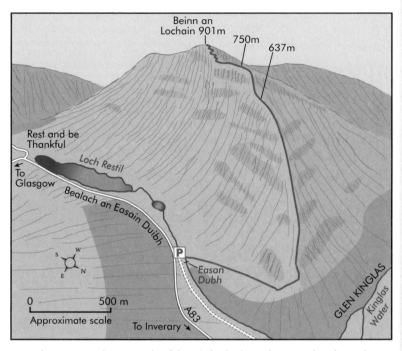

passes between some large tussocks of deer grass, the blades easily identified by their orange-coloured tips. Beyond the little 'top' at 637m, a 15m dip leads to even steeper ground where the path leaves the ridge and slants upwards to the right (north-west) before turning left to regain the ridge at a level section (750m). Take great care in this area if the weather is misty or wet, since there are tremendous drop-offs. On a clear day, there are great views of beetling crags, overhangs and gullies on the north-west side, with an extensive boulder field of huge blocks far below. Look out for the feature known as the Old Man's Face, immediately below the summit and a little to the right. On the left, there is a curious pond full of reeds on a tiny ledge, with the much larger Loch Restil and the road far below.

The ridge narrows dramatically, followed by very minor scrambling on a few slippery, mica-schist ledges, with sections of badly eroded path traversing the steep summit slopes. The path goes a little leftwards before zigzagging steeply upwards to reach the substantial cairn on the grassy summit at 901m, a magnificent perch and a good spot for dozing in the sun. There are good views all around, with Beinn Ime dominating to the east and, to the south-east, the Cobbler presenting its least interesting face. On a clear day, look for the prominent Paps of Jura 80km to the south-west.

It is worth following the path a short way to the very slightly lower, grassy southern summit (c900m). Although it's possible to continue southwards, down to the 834m top at gr NN218074, then descend eastwards on steep grass slopes (avoiding any little crags) towards the A83 at the Rest and be Thankful pass, it is more enjoyable to return to the road by the upward route. The steep north-east ridge looks particularly impressive when seen from above.

Sections of the north-east ridge may be difficult under snow and only experienced parties should consider an ascent in hard winter conditions.

4

BEN LEDI

Grand panoramas at the edge of the Highlands

Parking: Brig o' Turk, gr NN531074

Distance: 12km

Height Gain: 800m

Time: 4–5 hours

Terrain: Road, track, grassy hillside, broad grassy ridge

Standard: Easy to moderate

OS Maps: Stirling & The Trossachs (1:50,000 Landranger sheet 57), The Trossachs, Callander, Aberfoyle & Lochearnhead (1:25,000 Explorer sheet 365)

Ben Ledi, meaning either 'hill of easy slope' or 'hill of God', is a prominent and well-known peak on the edge of the Highlands. The more popular ways to the summit start from the A84 to the east, but these routes are steep, partly forested and often wet and muddy. The recommended route from the west gives better views and is considerably less busy.

From the A821 Callander–Aberfoyle road at Brig o' Turk (gr NN535066), turn off northwards onto the minor road. Park in the spaces provided at the end of the public road (gr NN531084), then take the right-hand fork, an asphalt-surfaced private road ascending through pleasant natural woodland, mainly silver birch. About 800m along this road, there is an odd, curved, dry-stone-dyke structure with a gravel interior, apparently a resting spot and viewpoint. Unnatural plantations on the western side and shoreline scars near the dam unfortunately mar the views of Glen Finglas reservoir and the Toman Dubh islet. The road continues up-and-down, past some trees draped with lichen and moss. Beyond Duart House, a barn and silo, there is Ben Ledi Cottage, where the summit may be seen high up on the right. After crossing a burn, turn right and follow the four-wheel-drive track into Gleann Casaig. Keep right, through two gates with stiles, passing two more barns 100m on the left.

Looking along Ben Ledi's north ridge

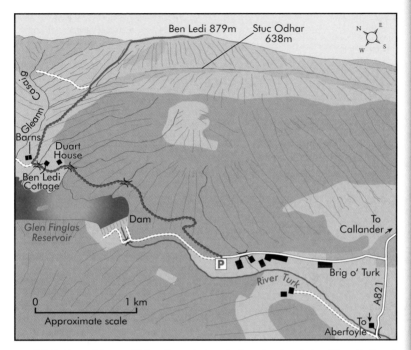

Keep left, ford a small burn and follow the track uphill, becoming less steep after the last ancient stunted trees.

About 1½km into the glen, cross two moderately sized burns in quick succession – both of them supplied with stepping-stones. Beyond the second burn, continue for around 100m to a crest then turn right onto a small path that leads up the grassy flanks of Ben Ledi. The path fades out but the direct route to the northern end of the summit ridge consists of easy grassy slopes (avoid straying to the right). After a while, there is a small burn (a tributary of the last burn crossed on the track), but it peters out in a tussock-covered area, part of Gualainn Bhuidhe.

On reaching the northern ridge of Ben Ledi at gr NN558105, turn right and follow a fairly steep path alongside rusty fence posts as far as a subsidiary top (Mullach Buidhe). From this top, there are great views of large rocks far below in the eastern corrie, and the path climbing up Stank Glen from the A84. The final section to the summit takes an easy path, following the old fence to a slight dip (from there, the fence posts go right, down a slope; do not follow these). The path continues along a fairly level, broad ridge before climbing gradually to the triangulation pillar and adjacent cairn on the summit (879m). The summit cairn was built to celebrate Queen Victoria's golden jubilee in June 1887. A rather obtrusive metal cross and plaque in a prominent location about 100m south is the memorial to Sergeant Harry Lawrie, killed while on duty with Killin mountain-rescue team when a rescue helicopter crashed near the summit of Ben More (Crianlarich) in February 1987.

From the summit, there are good views along the edge of the Highlands, including Callander, Loch Vennachar and Ben Lomond. The Highlands, which extend towards and beyond the northern horizon, include the Crianlarich hills, Meall nan Tarmachan and Ben Vorlich. To the north-east, steep slopes descend to Loch Lubnaig, one of many beautiful Scottish lochs blighted by unsightly industrial-scale forestry projects. To the north and north-west, a tempting ridge leads to Benvane but it can be hard going with deep grass and extensive areas of large tussocks; however, a fit party could include Benvane then descend to Glen Finglas by its southern ridge. Most folk will be content with returning by their outward route, giving great views across the Trossachs towards the Arrochar hills.

21

5

STUC A' CHROIN

An easy approach to a steep-sided peak

Parking: Braeleny, gr NN636108

Distance: 17km (excluding Beinn Each)

Height Gain: 825m (excluding Beinn Each)

Time: 4½–5½ hours (excluding Beinn Each)

Terrain: Track, paths, grassy ridge

Standard: Easy

OS Maps: Stirling & The Trossachs
(1:50,000 Landranger sheet 57),
Crieff, Comrie & Glen Artney (1:25,000
Explorer sheet 368)

The adjacent Munros Stuc a' Chroin and Ben
Vorlich, easily seen from Stirling on a clear day,
both have commanding positions near the edge
of the Highlands. Stuc a' Chroin is the more
interesting hill, with steep slopes around the
summit in most directions. The connecting ridge
between Stuc a' Chroin and Ben Vorlich is
exceptionally steep for over 100m so the
traverse is not recommended.

The approach to Stuc a' Chroin is easiest
from the south-east. From Callander, turn off the
A84 onto the single-track road signposted on
the eastern (southbound) side of the A84 to
'Bracklinn Falls'. This road continues 2½km
beyond the car park for the falls and ends at the
point where farm tracks lead to both
Drumardoch farm and Braeleny farm. Off-road
parking for up to six cars is available. Walk along
the private track for 500m to Braeleny farm and
pass through several gates. Continue uphill
(with a small burn crossing) then across a
featureless grassy moor for about 1½km. The
track descends towards the Keltie Water,
passing a small water-company hut with a weird
collection of gravestone-like markers.

The former Keltie Water bridge, just below
the confluence of the rivers from Gleann Breac-
nic and Gleann a' Chroin, vanished before March
2006 and hasn't been replaced. Ford the two
rivers just above the confluence, possibly
difficult in wet weather (note: the dam at gr
NN639138 can be crossed if required). Once

Stuc a' Chroin seen from the south-east

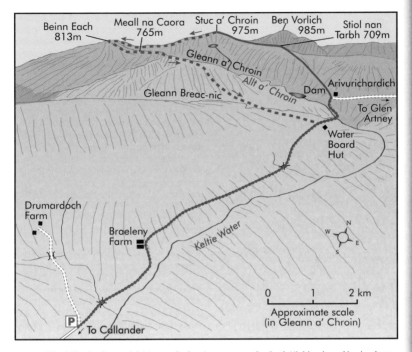

Beinn Each 813m
Meall na Caora 765m
Stuc a' Chroin 975m
Ben Vorlich 985m
Stiol nan Tarbh 709m
Gleann a' Chroin
Allt a' Chroin
Gleann Breac-nic
Dam
Arivurichardich
To Glen Artney
Water Board Hut
Drumardoch Farm
Braeleny Farm
Keltie Water
P To Callander

0   1   2 km
Approximate scale
(in Gleann a' Chroin)

across Allt a' Chroin, keep right to reach the track from the former bridge. Follow this track through a gate and past a stone barn to the stone cottage at Arivurichardich. Leave the track, keep left of the cottage and pass under a wooden beam. Keep right of a stone wall, then pass through a gap, rise up beyond a broken fence then onto the open hill beyond. A possibly hard-to-find path through the grass and heather a bit higher up the slope crosses a fence at gr NN642142 then continues slanting upwards, crossing a steep-sided gully (gr NN638150). Leave the grassy main path at gr NN636154 and follow another grassy path directly up the steep south-eastern flank of Stiol nan Tarbh, with bucket steps in places.

Good walking leads steadily along this easy, grassy and mostly well-defined ridge above 690m (the middle section is known as Aonach Gaineamhach) for 2½km, with some cliffs on the right and impressive views of Ben Vorlich. Above 900m, the ground gets steeper with lots of boulders; keep central up the steep slope where the path becomes indistinct. A final, easy, grassy section leads over a small bump to the summit (1m-high cairn at 975m, larger cairn on a lower top to the south-west) where great views

encompassing both Highlands and lowlands can be enjoyed on a clear day.

Most people return the same way but strong parties may consider completing the circuit of Gleann a' Chroin (not an easy option). The connecting ridge with the Corbett, Beinn Each, 2km south-west of Stuc a' Chroin, has numerous rocky knolls that have to be scaled or circumvented. This may take considerable time, especially in mist (allow 1½ hours from Stuc a' Chroin to Beinn Each, since there is at least 230m of re-ascent). Follow the old fence line down to Bealach Glas and over the unnamed 735m top to Bealach nan Cabar. The fence posts continue up steep craggy ground to Beinn Each's summit (809m). To return to Braeleny (1½ hours), follow a grassy ridge and yet another old fence line south-eastwards, over Meall na Caora (765m, 60m re-ascent) then over other tops further along the ridge (694m and 637m). Descend fairly steeply on grassy slopes from the extreme end of the ridge (Sgiath an Dobhrain, gr NN629139) into Gleann Breac-nic. Cross Allt Breac-nic (good ford at gr NN632132) and head for the track to Braeleny, the nearest point being the aforementioned water-company hut.

6

AN CAISTEAL

A fine ridge-walk and walkers' favourite

Parking: Glen Falloch, gr NN370240
Distance: 10km
Height Gain: 860m
Time: 5–6 hours
Terrain: Track, grassy hillsides, ridge with path, two places with easy scrambling
Standard: Moderate
OS Maps: Glen Orchy & Loch Etive (1:50,000 Landranger sheet 50), Loch Lomond North (1:25,000 Explorer sheet 364)

The Crianlarich hills, with steep, grassy flanks and bold ridges, attract many aspirant hill-walkers eager to cut their teeth. An Caisteal (the castle) and its fine northern ridge, Sron Gharbh (Twistin Hill), is the most recommended walk in the area.

Park in the lay-by just off the A82 Glasgow–Fort William road (gr NN369239), 2½km south of Crianlarich, and go through the gate at the lay-by's northern end. Follow the four-wheel-drive track around hillocks, through the cattle creep under the railway and across the wooden bridge over the River Falloch. Continue gradually uphill (south-eastwards) into Coire Earb, the deep glen between An Caisteal and Cruach Ardrain. Go through the gate opposite the extreme end of the plantation on the other side of the River Falloch and, within 300m, strike uphill to the right.

There is no path until the ridge is reached; long grass and very wet conditions underfoot are not unusual. Steep sections alternate with easier ground but, high up, it's very steep and the ground becomes drier – keep right and join the north ridge of Sron Gharbh at around 630m (gr NN373218).

There is a path going downhill in a northerly direction, but this should be avoided in descent; it peters out on steep and slippery grass slopes. Follow this path uphill (on the left,

The view north from An Caisteal

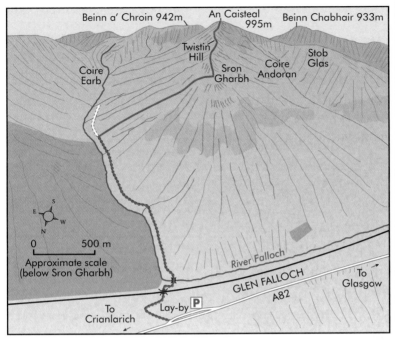

Beinn a' Chroin 942m An Caisteal 995m Beinn Chabhair 933m

Twistin Hill

Coire Earb

Sron Gharbh

Coire Andoran

Stob Glas

N S E W

0 500 m

Approximate scale
(below Sron Gharbh)

River Falloch

GLEN FALLOCH A82

To Glasgow

Lay-by P

To Crianlarich

southwards) to the broad top of Sron Gharbh (709m); from there, the now very clear path oscillates along to a col at 687m. Keep right and below the 723m top then, from a shallow col at 702m, ascend the ridge (Twistin Hill) to a section at around 750m with very steep drops into Coire Eich on the left (east). Continue upwards, alternating from the left to the right of the broad, grassy ridge. A shallow cleft slanting upwards and somewhat left leads to 870m, where a steep, gravel section of path brings hikers to an interesting area with deep holes, and a small geological fault just on the right. Beyond a 5m rise, there are several large holes, one in the middle of the path but easily hopped across. Next, an impressive, rock-girt cleft around 5m-deep (not shown on OS maps) cuts diagonally right and upwards across the ridge. Descend into the cleft's far southern end and scramble easily up the opposite wall. In wet conditions the mica-schist rock may be slippery but it is not exposed.

Proceed up the ridge to gr NN378196, where there is a choice of either a rock step in the centre (easy to miss on ascent) or a traverse path on the left. The traverse path continues to a small, easy, rock slab; climb the slab then follow a rather exposed traverse on very steep

ground that leads to an easy scramble through blocks, upwards on the right. There is a large cairn on the right where the path reconnects with the ridge. The alternative route on the ridge crest involves a 4m-high section with a marginally exposed rock slab sloping upwards from left to right. Scramble up the slab; it's fairly easy with no shortage of hand and footholds but people with limited reach may find descent awkward in wet conditions. Beyond the slab, follow the ridge up to the aforementioned cairn.

The ridge beyond the cairn becomes very well-defined, with steep sides; after a short descent, rise to the summit (995m), which is an extensive bumpy area with a couple of low cairns, short, cropped grass and little shelter. On a clear day, wide-ranging views include Ben Lomond, Ben More and Stobinian, Ben Nevis, Ben Lui and the Paps of Jura.

Descend the same way or take the less-frequented, steep-sided and rather craggy Stob Glas ridge, returning to the car park via the West Highland Way. The descent from Stob Glas to Derrydarroch cottage is less steep than the descent from the Sron Gharbh ridge but route finding on Stob Glas may require accurate compass work.

7

BEN LUI

An exhilarating ascent on a first-class mountain

Parking: Dalrigh, gr NN344292
Distance: 21km
Height Gain: 1030m
Time: 7–8 hours
Terrain: Track for 7km, then steep path, pathless slopes and ridges
Standard: Strenuous, moderate to difficult
OS Maps: Glen Orchy & Loch Etive (1:50,000 Landranger sheet 50), Loch Lomond North (1:25,000 Explorer sheet 364)

Ben Lui, one of the most attractive mountains in the southern Highlands, presents its steepest and most interesting face towards the A82 Glasgow–Fort William road just south of Tyndrum. The standard route from the A85 in Glen Lochy is relatively short but it is muddy and lacks interest compared to the recommended walk from the A82 via Cononish.

Turn off the A82 at the signpost for Dalrigh, 1½km south of Tyndrum, and park in the well-made parking area just 50m from the main road (gr NN344292). In 1306, a skirmish between Robert the Bruce's men and McDougall of Lorne led to the death of McDougall's men and it is said that Bruce's sword and other heavy weapons were abandoned in a nearby lochan. From the car park, turn right towards the main road then turn left towards Dalrigh. Keep right on a gravel track to avoid the houses then keep right again at a junction. Now on the West Highland Way, cross the Crom Allt's wooden bridge; Bruce's lochan may be seen over a small rise on the right, just beyond a cattle grid. The West Highland Way turns off to the right a little further on. Continue on the main track through an area with lots of Ice Age glacial deposits, known as drumlins, then pass underneath the Crianlarich–Oban railway, where rails have been used to strengthen the bridge walls. Keep right after the bridge and note the remnants of

Ben Lui dominates the view from Dalrigh, near Tyndrum

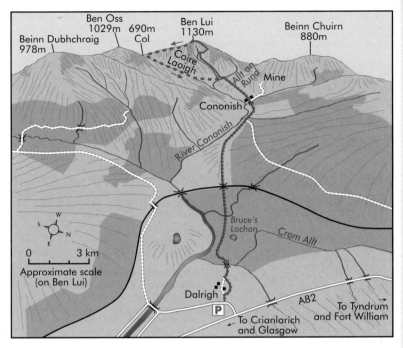

Ben Oss 1029m 690m Col Ben Lui 1130m Beinn Chuirn 880m
Beinn Dubhchraig 978m
Coire Laoigh
Allt an Rund
Mine
Cononish
River Cononish
Bruce's Lochan
Crom Allt
0   3 km
Approximate scale (on Ben Lui)
Dalrigh
P
To Crianlarich and Glasgow
A82
To Tyndrum and Fort William

Caledonian pine forest across the River Cononish on the left. Look out for a sign marking the Ben Lui nature reserve shortly after a gate. The track keeps close to the pleasant northern bank of the River Cononish as far as Cononish farm, where there are two houses and several fluorescent-green barns. Keep straight ahead and rise onto the southern shoulder of Beinn Chuirn. On the right, there are some modern buildings at Scotland's only gold mine, which is below the Eas Anie waterfall (when deemed economical the precious metal is extracted from quartz veins here). About 2km beyond the farm, the track descends about 30m to the Allt an Rund and comes to its end.

If the river is in spate, there is an easy crossing point a short way upstream. Once across, keep the walled enclosure (sheepfank) on the left and ascend the steep path by the Allt Coire Ghaothaich for around 350m. Central Gully and the summit lie straight ahead at the top of Coire Gaothaich, but the recommended route ascends very steep grass slopes with scattered rocks north-westwards (right) to pick up the excellent north-east ridge of the mountain. In winter, beware of avalanches in the corrie; an ice-axe and crampons may be required. Beyond an unnamed top at 960m,

there is a 12m dip then the ridge merges with the northern flank of the mountain and a steep pull upwards on mixed grass and stones leads to Ben Lui's north-west top and cairn (1127m). Walk about 140m south-eastwards past Central Gully's exit (beware of cornices in winter) to the summit cairn at 1130m. The phenomenal views stretch from Ben Lomond to Ben Nevis, with Ben Cruachan to the west and Ben Lawers to the east.

The quickest way down is to return via the north-east ridge, but it's easier and very pleasant to follow the broad, south-east ridge to the deep col between Ben Lui and Ben Oss at 690m. The upper section, down to a minor top at 987m, is fairly steep and stony, but the lower section has easier gradients. From the col, turn left and descend a steep slope into Coire Laoigh; continue on the left bank of the burn for 2km, then head northwards to the afore-mentioned sheepfank to join the outward route and the gravel track at the crossing of the Allt an Rund. Unfortunately, it's a long way along the track back to the car park!

8

STOB DIAMH

Wonderful views and well-defined ridges

Parking: Strath Orchy, gr NN132283
Distance: 11km
Height Gain: 1080m
Time: 6–7 hours
Terrain: Low-level tracks, grassy hillsides, grassy and rocky ridges
Standard: Moderate
OS Maps: Glen Orchy & Loch Etive (1:50,000 Landranger sheet 50), Loch Etive & Glen Orchy (1:25,000 Explorer sheet 377)

The magnificent circuit of Ben Cruachan's eastern corries (also known as the Dalmally Horseshoe, with Stob Diamh as the highest point) follows lofty, well-defined ridges, giving pleasant walking and wonderful views.

The area is steeped in Clan Campbell history and a visit to the nearby Kilchurn Castle, which dates from 1440, is recommended. The original keep was extended between the sixteenth and eighteenth centuries, but the castle fell into disuse after the 1745 Jacobite rebellion. It was hit by lightning in the 1770s but was still in good condition until the mid-twentieth century. Historic Scotland now maintains the substantial remains of the building.

Cars may be parked beside the B8077 Stronmilchan road, just off the A85 Tyndrum–Oban road, at gr NN133284 (about 1km due north of the castle). Go through the gate on the western side of the B8077 and follow the four-wheel-drive track heading north then north-west across open moorland below Monadh Driseig's crags. The track (formerly a narrow-gauge railway) serviced rock extraction at the quarries on the flanks of that hill and some railway sleepers can still be seen in the track bed. Just before reaching the first quarry, about 200m beyond a second gate, an indistinct track branches off to the right and descends to a bridge over the Allt Coire Chreachainn (gr NN127297). This bridge, which lies below steep slopes and is obscured by trees, is not easily seen from the four-wheel-drive track.

The Sron an Isean ridge of Stob Diamh

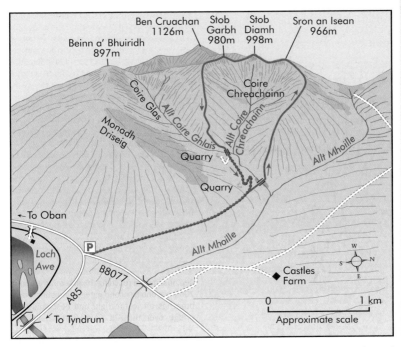

Once across the burn, head north-west up increasingly steep and somewhat wet, grassy slopes towards the blunt eastern end of the ridge leading to Sron an Isean, the eastern top of Stob Diamh. Above 200m, a steep and rather eroded path assists upwards progress. At around 400m, the route avoids some small bluffs with scattered trees by climbing very steeply up a grass slope in the central part of the hill's flank. Once clear of the steepest section, the ridge becomes quite well defined and gives more straightforward walking, mostly on grass but with some stony sections. At around 900m, the ridge narrows considerably, then a short but steep climb leads to the blocky summit of Sron an Isean (966m). Just beyond Sron an Isean's cairn, there is a great view of a little corrie lochan and (beyond) down Glen Noe to Loch Etive. The beautiful twin spires of Ben Cruachan's summit and the Taynuilt Peak dominate the scene behind the more rounded summit of Stob Diamh.

Continue south-westwards along an interesting, narrow-but-easy ridge covered with large granite blocks. In places, weaving in-and-out between the rocks is necessary. From the low point between Sron an Isean and Stob Diamh (at 910m), a path winds a straight-forward route up through steep rocks and broken outcrops to Stob Diamh's large summit cairn at 998m. Hands may be required for balance but there is no real scrambling. Views all around are wonderful: the ridge to Ben Cruachan, Ben Starav to the north, Ben Lui to the east, and, closer to hand, Beinn a' Chochuill and Beinn Eunaich to the north-east.

From Stob Diamh, continue southwards on a rock-strewn ridge with grassy patches to reach a dip at 930m, then climb fairly steeply across rocks to Stob Garbh (980m). Continue southwards, with a steep drop of around 30m followed by patches of loose rock and grass. Beyond a dip at 935m, a short rise leads to a broad section of ridge at 947m. From there, a mainly grassy ridge heads east-south-east – avoid the south-pointing ridge towards Beinn a' Bhuiridh, unless wishing to add that very steep-sided Corbett to an already long day. The east-south-east ridge of Stob Garbh continues fairly steeply downwards to a small level section at 450m. Below this, keep right to avoid some crags then cross easy-angled ground to reach a bridge across the Allt Coire Ghlais at gr NN120295. Beyond the bridge, the afore-mentioned four-wheel-drive track leads past the largest quarry and back to the main road.

9

MEALL NAN TARMACHAN

A marvellous ridge-walk with four prominent tops

Parking: Loch Tay to Glen Lyon road, gr NN604383
Distance: 12km
Height Gain: 770m
Time: 5–6 hours
Terrain: Mostly good paths or tracks, some narrow ridges and steep sections
Standard: Moderate, with one short, dangerous section (easily avoided in snow-free conditions). Crampons may be required in winter
OS Maps: Loch Tay & Glen Dochart (1:50,000 Landranger sheet 51), Ben Lawers & Glen Lyon (1:25,000 Explorer sheet 378)

Meall nan Tarmachan is a favourite with many hill walkers and is rated one of the finest ridge traverses in the southern Highlands.

Park cars just off the Ben Lawers to Glen Lyon road at gr NN605383 then follow the track over the burn from Lochan na Lairige, with more parking possibilities just before a locked gate and turning area. Beyond the gate, continue for about 400m along the track and keep a good look out for a fairly obvious path on the right. This well-maintained trail ascends steep, grassy flanks directly uphill to a gate at an electric fence, continuing further to a shoulder at an altitude of 700m. The path takes a right-angled turn and goes steeply northwards to a 923m top, then turns westwards to descend to a stile. Beyond the stile and a dip at 890m, the path goes up a rather steep open gully on stone stairs, with easier ground higher up; a final short ascent up a grassy slope on the left leads to the small summit cairn (1044m). The summit is a grand viewpoint, with the fine-looking Tarmachan ridge extending to the south-west (Ben More and Stobinian prominent in the distance), and the grand peaks of the Ben Lawers group dominating to the north-east. Southwards, beyond the silvery waters of Loch Tay, there is Ben Vorlich, Stuc a' Chroin and Ben Ledi.

Although some Munro baggers may be tempted to return to the road once they have

A narrow ridge on Meall Garbh of Meall nan Tarmachan

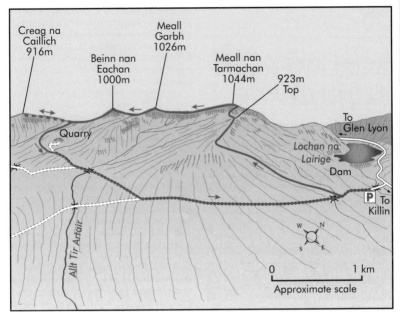

Creag na Caillich 916m
Beinn nan Eachan 1000m
Meall Garbh 1026m
Meall nan Tarmachan 1044m
923m Top
Quarry
To Glen Lyon
Lochan na Lairige
Dam
To Killin
Allt Tir Artair
0   1 km
Approximate scale

gained their objective, it is far better to continue westwards along the Tarmachan ridge, an entertaining route with an exciting narrow section. Initially, a gradual descent on grass and sections of slightly eroded path leads south-west to a col at around 950m. An earthen path then passes various rocky outcrops and small lochans before rising to the spectacular pointed summit of the 1026m top, Meall Garbh. The summit is immediately followed by a short scramble down to an almost horizontal ridge less than 1m wide but around 80m long. The north side of this ridge is vertical. Follow the path traversing the southern side, just below the crest. Beyond the level section, the path descends a wider ridge to the west, but there is a nasty surprise with a precipitous and badly eroded section low down. A particularly exposed section with slabs and unpleasant ledges strewn with gravel lies at the lower end of this ridge, so descending here in poor weather or in wet or wintry conditions is not recommended. Even experienced hikers may choose to descend a steep, mainly grassy, slope about 100m to the north, but this may also be dangerous if wet or icy – in that case, consider turning back.

Beyond the col at 910m, the path continues easily over various grassy hillocks, with some rocky outcrops and a few tiny lochans. A steep slope and earthen path rises to the 1000m summit of Beinn nan Eachan, from where there are fine views of the rarely visited north-western corries. Another steep path descends surprisingly easily to the next col (840m), between Beinn nan Eachan and the 916m top, Creag na Caillich. Top collectors may be tempted to follow the wide, grassy ridge (with a few scattered crags) to pop another tick in the book while purists may just want to complete the ridge traverse.

From the 840m col, a faint path that is boggy in places leads south-eastwards into Coire Fionn Lairige. Keep right, below the impressive cliffs of Creag na Caillich, then slant down to the left, passing below the quarry (gr NN574374) to gain the quarry access track at gr NN577370. In May, keep an eye open for alpine flowers, which are unusually prolific just south of the quarry. Once on the track, it's a rather tedious 4km walk back to the car park, but this doesn't detract from a great day on one of Scotland's finest hills.

10

BEN LAWERS and BEINN GHLAS

Two Munros, both with panoramic views

Parking: Ben Lawers visitor centre, gr NN609379

Distance: 9km

Height Gain: 985m

Time: 5–7 hours

Terrain: Paths on grassy and stony hillsides and ridges

Standard: Moderate

OS Maps: Loch Tay & Glen Dochart (1:50,000 Landranger sheet 51), Ben Lawers & Glen Lyon (1:25,000 Explorer sheet 378)

The highest mountain in Britain south of Ben Nevis, Ben Lawers is a fine hill dominating a 13km-long ridge. The area around Ben Lawers is a national nature reserve, managed jointly by the National Trust for Scotland and Scottish Natural Heritage. Dalradian mica-schist bedrock has weathered to give lime-rich soils, encouraging arctic and alpine plants that are rarely found elsewhere in the country. In full winter conditions, ascending Ben Lawers may require ice axe and crampons and the weather may be extremely unpleasant. The ridge between Beinn Ghlas and Ben Lawers is particularly notorious for high winds.

The most obvious way to climb Ben Lawers, a circuit of Lochan nan Cat via An Stuc, is not advised due to difficult ground east of An Stuc and lack of parking in Lawers village. There is a better alternative. From the A827 Killin–Aberfeldy road, take the minor road leading over Lairig an Lochain (a pass) destined for Bridge of Balgie in Glen Lyon. In winter, due care should be taken since the road is not regularly gritted or snow-ploughed. Drive to the National Trust visitor centre at 430m, where there is a large car park with a voluntary parking charge. The visitor centre may be of some interest to anyone unfamiliar with the area.

A gate at the eastern side of the car park leads to the start of a nature trail, a gravel or

Ben Lawers from Beinn Ghlas on a stormy winter's day

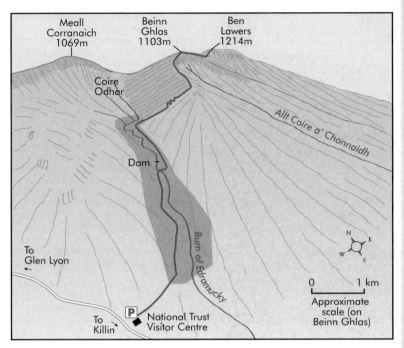

Meall Corranaich 1069m   Beinn Ghlas 1103m   Ben Lawers 1214m

Coire Odhar

Allt Coire a' Chonnaidh

Dam

To Glen Lyon

Burn of Edramucky

N E S W

0   1 km

Approximate scale (on Beinn Ghlas)

To Killin

P National Trust Visitor Centre

earthen path with some wooden 'duck' boards bringing walkers to another gate. Pass through this gate into a plantation of young trees, mostly native woodland, where there are some low ruins of ancient shielings. The path ascends by the side of a small, oddly named watercourse, the Burn of Edramucky; keep right at a sign just below a little dam (part of the Glen Lochay hydroelectric scheme). Cross the burn easily and keep left at another sign. The path, often quite deeply eroded, ascends gradually across moorland then curves right, crosses more boards and leaves the plantation through another gate. Now the climb begins in earnest, with the path zigzagging steeply up grass slopes to reach the south ridge of Beinn Ghlas at 830m.

The path widens and crosses a level, stony area; then there is a short, steep section with some exposed rock and minor scrambling. A steady ascent leads to a 20m-high steep section where the path keeps left of the ridge then it climbs sharply to regain the ridge on the right. In winter, this section is often buried in deep snow and an ice axe and crampons may be required. Stony ground and some flat areas lead past various knolls to the summit (1103m, tiny cairn), where there is an impressive drop to the north.

The views of Ben Lawers and Meall Corranaich from the top are particularly fine.

Continue north-east along a well-defined and sometimes narrow ridge which is not steep but may be corniced above its craggy, northern side. The path descends over grass and scattered stones to the col below Ben Lawers, at 1000m. From this col, the ascent of Ben Lawers is quite steep and at first the path ascends between rocky outcrops, with lots of loose stones. The easier upper half of the ascent leads to the summit, where there is a large cairn, a direction indicator and a concrete triangulation pillar (1214m). The ridge to Meall Garbh via An Stuc is most impressive from the summit. Lochan nan Cat, a curious, pear-shaped loch below gloomy crags, lies 500m below. Look out for Ben Nevis, about 50km to the north-west. The bulky cairn was built in an attempt to bring the height of the hill to 4000 feet!

Return to the visitor centre via Beinn Ghlas. It is tempting to take the path that traverses below Beinn Ghlas to the north, but it is not necessarily a faster route and on a clear day, keeping high keeps the views too.

11

STUCHD AN LOCHAIN

A distinctive peak with a curious lochan far below

Parking: Pubil, gr NN465420
Distance: 8km
Height Gain: 655m
Time: 4–4½hours
Terrain: Track, grassy and heathery hillsides
Standard: Easy
OS Maps: Loch Tay & Glen Dochart (1:50,000 Landranger sheet 51), Ben Lawers & Glen Lyon (1:25,000 Explorer sheet 378)

Glen Lyon is one of Scotland's finest glens and the drive to the foot of Stuchd an Lochain is a delight in itself. The dome-shaped summit, which lies above the mysteriously dark Lochan nan Cat and is an exceptionally fine viewpoint on a clear day, was reputedly first climbed by Colin Campbell of Glen Lyon in 1590. Many people ascend the hill from Giorra Dam (Loch an Daimh) but this route is overused, steep and slippery. It is much more pleasant to approach from Pubil, near the Glen Lyon dam and south-west of the hill.

Follow the single-track road through Glen Lyon to Pubil, 1km east of Lubreoch Dam (Loch Lyon). There is limited space for parking on roadside grass at the eastern entrance to Pubil. Pass through the gate (usually open) and walk along the track, past the end of the row of stone cottages to reach the intriguing and rather comical-looking lodge. Keep right below the lodge and continue to a gate where a clip opens a chain. Follow a gravel track, climbing steeply up the grassy and bracken-covered hillside past a young plantation. The sudden gain of altitude rewards with great views across Lubreoch Dam to Beinn Heasgarnich, and down Glen Lyon to Meall Ghaordaidh. The track double bends above the plantation and passes below a large pile of rock debris, evidence of excavations relating to the hydroelectric schemes. Just before a small dam at 500m on the Allt Phubuill, the track

Lochan nan Cat from Stuchd an Lochain

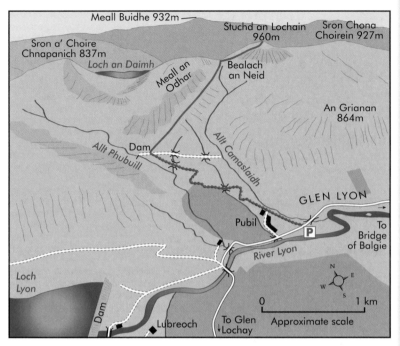

Meall Buidhe 932m

Stuchd an Lochain 960m

Sron Chona Choirein 927m

Sron a' Choire Chnapanich 837m

Loch an Daimh

Meall an Odhar

Bealach an Neid

An Grianan 864m

Allt Phubuill

Dam

Allt Camaslaidh

GLEN LYON

Pubil

P

To Bridge of Balgie

River Lyon

Loch Lyon

Dam

Lubreoch

To Glen ↓Lochay

Approximate scale

0   1 km

levels out and there is a junction with a branch heading east to a dam on the Allt Camaslaidh. A concrete cap at the junction marks a tunnel diverting water between the dams.

Head north-east onto the open moor, cross a decrepit wooden bridge over a ditch then continue on easy, grass slopes. Follow a grassy and occasionally boggy argocat trail that goes uphill for a while, then trends right (east). Leave the trail and continue easily north-east on grass, aiming for the highest point on the skyline. Once the summit dome of Stuchd an Lochain appears on the right, head directly for the obvious col on its left-hand side (Bealach an Neid). The walking remains good on generally dry grass and heather, but there are some fairly boggy sections. Alpine flowers may be seen in this area during spring and early summer. Cross a dilapidated fence then continue over slightly rougher ground and some peat hags to reach the col at gr NN475447.

Rusty, iron fence posts and loose wires mark the way to the top of Stuchd an Lochain, a grass slope without a path that gets steeper and more mossy with scattered stones higher up. There are wonderful views of Ben Nevis and its satellites beyond the crags of Meall an Odhar, the west top of Stuchd an Lochain. A little higher up, Buachaille Etive Mor comes into view beyond

Sron a' Choire Chnapanich (also called Stob a' Choin). The fence-line skirts about 10m below and south-west of the summit at its closest approach. The summit, mostly grassy with some outcrops of mica-schist, sports a half-metre-high cairn (960m) on the edge of a steep drop to the almost circular Lochan nan Cat, 270m below. This is an impressive place, with fine views all around, including Ben Lawers, Ben Alder and the distant Cairngorms. The cliff edge of Sron Chona Choirein (to the east) often holds snow until early summer. A well-worn path from the east via Sron Chona Choirein brings most walkers to the summit.

Return to Pubil by the outward route. Alternatively, follow the south-west ridge of Meall an Odhar to the dam on the Allt Phubuill or go southwards from Stuchd an Lochain to An Grianan and follow its grassy western ridge to the Allt Camaslaidh dam and the track to Pubil. The direct descent via Allt Camaslaidh is not recommended due to boggy areas near the burn.

12

SCHIEHALLION

Ascend one of Scotland's most dramatic peaks

Parking: Braes of Foss, gr NN753557

Distance: 10km

Height Gain: 755m

Time: 4–5 hours

Terrain: Footpath, stony summit ridge

Standard: Easy

OS Maps: Loch Tay & Glen Dochart
(1:50,000 Landranger sheet 51),
Pitlochry & Loch Tummel (1:25,000
Explorer sheet 386)

Graceful Schiehallion presents a cone-shaped profile when viewed from Loch Rannoch and, unsurprisingly, it has appeared in many calendars. It is very popular with walkers and around twenty thousand people attempt the ascent each year. The John Muir Trust bought Schiehallion in 1999 and £600,000 was spent on footpath works between 2002 and 2007. A new path was constructed to the south of the former route, which was in very poor condition due to the high number of visitors. The walking route basically follows Schiehallion's eastern ridge, which is for the most part fairly easy angled and is a good introduction to hill walking if the weather is fine.

Intriguingly, Schiehallion has an important place in the history of physics. In the eighteenth century, the astronomer royal, Nevil Maskelyne, used Schiehallion's near perfect shape to obtain approximations for both the mass of the earth and the gravitational constant, G, an elusive and tiny quantity that first appeared in Isaac Newton's theory of gravitation. Maskelyne measured the tiny sideways gravitational pull of the hill on a pendulum, taking observations over four months during 1774 at observatories built on platforms on Schiehallion's northern and southern slopes. The mathematician Charles Hutton invented contour lines while determining the mountain's volume and centre of mass.

Loch Rannoch and Schiehallion

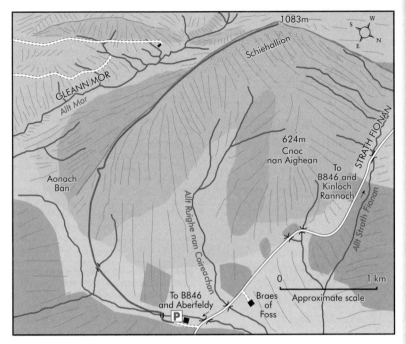

Schiehallion consists mainly of Dalradian quartzite, which fractures into large blocks or boulders often with a whitish and grainy appearance. There is also a strip of limestone running across the hill's southern and eastern flanks, where there are comparatively few watercourses and even a small cave.

Cars may be parked in the area provided 200m east of Braes of Foss on the minor road between Aberfeldy and Kinloch Rannoch. A good gravel path heads southwards across level ground to a gate and an information sign then it passes between two blocks of trees, crosses a burn (footbridge) and continues steadily uphill through bracken and heather. Beyond another footbridge, there is a sheepfank and a steeper rise on grass and heather slopes. The path's dry, gravel surface encourages swift progress, with sections of stone stairs where the ascent is steepest. The gradient eases on a heathery flank with occasional rocks then it becomes steeper again with zigzags, some stone stairs and traverses. The path continues along another broad and stony but easy-angled ridge, becoming steeper with a poorer path leading to a 1½m-high cairn at 940m. From this cairn, the summit ridge can be seen ahead, rising a little to the right.

The ridge levels out and the path continues past a stone ring shelter, with a steep stony section leading to another stone ring 4m in diameter but on easier ground. Continue by path across bouldery or stony areas to a level section with a 1m-high cairn. A steady ascent leads upwards to the final steep-sided and well-defined ridge with broken rock, outcrops and a bouldery crest; no place for nervous novices in bad weather or snow, but it is generally easier just to the right (north) of the ridge line.

The summit is marked with a surprisingly small half-metre-high cairn. The best viewpoint is about 10m to the west of the cairn, past some large blocks, with a splendid panorama across Rannoch Moor to the Glen Coe hills and Ben Nevis. Beyond vast heathery moors to the north and north-east lie the Cairngorms and Lochnagar and south-eastwards the eye may be drawn as far as Fife.

Return to the car park by the same route.

13

BEINN DORAIN

Fabulous landscapes seen from a distinctive summit

Parking: Bridge of Orchy railway station, gr NN300395

Distance: 10km

Height Gain: 930m

Time: 4½–5½ hours

Terrain: Gravel, stony or boggy paths

Standard: Moderate

OS Maps: Glen Orchy & Loch Etive (1:50,000 Landranger sheet 50), Loch Etive & Glen Orchy (1:25,000 Explorer sheet 377)

Beautiful Beinn Dorain presents a striking cone-shaped profile towards the A82 at the pass north of Tyndrum, but this appearance is misleading since it's really the southern end of a ridge stretching 10km from Beinn a' Chreachain. The walk is straightforward but the entrance to Coire an Dothaidh can be very boggy and unpleasant.

Turn off the A82 Glasgow–Fort William road at the Bridge of Orchy Hotel, take the road heading eastwards and drive uphill past some houses towards the railway station. From the station car park, use the pedestrian underpass to reach the other side of the tracks, ascend steps and go through a gate then cross the West Highland Way. Follow an easy path heading eastwards towards Coire an Dothaidh, rising uphill past a mobile-phone base station. It's a mainly gravelly and stony path, wide and eroded with boulders in places, that steadily ascends grassy slopes to the right (south) of the pleasant burn Allt Coire an Dothaidh. The burn, which has scattered trees on its banks, becomes quite deeply cut into the hillside above 290m and there is a waterslide at 390m, near the upper end of the fence on the burn's northern side.

On the final approach to Coire an Dothaidh (between 500m and 550m), the path is up to 10m wide in places; following wet weather, take care while crossing unpleasant quaking bogs and sections of deep mud. On entering the corrie,

Beinn Dorain and Auch Gleann from the A82

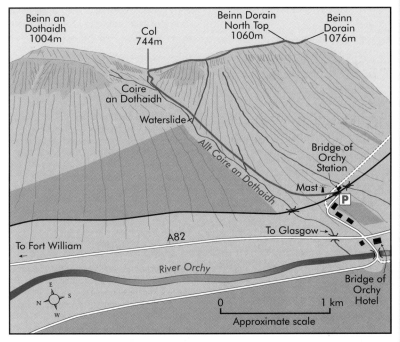

which has impressive crags on both sides, the gradient decreases and the path passes scattered rocks and some huge boulders. The path then directly ascends the corrie headwall and becomes very steep, eroded, stony, bouldery and rather loose. There is often a burn flowing down the path in this section. Keep left of a crag, continue upwards to the right above it then ascend to the left to reach easier ground beyond a broken boulder around 4m high. Continue steadily upwards to the 744m col and little lochan between Beinn an Dothaidh and Beinn Dorain. This is a pleasant spot for a break, with good views of the Cruachan group, Ben Starav, Stob Coir' an Albannaich and Stob Ghabhar.

To reach Beinn Dorain, turn right (south), keeping left of broken slabs at first. A steeper ascent through broken slabs and outcrops (use hands for balance) leads to an easier flank with a stony or slabby path. Easily descend a small crag (2m) then bear right (south-west) onto a sloping, grassy shelf, passing a circular lochan. The mainly gravel or stony path then bears left (south), rising gradually at first, followed by a steeper ascent just to the right (west) of the small broken outcrops and crags on the Am Fiaclach ridge. At 990m, there is a level, grassy shoulder to the right of the main ridge but beware of a false path leading onward to steep slopes. On reaching this shoulder, look for a path on the left and ascend to a broad ridge at 1010m that leads in a southerly direction, mainly rising steadily but with some flatter areas. Follow a gravelly, earthen or stony path, with one section crossing large, flat stones, past outcrops, mossy grass and an oddly located 1m-high cairn, to reach the well-constructed 2m-high cairn on Beinn Dorain's north top (c1060m).

From the north top, continue southwards on a mixed earthen and stony path, descending fairly steeply for about 15m to a col (with great views leftwards to gloomy crags, scree and Auch Gleann far below) then rising to the summit across some easy slab on a well-defined ridge. The broad, grassy top has a rock plinth with a 1m-high cairn (1076m); it is a great viewpoint, with views ranging from Ben More (Crianlarich) to the Paps of Jura and Ben Nevis.

Return by the outward route. Including Beinn an Dothaidh from the 744m col adds 1½ hours (a steep path rises to 900m, then grassy slopes lead to the summit cairn at 1004m).

14

BEINN ACHALADAIR and BEINN A' CHREACHAIN

Splendid ridge-walking linking two Munros

Parking: Achallader farm, gr NN322443
Distance: 16km
Height Gain: 1240m
Time: 7½–8½ hours
Terrain: Paths, tracks, grassy hillsides and ridges
Standard: Moderate to difficult
OS Maps: Glen Orchy & Loch Etive (1:50,000 Landranger sheet 50), Loch Etive & Glen Orchy (1:25,000 Explorer sheet 377)

These finely-shaped hills north of Bridge of Orchy give great walking on grassy ridges with some impressive mica-schist cliffs on their northern flanks.

Turn off the A82 Glasgow–Fort William road 4km north of Bridge of Orchy and follow the track to the parking area at Achallader farm. Achallader saw a vicious clan battle in 1497 but the tower house by the farm wasn't completed until 1600. The building was sacked in 1646 and again during the 1689 Jacobite Rebellion.

Follow the 'To Hill' signs through the farmyard, go through a gate and take a four-wheel-drive track uphill to a bridge over the railway. Continue on a boggy argocat trail alongside a deer fence following a shelf above Allt Coire Achaladair; the trail improves to become a gravel footpath with occasional soft areas. Hop across some minor burns flowing from Beinn an Dothaidh (right), then cross Allt Coire Achaladair where a crag on the right forces the path into the burn. Follow the path on the left bank uphill to a fork, cross the left branch and ascend steep ground between the two branches (if it is icy, easier grassy ground ascends left of the left branch). Above the steep slopes, in flat-floored Coire Daingean, cross the burn, pass various ponds and bumps then ascend steep grass to the southern end of Beinn Achaladair's ridge, just left (north) of the 760m col with Beinn an Dothaidh.

Cloud inversion from Beinn a' Chreachain

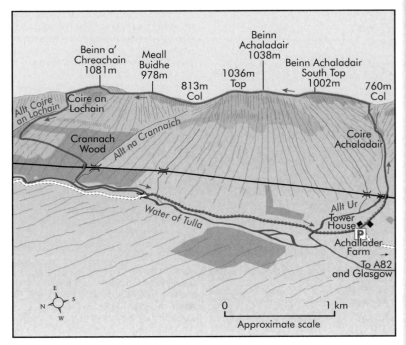

Beinn a' Chreachain 1081m
Meall Buidhe 978m
Beinn Achaladair 1038m
Beinn Achaladair South Top 1002m
1036m Top
813m Col
1036m Top
760m Col
Coire an Lochain
Allt Coire an Lochain
Crannach Wood
Allt na Crannaich
Coire Achaladair
Water of Tulla
Allt Ur
Tower House
Achallader Farm
To A82 and Glasgow

N E S W

0   1 km
Approximate scale

A path across excellent short grass leads steadily upwards for nearly 1½km to the small cairn on Beinn Achaladair's south top (1002m). From there, descend easily northwards for 50m to a col then continue upwards to the fairly narrow and stony summit ridge, with precipitous drops on the left. There is a small cairn at gr NN344432 (1038m), but the better viewpoint and recommended lunch stop is by a larger 1m-high cairn (1036m) 300m north-east.

Descend stony, pathless slopes eastwards, with the gradient easing as the ridge curves left. Follow the ridge down to around 930m. A steep drop between crags to the 813m col below may be circumvented by traversing right for about 200m horizontally, then descending straightforward grassy slopes to an old fence leading northwards to the col.

From the col, a steep path leads up the grassy south-west flank of Meall Buidhe; the highest point (978m) is at the western end of a broad and almost level ridge. From the eastern end, descend to a dip (924m) that overlooks a gully above Lochan a' Chreachain. Beyond a small top there is another dip (930m), then steep slopes of grass and scattered rocks (intermittent path) lead up the dome-shaped Beinn a' Chreachain. Beyond the junction with the north-

east ridge, keep right on easier-angled, stony ground for the 1m-high summit cairn (1081m). Fine views include Beinn Achaladair and Meall Buidhe, Rannoch Moor with the Black Mount hills beyond, Ben Nevis to the north-west, and, to the south-east and beyond Loch Lyon, the Ben Lawers group.

The recommended descent follows a path down the mainly grassy and occasionally narrow north-east ridge. Turn left at the broad 940m col and descend grass (steep at first) into Coire an Lochain, with great views of cliffs across the water. Keep the lochan well left and cross the burn draining it (Allt Coire an Lochain) easily at gr NN368451. Continue across grass to the deer fence (stile) at gr NN366455. Cross another stile at gr NN362459, then follow the northern edge of this fence (westwards) and gradually descend to the Caledonian-pine dominated Crannach Wood. Cross several small burns, cross the railway at a foot bridge (gr NN349455) then descend to the Water of Tulla. Cross the Allt na Crannaich easily on the left then proceed southwest on a path alongside the Water of Tulla. This path meets a four-wheel-drive track that continues to the ford on Allt Ur (deep in wet weather), 400m before Achallader farm.

15

STOB A' CHOIRE ODHAIR

Magnificent outlook across Rannoch Moor

Parking: Victoria Bridge, gr NN270419

Distance: 12km (excluding Stob Ghabhar)

Height Gain: 780m (excluding Stob Ghabhar)

Time: 4½–5½ hours (excluding Stob Ghabhar)

Terrain: Track, paths, stony upper slopes

Standard: Easy

OS Maps: Glen Orchy & Loch Etive (1:50,000 Landranger sheet 50), Loch Etive & Glen Orchy (1:25,000 Explorer sheet 377)

Stob a' Choire Odhair, the easiest of the Black Mount hills, is easily seen from the A82 while driving across Rannoch Moor. The hill appears to be a subsidiary top of the considerably higher Stob Ghabhar, but it's a Munro in its own right and is also a magnificent viewpoint.

From Bridge of Orchy Hotel on the A82 Glasgow–Fort William road, take the single-track road to Inveroran and Forest Lodge, past fine stands of Caledonian pine. Beyond Inveroran Hotel, the modern road follows the route of the former military road, which was completed in 1753 to aid subduing rebellious clans. There is a car park on the left, 400m before the turning area, at Forest Lodge. From the car park, follow a footpath past some plantation pines, return to the road and cross Victoria Bridge to reach the lodge. The attractive woodland around Forest Lodge (a group of traditional, dressed-stone buildings with slate roofs) includes rhododendrons, moss-covered alders and Caledonian pines. At the lodge, turn left onto the private, four-wheel-drive track to Clashgour farm, direction indicated 'Loch Etive'. Go through the gate at the edge of the woods and continue along the track, mainly following the river bank. Beyond a plantation on the right, the odd little green-painted corrugated iron Clashgour Hut appears ahead; this Meccano-type hut was a

Rannoch Moor with brockenspectre and glory, from Stob a' Choire Odhair

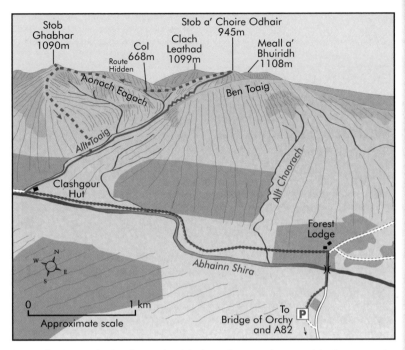

Stob Ghabhar 1090m
Col 668m
Route Hidden
Clach Leathad 1099m
Stob a' Choire Odhair 945m
Meall a' Bhuiridh 1108m
Aonach Eagach
Ben Toaig
Allt Toaig
Allt Chaorach
Clashgour Hut
Forest Lodge
Abhainn Shira
0   1 km
Approximate scale
To Bridge of Orchy and A82

four-pupil primary school until 1933, but it is now used for overnight stays by mountaineering clubs.

A few metres beyond the hut, turn right on a good quality gravel path that is wide enough to take argocat vehicles. The path follows the east bank of Allt Toaig, past some alders, a rising curve followed by a curious, long, straight section. Above 300m, the gradient increases a little and the path arrives at the ford over Allt Caolain Duibh, a fair-sized burn that descends a steep-sided gully from the upper slopes of Beinn Toaig. Cross the burn and look out for a small path about 20m beyond the ford; it is not shown on any map and is very easy to miss. The path rises up a steeply angled shoulder, with a substantial drop into the Allt Caolain Duibh on the right. Above 550m, the path zigzags up the steepest slopes; above 700m, it crosses less steep ground with grass and scattered rocks. Fine views of Stob Ghabhar improve with gaining height. The path becomes fainter and intermittent on crossing loose rocks, but the route to the bouldery summit (945m) with its 1m-high cairn is straightforward. From the top, there are wonderful views of Stob Ghabhar, Clach Leathad, Meall a' Bhuiridh, Bidean nam Bian and the Bridge of Orchy hills.

Return to the car park by the same route. Alternatively, Stob Ghabhar may be added to the day (allow two to three hours more), but the route described here is not recommended in wet or wintry conditions. Descend the rocky, west-pointing ridge of Stob a' Choire Odhair to the 668m col at the head of Coire Toaig. From there, ascend 130m to the foot of the steep northern flank of Stob Ghabhar's Aonach Eagach ridge; a shallow, grassy rake with an occasional path rises steeply for 130m to the ridge. Follow the Aonach Eagach (not as notched as its name suggests) westwards over the top of Couloir Buttress, down to a dip, then over a narrow section. The ridge levels out and curves north-wards (this section is often spectacularly corniced in winter), then follows an old fence line upwards to the rock-strewn summit (1090m). Superb views include Coirein Lochan and the sweeping northern and western ridges of the mountain.

The shortest route down from Stob Ghabhar returns to the eastern end of the level section of ridge between Stob Ghabhar and Aonach Eagach (gr NN234453) then descends steep slopes to the south-east, crossing Allt Toaig just north of the forest edge.

16

BLACK MOUNT HILLS

Grand peaks proudly guarding the entrance to Glen Etive

Parking: Glencoe Ski Centre, gr NN266525
Distance: 10km
Height Gain: 1120m
Time: 5½–7 hours
Terrain: Grassy or stony slopes or ridges, occasional steep broken crags, paths in places
Standard: Moderate to difficult
OS Maps: Ben Nevis, Fort William & Glen Coe (1:50,000 Landranger sheet 41), Glen Coe & Glen Etive (1:25,000 Explorer sheet 384)

At the beautiful Lochan na h-Achlaise on Rannoch Moor, the Black Mount hills of Meall a' Bhuiridh and Creise create a perfect background and fine reflections on calm days. The safest and easiest way to Creise involves traversing Meall a' Bhuiridh twice. The alternative is ascending Sron na Creise from the northern end of Glen Etive, but this is not advised as it is steep and loose, with some unpleasant scrambling high up.

Turn off the A82 Glasgow–Fort William road 1km east of Kingshouse Hotel and follow the single-track road to Glencoe Ski Centre (formerly White Corries), where there is a huge car park. Keep right of the chairlift and follow the road into an upper parking area. Just beyond the two buildings, at the head of this area, ascend a steep bank and follow a footpath just to the right of the chairlift. Beyond a grassy section, cross a small burn and ascend increasingly steep slopes between this burn and a larger one with small waterfalls to the right. The gravel path includes very steep, stony and bouldery sections, with some patches of exposed rock. After passing underneath the chairlift, with the left-hand burn immediately on the left, the path becomes grassier and the gradient gradually eases. The path becomes gravelly again, passes underneath the chairlift then keeps right of two buildings (including a skier's cafe), with some

Clach Leathad and Meall a' Bhuiridh from Rannoch Moor

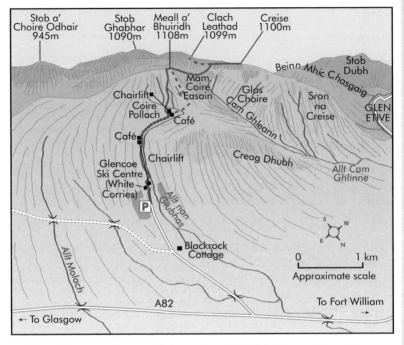

wooden sections over soft ground. Follow a gradually rising gravel track on the right-hand side of a snow fence towards some buildings at the back of Coire Pollach. The largest wooden hut is a cafe; there is also a ski school and the turning point at the lower end of the 'Cliffhanger Chairlift'.

Hop across the burn and pass underneath the chairlift. Keep left of a second burn and a ski tow but keep right of a small, craggy gully and the chairlift. Ascend straight uphill on steep grass and heather to slopes where a path zigzags between outcrops. As the gradient eases near the top of the ski tow, the ground becomes stonier and tedious, and two huts will be seen to the left. A line of large blue posts, one with a curious sign reading 'Happy Valley', leads up a long, stone-and-boulder slope to the half-metre-high cairn on the bouldery summit of Meall a' Bhuiridh (1108m). There are great views of Rannoch Moor from the top.

Continue west-south-west down a stony ridge towards the 932m col, Mam Coire Easain; it is broad and bouldery at first but becomes better defined lower down. The ascent of Creise begins easily enough but it soon becomes steep, broken and loose, with outcrops that are often damp. Crampons and ice axe may be required in full winter conditions. Although a path follows the easiest line, hands may occasionally be required for balance, with a particularly steep 20m-high section at the top. A small cairn (1070m) on a small bump on the plateau between Creise and Clach Leathad marks the route. Turn right (north) on a path across easy mixed grass and stones for Creise, descend gradually to a 1060m col, then continue northwards to the double-topped summit (both cairned), with grass and small outcrops. The highest point (1100m), marked by a 1m-high cairn on an outcrop, is the northernmost. The views of Bidean nam Bian and Buachaille Etive Mor are particularly fine from here.

Return to the car park by following the upward route. From the 1070m 'top', it is also possible to take a short detour southwards to a col (1033m), then ascend mixed grass and rocks to the bouldery summit of Clach Leathad (1099m), where there is a large cairn. Take care on the descent from the 1070m top to Mam Coire Easain. From Meall a' Bhuiridh, the stony north ridge (west of the skiing area) gives an easy descent, with grassy flanks low down. At around 750m, bear right (east) into Coire Pollach and join the upward route.

17

BEN STARAV GROUP

A majestic summit overlooking placid Loch Etive

Parking: Glen Etive (Coileitir track end), gr NN136468

Distance: 12km

Height Gain: 1110m

Time: 7–9 hours

Terrain: Gravel track; boggy/gravel/stony paths; grassy/stony/bouldery ridges

Standard: Moderate to difficult

OS Maps: Glen Orchy & Loch Etive (1:50,000 Landranger sheet 50), Loch Etive & Glen Orchy (1:25,000 Explorer sheet 377)

The lower part of Glen Etive is dominated by the impressive Ben Starav, which soars 1078m above the fiord-like Loch Etive and faces the spectacular Trilleachan Slabs on Beinn Trilleachan. The route along the north ridge gives the finest views.

Parking spaces by Glen Etive's single-track road fill up early. There are several suitable spots around gr NN136468, where the track to Coileitir and Glenceitlein descends a steep bank (locked gate, bypass on foot). The track crosses grassy moorland with some trackside trees to reach a bridge over River Etive, with an impressive pool under the bridge. Cross the bridge, keep right at the junction 100m further on, then pass Coileitir cottage and its outbuildings. The path crosses boggy ground with the help of a few wooden sleepers then follows the Etive's bank for about 300m.

Turn left onto a footpath following the left bank of the Allt Mheuran to a bridge, cross this and continue gradually uphill, close to the attractive tree-lined burn with its pink granite boulders, slabs and little waterfalls. Beyond zigzags on steeper ground, the path keeps left along the base of Ben Starav's northern ridge but a rather eroded, hill-walkers' path trends right up the broad ridge itself. This path ascends steep and unrelenting grassy slopes with occasional rocks and outcrops, although the

Ben Starav dominates lower Glen Etive

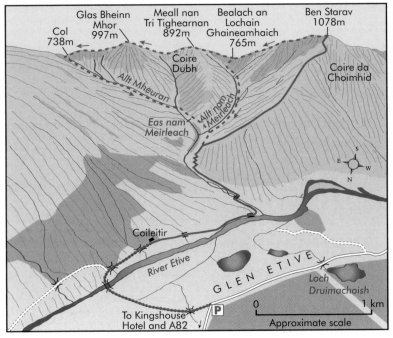

gradient eases above the 400m level. At a small, craggy outcrop on the ridge at 560m, keep to the right on steep grass. Above the outcrop, at 580m, there is a less steep area; beyond this, a fairly obvious path leads straight up the centre of the now well-defined ridge, very steep for 220m of ascent. The ridge widens and flattens out at 860m, with stones becoming much more prevalent. There is a rise of 40m then the ridge becomes more level and well-defined, with precipitous cliffs on the left. At the next steep section (950m), the path through the rocks keeps right, climbing steadily and regaining the ridge where it narrows at 1000m. This section is very steep and slippery, with lots of granite boulders to negotiate; keep to the ridge crest. The summit (1078m), which appears suddenly, has a moderately sized cairn of granite blocks; the triangulation pillar has disappeared. Wide-ranging views include Ben Nevis and Bidean nam Bian (northwards), Glas Bheinn Mhor and Stob Ghabhar (eastwards), and Ben Cruachan (southwards).

Either return to Glen Etive by the north ridge or take the interesting ridge over Stob Choire Dheirg (1068m). Descend southwards (about 25m), continue across almost level ground to the 1068m top then descend north-east-wards to the 1020m top, down and along an arete as narrow as 1m, with a crest of granite blocks. The ridge path continues eastwards, dropping steadily on mixed grass and rocks to a col, Bealach an Lochain Ghaineamhaich (765m). The easiest way down to Glen Etive is to follow a path descending steep ground to the left (north), into Coire Lochain Ghaineamhaich. This path consists of worn 'stairs' in places but it improves lower down; keep left of the burn and connect with the reasonably good Allt nam Meirleach stalkers path, which ultimately leads to the Allt Mheuran bridge.

On long summer days, there may be time to continue over Meall nan Tri Tighearnan (892m) and Glas Bheinn Mhor (997m). This route adds up to two hours to the walking time, with 300m more climbing and an extra 4km distance. A gravelly path goes along the mainly pleasant grassy ridges but the descent to the 738m col east of Glas Bheinn Mhor is quite steep and stony. There is a path on the north (right) side of the Allt Mhueran, but it is usually wet. Cross to the left side of the Allt Mhueran well above Eas nam Meirleach (the Robbers' Waterfall) to link with a path leading to the Allt nam Meirleach descent path from Ben Starav.

18

BEINN TRILLEACHAN

Extraordinary rock formations on a unique mountain

Parking: Head of Loch Etive, gr
NN111453
Distance: 9km
Height Gain: 1000m
Time: 5½–6½ hours
Terrain: Boggy path, craggy/grassy
hillsides, slabs
Standard: Difficult
OS Maps: Glen Orchy & Loch Etive
(1:50,000 Landranger sheets 50),
Loch Etive & Glen Orchy and Glen Coe
& Glen Etive (1:25,000 Explorer sheets
377 and 384)

The smooth granite Trilleachan Slabs overlook the head of Loch Etive and attract rock climbers from around the world. Although less well known, the hill above the slabs (Beinn Trilleachan) is distinctly unusual and gives a tough walk that is fine in summer but not advised in severe winter conditions.

Follow the single-track road down attractive Glen Etive from the A82 near Kingshouse Hotel. On reaching Loch Etive, about 500m before the end of the road, park on the left (south-east) in an area used by wild campers (gr NN111453). There is a particularly fine view of the slabs from this lovely spot.

A boggy path follows the edge of a larch plantation to the north-north-west; it gradually becomes steeper with ankle- or knee-deep swamps a frequent hazard. Above 70m, steeper ground includes some drier sections of bracken but it is generally very wet with scattered granite boulders amongst long grass and bog myrtle. At 180m, the persistently boggy path keeps left of some outcrops then continues uphill with a more gradual gradient. Views of the two Buachailles and Stob Dubh are particularly fine. On the left, the steep, craggy flank of Meall nan Gobhar has a pleasant cover of scattered trees but the gradient looks intimidating. Continue west-north-west across boggy ground above the plantation's fence.

The River Etive delta from Beinn Trilleachan

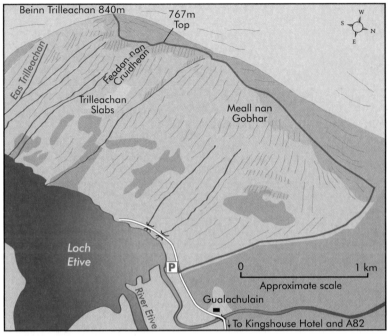

At gr NN105463, turn left off the path and zigzag steeply upwards through long grass with bog myrtle, scattered boulders and patchy slab. The gradient eases slightly then increases again, with small crags between 430m and 480m. Look for an intermittent path just left of a dead tree and follow it upwards on steep grass between outcrops. Between 480m and 600m, there is less steep ground with reasonably dry grass, occasional outcrops and sections of slab that can be crossed on foot. There is a great view of River Etive from a small flat area at 600m. Above 600m, gentle uphill slopes lead to a pond; continue on steeper grass slopes with some heather and a scuffed path. Above 710m, the gradient eases with intermittent slab, small outcrops and a scuffed path across grass, deer grass and heather. Beyond a vertical-sided gully at 730m, ascend to a 450m-long, gently sloping area giving very good walking on a mix of granite slabs, grass and heather. The 767m top, marked with a half-metre-high cairn, gives great views of Glen Etive, Ben Starav and Ben Cruachan.

The main dome-like summit of Beinn Trilleachan lies just over 1km to the south-west, but the route is neither easy nor obvious. From the 767m top, the descent south-west to the 693m col at the head of Feadan nan Cruidhean is quite tricky, with slabs and short, vertical faces to negotiate. Intermittent paths descend to the right (west) but there are awkward sections low down so it's best to keep left initially. Head southwards from the 767m cairn and descend between broken slabs and boulders, zigzagging when required. A path heads across broken ground down to the 693m col, following a shelf slanting downwards to the right (west). Leave the shelf and cross outcrops and slabs to reach a 1½m-high wall just above the col; it's exposed on the left (with a narrow ledge) but there is an easier way 10m to the right.

A path follows the broad ridge south-south-west from the col, rising gradually then vanishing in an area of flat slab with occasional juniper. Descend around 10m to a dip then ascend the summit dome; it is mainly grassy with some slab and a path at first but the gradient eases and the path disappears. Steeper grass with an indistinct path leads to an area of mixed grass, slab and occasional outcrops. At the summit (840m), which is mainly grassy with some broken slab, there is a well-built, 1½m-high cairn and great views of the two Buachailles, Ben Starav and Ben Cruachan.

Return to Glen Etive by the upward route.

19

BEINN FHIONNLAIDH

Breathtaking combination of mountain and coastal scenery

Parking: Elleric, Glen Creran, gr NN036489

Distance: 14km

Height Gain: 960m

Time: 4½–6 hours

Terrain: Roads and tracks for 2km, then mainly pathless grassy slopes and ridges with patchy rock

Standard: Moderate

OS Maps: Glen Orchy & Loch Etive (1:50,000 Landranger sheet 50), Glen Coe (1:25,000 Explorer sheet 384)

Of the two Munros named Beinn Fhionnlaidh, this one – which lies in Glen Creran, between Oban and Fort William, just off the A828 – is far south of its namesake at the remote western end of Loch Mullardoch in the north-west Highlands. It is a magnificent hill with a curious whaleback shape, consisting of metamorphic phyllites and mica-schists, with a summit that cannot be seen from its western end. Look out for golden eagles and mountain hares during the walk.

The route from Glen Creran is recommended compared to the steeper and partly forested approach from Glen Etive. Drive to Glen Creran and leave vehicles in the car park at the end of the public road. Follow the private asphalt road on the right, past the cottage at Elleric and onwards to Glenure House. Before reaching Glenure House (clearly a landlord's property), take the left-hand track behind the farmhouse on the left and immediately pass through a sheepfank. The track crosses a burn just before reaching stands of pine trees; turn right shortly after the bridge and follow a steep and muddy four-wheel-drive track through the forest and onto the open hill above. The track ends abruptly in a boggy area. Look out for a faint footpath continuing beyond the bog, keeping a

Ben Starav (right) and its neighbours, from Lochan Cairn Deirg, Beinn Fhionnlaidh

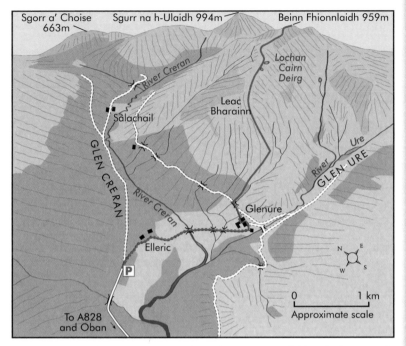

Sgorr a' Choise 663m — Sgurr na h-Ulaidh 994m — Beinn Fhionnlaidh 959m — Lochan Cairn Deirg — Leac Bharainn — River Creran — Salachail — GLEN CRERAN — River Creran — Glenure — River Ure GLEN URE — Elleric — P — To A828 and Oban

0 — 1 km — Approximate scale

fairly obvious little ridge to the right. This path heads uphill and almost due east, along the southern flank of Beinn Fhionnlaidh. At around gr NN057485, turn off this path and strike directly north-east up the hillside, towards the area named Leac Bharainn on the Landranger map. The grassy slopes offer easy and fairly dry conditions underfoot.

At around 400m, this route reaches the broad main ridge of Beinn Fhionnlaidh, which is carpeted with short grass and heather and is a delight for walkers. At 630m, the route passes just north of Lochan Cairn Deirg, a curious 'hanging lochan', with great views of the Ben Starav group beyond. Steeper slopes and a patchy path lead past a salmon-pink, felsite sill at around 700m. Beyond 800m, there is a wide but undulating ridge with grassy patches and a variety of oddly inclined and broken schist slabs. There are good views of Ben Nevis, peeking out from between the closer Glen Coe hills. Above 850m, there is more stony ground with mixed grass and moss, slabs and loose rocks, but it is still straightforward walking. With such gradual gradients, it seems a long way to the summit (959m), where there is a cylindrical triangu-

lation point surrounded by a circular stone wall. Beware of the steep northern cliffs of the mountain, especially in misty or white-out conditions. Continue eastwards a little for marvellous views down the eastern ridge of the hill, with Buachaille Etive Mor and Creise prominent in the background.

The views from the summit are amongst the best from any of the Munros on Scotland's western seaboard. Looking south-west down Loch Creran and across the Firth of Lorne towards Mull is particularly fine. Close at hand are the significant peaks of Beinn a' Bheithir (north-west), Fraochaidh (west), Beinn Sgulaird (south-west) and Bidean nam Bian (north-east). On a clear day, the scene includes an impressive selection of Scotland's finest hills. Look out for the Sgurr of Eigg, the Paps of Jura, Carn Eighe and Mam Soul, Ben Alder, Ben Lawers, Knoydart's Sgurr na Ciche, Blaven on Skye, Ben More on Mull, and the Strathfarrar hills behind Mullach nan Coirean in the Mamores.

Return to the car park by retracing steps down the western ridge of the hill, which gives great views of sea lochs, islands and mountains all the way down.

20

BEINN A' CHRULAISTE

Awe-inspiring views of Buachaille Etive Mor

Parking: Kingshouse Hotel, gr NN260546

Distance: 8km

Height Gain: 610m

Time: 3½–4½ hours

Terrain: Path, grassy and stony hillsides and ridges

Standard: Easy

OS Maps: Ben Nevis, Fort William & Glen Coe (1:50,000 Landranger sheet 41), Glen Coe (1:25,000 Explorer sheet 384)

Pudding-shaped Beinn a' Chrulaiste can hardly be described as an attractive-looking mountain but the summit area provides phenomenal views, including the wide expanse of Rannoch Moor and the spectacular front end of Buachaille Etive Mor.

Leave cars in the large car park by the Kingshouse Hotel, just off the Glasgow–Fort William A82 road. The hotel – affectionately known to climbers as 'The Kingy' and one of Scotland's oldest established inns – was built in the early 1750s and used as a barracks by the King's troops following the disastrous 1745 Jacobite rebellion. Cross the bridge (now closed to vehicles) over the river just north of the hotel; the river bank is used as a wild camping area by walkers and climbers. The single-track road beyond the bridge was formerly the main Glasgow–Fort William road (opened in 1933). Follow the road for 250m beyond the bridge, as far as the right-angled bend where the track to Black Corries Lodge branches off to the right (east). A sign here indicates 'Rannoch by Loch Laidon'.

Pass through the gate for Black Corries Lodge then, facing towards the lodge, turn left (north) and follow a very boggy path for around 600m across moorland, towards the Allt a' Bhalaich. The path, which continues along the left (west) bank of this burn, becomes narrow as it passes through varied terrain including boggy and muddy areas but also more pleasant

Beinn a' Chrulaiste from Buachaille Etive Mor

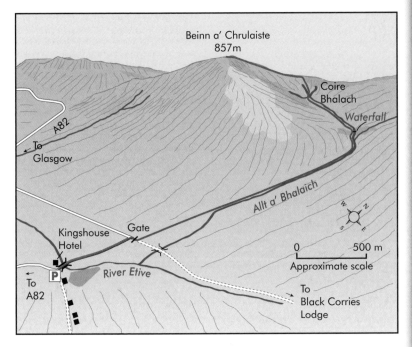

sections of short grass and heather. The Allt a' Bhalaich itself is a lively burn that descends granite steps and slabs and there is a waterfall at the lip of the corrie (430m).

From the lip of the corrie it is possible to head west and ascend the steep, eastern flank directly to the summit of Beinn a' Chrulaiste, but this is very hard work and is not recommended. The route into Coire Bhalach is more pleasant, the path following a rushing burn with many small waterslides and falls. Once on the flat floor of the corrie (550m), an interesting place of grassy areas and scattered large rocks, the path fades out. The steep and craggy eastern face of Beinn a' Chrulaiste rises abruptly on the left. Ascend moderately steep heather and grass slopes straight ahead (north-west) to reach the foot of the hill's broad north ridge (at gr NN248575). There is some good walking on short grass and heather but once the left turn is made to ascend the ridge there is steeper ground with loose rock, followed by easier and more pleasant patchy rock slab, gravel, moss and grass.

Although there is no path on the ridge, the route heads almost due south and is easy to follow. The ridge becomes more level on approaching the stony summit, where there is a partial ring cairn of granite rocks around a cylindrical triangulation pillar (857m). There is also another 1m-high cairn about 20m east-south-east of the triangulation pillar.

Views are exceptional, with Buachaille Etive Mor dominating the scene to the south-west, Creise and the White Corries ski area (south), Glen Coe (west) and the Mamores and Ben Nevis (north). Eastwards, there is the broad and desolate Rannoch Moor, a treeless wilderness of lochs, rocks and heather. On a clear day, look for Schiehallion on the eastern horizon.

Although descent is easiest by the upward route, there are other options. The steep, eastern flank is the quickest way down, but it is not particularly pleasant. There is also the western flank via Stob Beinn a' Chrulaiste, but it is rather steep below 600m and return to Kingshouse Hotel requires a 4km hike along the West Highland Way. Alternatively, head for the col at the head of Coire Bhalach (gr NN253575) via the upward route, then continue over the two tops of Meall Bhalach; ground conditions are wet, rough and hard work in places. The direct descent to Kingshouse Hotel from Meall Bhalach's eastern top (705m) is fairly steep but straightforward. Allow an extra hour to descend by this route.

21

BUACHAILLE ETIVE MOR

Superb ridge traverse on the queen of Scottish mountains

Parking: Altnafeadh, gr NN221563

Distance: 13km

Height Gain: 1170m

Time: 8–9 hours

Terrain: Varied paths including steep and loose mountain ridge routes, some scrambling

Standard: Moderate to difficult

OS Maps: Ben Nevis, Fort William & Glen Coe (1:50,000 Landranger sheet 41), Glen Coe (1:25,000 Explorer sheet 384)

Affectionately known as the Buachaille, this beautiful mountain's sharp summit is an impressive sight from Kingshouse on Rannoch Moor. There are Munros at either end of the 4½km-long ridge, a delightful traverse giving some of the best hill walking in Scotland.

Leave cars by the A82 Glasgow–Fort William road at Altnafeadh then follow a gravel track to a wooden footbridge over the River Coupall, cross this and continue past the SMC's Lagangarbh cottage on a gravel or stony path. At a junction, keep right then rise with increasing gradient to ford Allt Coire na Tulaich (at 400m; normally easy). Beyond the burn, there is a small rock step followed by stone stairs. Continue into the impressive Coire na Tulaich, with cliffs on either side of a section of dry stream bed, steep sections of stone stairs and boulders, and a path changing from one side of the burn to the other. Two short, easy scrambles on the right lead to a ledge 10m above the burn, with sections of boulders and broken slab. Cross a small burn, scramble up a broken slab and ascend more stone stairs. At 600m, leave the path and traverse easily right on mixed grass and stones, cross the small burn again (look out for butterwort) and pass between outcrops to reach a flat area below an imposing crag at gr NN215548.

Buachaille Etive Mor from Meall a' Bhuiridh

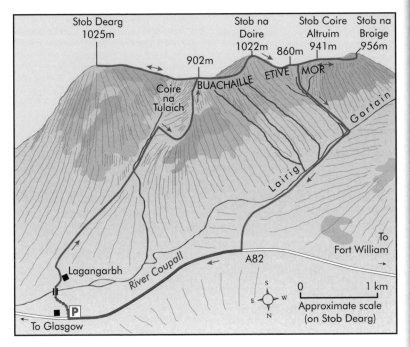

Keep right (west) of this crag then ascend steep grass to pick up a gravel path. An easy scramble leads to a short level section with rock outcrops (740m). Scramble occasionally on pink-coloured rock outcrops and easily cross broken slabs with loose rock to reach the mainly grassy 902m top. Keep left of the cairn on rough, stony ground and descend to the stony col at the head of Coire na Tulaich (two large cairns). A rough, stony path continues eastwards towards Stob Dearg, with vast amounts of pink and grey rhyolite scree littering the hillside between broken outcrops and slabs. The path improves, rising past several large cairns and crossing a stony area to reach a half-metre-high cairn on the 1022m false summit. A stony ridge with outcrops, as little as 2m wide, leads to an open area with the 1m-high summit cairn (1025m, gr NN224543) and adjacent ring shelter. There are great views down Glen Coe and northwards to the Mamores and Ben Nevis. Carefully continue a little further east for a fantastic view down the cliff face to the Crowberry Tower.

Return westwards to the 902m top, keep left of the cairn and pick up a good ridge path across grassy ground with some slabs and outcrops. Beyond the tiny pond at the Feadan

Ban col, cross a bump and an easy rock step, then follow a stony path up the boulder-strewn shoulder of Stob na Doire (1022m, cairn). The grassy top is another great viewpoint. A steep path descends the bouldery west ridge with zigzags, improving low down where there is a grassy col (820m). Another steep path leads to the 860m top then a steady rise over grass and scattered rocks leads to Stob Coire Altruim (941m). The ridge to Stob na Broige (956m, 1m-high cairn and adjacent ring shelter), the Buachaille's second Munro, is well defined and straightforward, with grass and scattered rocks and a moderately steep pull to the summit.

Return to the dip west of the 860m top (half-metre-high cairn) and descend a steep gravel path into Coire Altruim. Straightforward rock steps at around 660m lead to some steep scrambling just left of a waterfall at 610m. Cross the main burn (580m) then follow a tedious path with stone stairs down to the Lairig Gartain, cross the main burn there and pick up a poor peaty, boggy, rough and eroded path heading for the A82. There is no let-up, the final section is rough and unpleasant but, once on the road, it is an easy walk back to Altnafeadh.

22

BIDEAN NAM BIAN

Glen Coe's finest peaks and corries

Parking: Glen Coe, NN168569
Distance: 9km
Height Gain: 1300m
Time: 6–8 hours
Terrain: Gravel paths, rough mountain paths, steep grassy or bouldery hillsides and ridges
Standard: Difficult
OS Maps: Ben Nevis, Fort William & Glen Coe (1:50,000 Landranger sheet 41), Glen Coe (1:25,000 Explorer sheet 384)

Glen Coe's highest peak, Bidean nam Bian, lies amidst a multi-topped massif including vertical rock walls, narrow ridges and some very rough terrain. There are few easy options to reach the summit, the most straightforward being via Stob Coire nan Lochan, a fine peak visible from the glen.

Leave cars in the large parking area by the A82 Glasgow–Fort William road at gr NN168569 and descend from its south-western corner towards the former road through Glen Coe, now just a gravel track. Cross the track and continue on a gravel footpath that heads towards Coire nan Lochan. A wooden footbridge leads across a deep pool in the River Coe; a steadily rising path across grass leads to a steeper ascent with occasional stairs and flagstones. Above 190m the path makes a gradual, rising traverse to the right and, beyond some flagstones, steep, stone stairs lead to another gradual section. Cross an open and rather eroded gully then ascend around 100m on sections of steep, stone stairs separated by stretches of gravel. More gravel or bouldery sections and stone stairs lead steeply into the depths of the impressive corrie, with soaring cliffs on both sides and fine views of Stob Coire nan Lochan ahead.

At 500m, the path approaches the burn then crosses a broken slab near a 5m-high waterfall with a plunge pool. Keep left and ascend a steep slab (no scrambling required) to pick up a stony

Bidean nam Bian from Stob Coire nan Lochan

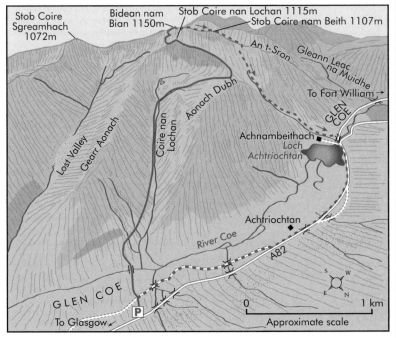

or gravel path above. The path, which passes pleasant waterfalls, includes sections of stone stairs; above 550m, it is badly eroded and boulder-strewn in many places. At 620m, just beyond a fork in the main Coire an Lochan burn, leave the path, cross the main burn and follow the left bank of the right branch, which rises steeply to the west. A gravel or bouldery path leads upwards to an easy 1½m-high rock step at 730m. Above the rock step, the path disappears on easier grass between boulders. Continue north-west towards the rough 856m col between Aonach Dubh and Stob Coire nan Lochan; steeper ground with some scree leads to less-steep slopes again, with grass, boulders and outcrops. There are great views of Stob Coire nan Lochan's cliffs on the way to the col.

From the col (gr NN150557), turn left (south-west) onto a broad, steadily rising ridge that becomes increasingly bouldery, although there are sections of path. The route passes the top of Pinnacle Buttress (taking due care, look down a gully on the left to see the 10m-high pinnacle). More boulders, outcrops and broken slab (steep in places) lead past several vertical-walled gullies to a relatively flat but boulder-strewn area at 1050m. Views of Bidean nam Bian improve on gaining height. Sections of

path may be found amongst the boulders on Stob Coire nan Lochan's steep, 50m-high summit cone, which is crowned by a 1m-high cairn (1115m). Excellent views include Bidean nam Bian, Buachaille Etive Mor, Ben Nevis and the Aonach Eagach.

To reach Bidean nam Bian, descend a broad, stony ridge south-westwards to a col at 1000m then continue upwards on a steep, well-defined bouldery ridge, with sections of path. Hands may be required for balance. At a level area (1085m), the route bears left (south), a change in direction that should be noted for any descent in misty conditions. A steep, bouldery ascent of around 60m leads to the 1½m-high cairn on the summit (1150m), an excellent perch with wonderful views including Glen Etive and the peaks of Appin.

It is advisable to return by the outward route. The steep and loose descent into the Lost Valley is not recommended. Otherwise, continue westwards over Bidean nam Bian's 1141m top and Stob Coire nam Beith, then descend steeply eastwards from Bealach An t-Sron into Coire nam Beitheach. Following the unrelenting, knee-jarring path to Glen Coe at Achnambeithach, a further 3km leads back up the glen to the car park.

23

AONACH EAGACH

Mainland Scotland's most exciting high-level ridge

Parking: Glen Coe, NN173568
Distance: 10km (3km by road)
Height Gain: 1240m (90m by road)
Time: 7–9 hours
Terrain: Steep paths and pathless hillsides; narrow grassy, stony and rock ridges
Standard: Very difficult; scrambling and 'easy' rock climbing; mountaining skills required in winter conditions (grade II/III)

OS Maps: Ben Nevis, Fort William & Glen Coe (1:50,000 Landranger sheet 41), Glen Coe (1:25,000 Explorer sheet 384)

Glen Coe's exciting Aonach Eagach, the most difficult ridge connecting peaks on the Scottish mainland, involves sections of persistent scrambling and low-grade rock climbing. Walkers attempting the ridge must be competent, experienced and agile; otherwise, ascend Am Bodach only.

Leave cars in a small parking area by the A82 eastbound at gr NN173568, or use the larger Lost Valley car park 250m west. Ascend steeply on a good gravel or rock-paved path, with some easy rock outcrops, steep, stone stairs and wonderful views southwards to Stob Coire nan Lochan and the Lost Valley. Keep right at a junction (450m); follow the path descending 5m to the Allt Ruigh then rise into Coire an Ruigh. Cross scree and ascend through easy rock outcrops and scree to a reasonable path that leads to the burn junction at gr NN175576. Keep to the left bank of the left branch on a steep, stony path; a steeper gravel/scree section ascends the final 20m to the ridge, with a 1m-high cairn at 816m (gr NN172582). There is a great view north, across the red-coloured screes of Garbh Bheinn to the grey scree on the Mamores, and the huge bulk of Ben Nevis behind.

Turn left on a clear path ascending a well-defined ridge with outcrops of hard, purple-coloured andesite lava. This ridge widens to become a rocky flank. Avoid a flat, mainly grassy

Looking west along the Aonach Eagach

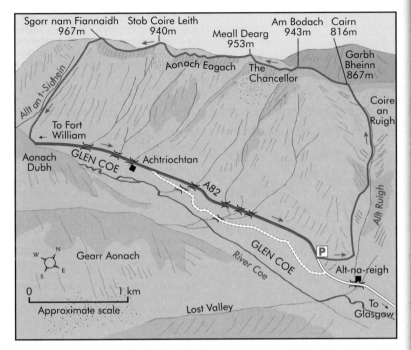

area on the left, with a 1m-high cairn; keep right and rise 5m to the 1m-high cairn on the summit of Am Bodach (943m). The view southward into deep gullies and across the trench of Glen Coe is spectacular.

A gravel path then leads westward along a narrow grass-covered ridge, as little as 1m wide and with gullies on both sides. Rise 3m, then descend steeply; keep right, initially an easy scramble then a gravel path. Keep right again, descending a near-vertical 15m-high cliff by means of precarious but clean ledges, with continuous scrambling. Keep left at the bottom, easier for a bit then tricky to bypass a block, with small holds and great exposure. Easier ground leads to the col at 866m, then a wider ridge of grass and scattered rock leads to the Chancellor, a top at 924m. A steep, loose descent to another col (896m) is followed by a more gradual rise to the stony summit of the Munro Meall Dearg (953m, cairn).

From Meall Dearg, a broad ridge descends gradually westwards (500m horizontally), then the fun begins again. Descend sharply to an airy rocky col at 880m then traverse the ridge on the Glen Coe side, where there are good holds for both hands and feet. An impressive, though easy, scramble leads up a chimney for around

10m to an exposed ridge with cliffs on both sides. Scramble over or past the pinnacles that follow; an unpleasant 'nose' is followed by another airy col with an exposed ridge (path just off the northern side). Scramble past an exposed pinnacle in the col then follow an extraordinary wall-like ridge only 20cm wide. The next pinnacle involves 15m of 'moderate' rock climbing if tackled directly; it's slightly easier on the left. More scrambling leads downwards then cross another pinnacle before ascending to Stob Coire Leith (940m), with great views back along the ridge. Allow at least $1\frac{1}{4}$ hours from Meall Dearg to Stob Coire Leith.

A broad but well-defined ridge with a good path goes westwards, down to a dip (870m), then it rises to the triangulation point on the Munro Sgorr nam Fiannaidh (967m). Descending to Glen Coe via the loose path immediately west of Clachaig Gully is considered dangerous and is not advised. It is best to descend in a south-westerly direction from Sgorr nam Fiannaidh for 70m (on scree), then go southward, mainly on grass between rock outcrops and small crags, down to the A82. A 3km walk up the glen leads back to the start.

24

RING OF STEALL

First-class ridge-walking in the heart of the Mamores

Parking: Head of Glen Nevis road, gr NN168691

Distance: 13km

Height Gain: 1600m

Time: 8–10 hours

Terrain: Gravel paths, steep gradients, narrow ridges, some scrambling

Standard: Strenuous, difficult

OS Maps: Ben Nevis, Fort William & Glen Coe (1:50,000 Landranger sheet 41), Ben Nevis (1:25,000 Explorer sheet 392)

The Mamores, characterised by steep flanks and narrow, interconnecting ridges, are rightly considered among the finest hills in Scotland. The central section, which can be broken into two or three separate days, can also be completed in a natural circuit, the so-called 'Ring of Steall'. In winter, sections of this traverse require mountaineering skills and are therefore not recommended for novices.

Drive to the head of Glen Nevis and follow the scenic footpath to Steall Meadows as described for the Ben Nevis walk. If the River Nevis is high, cross the wire bridge to Steall Cottage, which may be very difficult for people with poor balance and limited reach (otherwise, use the stepping stones just upstream). Cross Allt Coire a' Mhail below the thundering An Steall waterfall (no bridge), then pick up a path heading eastwards for 250m. This path turns right into Coire Chadha Chaoruinn and ascends steeply, with very tight zigzags. Cross the burn in this corrie, then more zigzags lead to a lofty perch at 630m, with great views over the An Steall waterfall. Although not shown on any map, a path leads directly up the steep north-west flank of An Gearanach, with easier ground above 850m. The path goes over a minor grassy top then continues straight up the scree-covered summit cone to the Munro's summit cairn at 982m. Views are magnificent, with Ben

Ben Nevis, An Gearanach and Aonach Beag from An Garbhanach

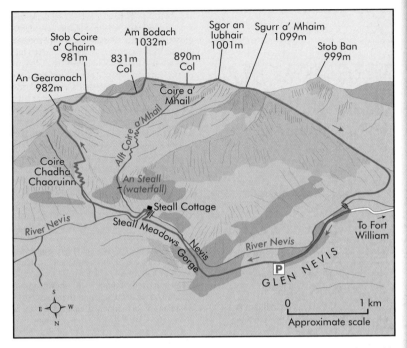

Nevis, Carn Mor Dearg, the Aonachs and the Grey Corries to the north, and the Mamores stretching to the south, east and west.

From An Gearanach, a narrow ridge of quartzite blocks, slabs and little pinnacles descends to a low point at 950m then rises to An Garbhanach (975m), with some airy sections of easy scrambling. It is best to keep on the eastern (left) side of the crest. A steep scree path descends southwards from An Garbhanach, slightly on the right (west) side of the ridge, to reach the broad Bealach a' Chadha Riabhach (857m), then continues upwards to the cairn on top of the second Munro, Stob Coire a' Chairn (981m). Follow the main ridge of the Mamores south-west over easier ground, up and over the 909m top, which has an excellent narrow ridge. Continue south-west along a grassy ridge flanked with scree, to the 831m col below the Munro Am Bodach. Although it's not too difficult to negotiate the rocky ridge directly towards the 1032m summit, the final 20m is very steep, loose and slippery, so take care in wet weather and in winter.

The broad ridge west of Am Bodach is stony and rather unpleasant for walking. Beyond a col at 890m, the ridge ascends to the cairn on Sgor an Iubhair (1001m), formerly a Munro but now just a round, baldy dome with little to recommend it. Proceed north-west-wards, down steep stony slopes to a 924m col, then head northwards along the superb, narrow, grassy spine of the Devil's Ridge, over the top of Stob Coire a' Mhail (991m), past several rock pinnacles and onwards to Bealach a' Chip at 940m. The Devil's Ridge, which may be corniced in winter, is mostly very easy walking; the pinnacles are easily turned by descent on the west (left). Do not attempt to traverse the eastern base of the pinnacles, since the route deteriorates into unpleasant ledges covered in loose rock.

From Bealach a' Chip, there is a 160m haul to the top of the Munro Sgurr a' Mhaim (1099m) but, fortunately, this side has little of the ball-bearing-like quartzite scree found elsewhere on the mountain. From the summit's ring shelter, follow the north-west shoulder downwards, towards Achriabhach (Glen Nevis). Quartzite scree soon gives way to steep grass slopes but there is a reasonable path. A little distance can be saved by keeping right near the base of the hill, then heading for the bridge over River Nevis at gr NN158684. A further 1km along the road leads uphill to the car park.

25

NA GRUAGAICHEAN
and BINNEIN MOR

Magnificent views from well-defined ridges and peaks

Parking: Mamore Lodge Hotel, Kinlochleven, gr NN186630

Distance: 13km

Height Gain: 1160m

Time: 5–6 hours

Terrain: Track, stalkers paths, well-defined and narrow ridges

Standard: Moderate

OS Maps: Ben Nevis, Fort William & Glen Coe (1:50,000 Landranger sheet 41), Ben Nevis (1:25,000 Explorer sheet 392)

The highest peak in the Mamores, Binnein Mor, is connected to its neighbour Na Gruagaichean with a fine ridge that gives wonderful walking and great views.

About 1km west of Kinlochleven a private, single-track road turns off the B863 Kinlochleven–North Ballachulish road and climbs 200m to Mamore Lodge Hotel (parking charge). Take the gravel track on the left, turn right, avoid Stalker's Cottage by a footpath on the right, then continue through birch woods to the bridge over Allt Coire na Ba (gr NN191639). Cross the bridge, then turn left and follow a gravel track (gate) past sheep pens and into grassy Coire na Ba for 1¼km. There are several minor burn crossings and a steep section with a waterfall on the left.

The track becomes a fairly muddy path and levels out on the corrie floor (420m). Cross a burn, follow its left-hand bank uphill then continue onwards to another burn. Beyond a strange section of tussocks, head fairly steeply upwards to the right onto a wide sloping grassy shelf, boggy and wet at first but improving further on. Continue ascending south-eastwards to a bend then turn left (north) and traverse above steep slopes and small crags. Zigzags ease progress on steep ground leading to the grassy col (783m) and great viewpoint between Stob Coire a' Chairn and Na Gruagaichean.

Binnein Beag seen from Binnein Mor

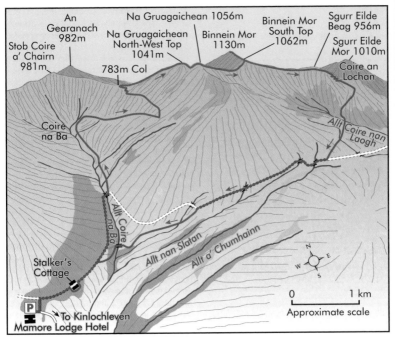

Turn right and ascend a broad grassy ridge to a flat area (850m). A steep path then zigzags eastwards, ascending patchy grass with many loose quartzite boulders. The gradient eases at 970m, with a 50m-long narrow ridge of mixed grass and quartzite blocks. More zigzags lead up the steep grass cone of Na Gruagaichean's north-west top, with slabby cliffs to the left and strange slices of mica-schist underfoot. The half-metre-high summit cairn (1041m) lies at the northern end of a near-horizontal steep-sided grass ridge around 5m wide. From the far south-east end, descend a steep, loose earthen/stony path (vertical drops on the left), avoiding a nasty rock step by keeping right then passing below it.

A loose path initially goes straight up the main summit, passing easily through a pink-coloured rock band (a felsite dyke), then keeping right through loose quartzite. Regain the loose quartzite 'ridge' on the left and ascend easily to the half-metre-high summit cairn (1056m). Look backwards for an astonishing view of the tent-like north-west top.

Eastwards, quartzite boulders and a scree path descend to an easy, but airy, almost level quartzite-boulder ridge that narrows to 1m (path on southern side). Beyond a grassy col, the ridge widens, with a gravel path rising through mixed boulders and grass to Binnein Mor's south top (1062m, small cairn). A broad, gravelly ridge heads north to the next col (1040m). The ridge narrows, steepens upward (stony), eases off (grassy), then becomes steep again with mixed grass and quartzite boulders. Binnein Mor's airy summit (1130m) has a small cairn at the southern end of a narrow quartzite boulder ridge. Views are magnificent, especially across Binnein Beag.

Return to the south top and descend the broad, grassy shoulder south-eastwards to Sgurr Eilde Beag. Either cross over this top or traverse easy moss, stone or grass slopes to reach a pink felsite dyke at gr NN221651. A half-metre-high cairn 10m below the dyke marks a good gravel path that zigzags down to meet a rough stony path connecting Coire an Lochan with the Luibeilt–Mamore Lodge track. Turn right on reaching this path and follow it steeply down to Allt Coire nan Laogh, then it is easier but a bit boggy down to the track. Continue westwards on the track as far as gr NN198633; leave the track, pass through the deer fence (gate) and follow a rough and rocky path down to Allt Coire na Ba. Cross the footbridge and ascend steeply to regain the track near Stalker's Cottage, only a short distance from the hotel.

26

BEN NEVIS and CARN MOR DEARG

An exciting route to Scotland's highest and most-visited mountain

Parking: Head of Glen Nevis road, gr NN168691

Distance: 15km (12km if excluding Carn Mor Dearg)

Height Gain: 1415m (1245m if excluding Carn Mor Dearg)

Time: 9–10 hours

Terrain: Good path in Glen Nevis, then grassy hillsides, boulder slopes and narrow ridges

Standard: Strenuous, difficult

OS Maps: Ben Nevis, Fort William & Glen Coe (1:50,000 Landranger sheet 41), Ben Nevis (1:25,000 Explorer sheet 392)

Ben Nevis – the highest mountain in Britain and known affectionately as the 'Ben' – attracts around 150,000 hikers and climbers every year, mainly via the tourist path from Achintee or Glen Nevis SYHA hostel. The more scenic and quieter alternative described here includes the optional arête (ridge) scramble to Carn Mor Dearg, the Ben's neighbour to the east. In winter conditions, when the summit and the aforementioned ridge may have dangerous snow cornices, the route is not recommended for novices.

In June 2000, the Ben and peaks to the east (including Carn Mor Dearg), were purchased by the John Muir Trust, a conservation organisation whose aims include keeping the mountain free of hotels and railways. The mountain is the core of a huge former volcano that was active around 350 million years ago; geologically, it's a ring-complex consisting mainly of quartz diorites and granites.

From Fort William, drive to the car park at the end of the Glen Nevis road and walk through the Nevis gorge as described for the Aonachs. Just before the bridge to the Old Steall ruins (gr NN187688), follow Allt Coire Giubhsachan's western bank up to the corrie's level floor at 500m. Now head easily uphill in a westerly direction for about 80m, to reach Bealach Cumhann (670m, gr NN178700; please note: the direct ascent/descent from the Nevis gorge

Ben Nevis from the Caledonian Canal basin, Corpach

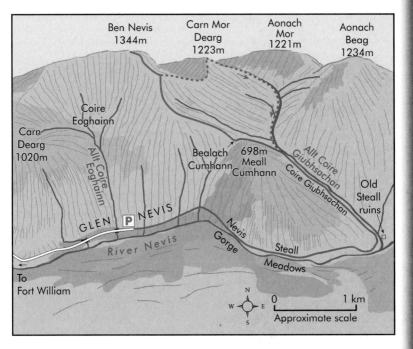

Ben Nevis 1344m
Carn Mor Dearg 1223m
Aonach Mor 1221m
Aonach Beag 1234m
Coire Eoghainn
Carn Dearg 1020m
Allt Coire Eoghainn
Bealach Cumhann
698m Meall Cumhann
Allt Coire Giubhsachan
Coire Giubhsachan
Old Steall ruins
GLEN P NEVIS
Nevis Gorge
Steall Meadows
River Nevis
To Fort William
N W E S
0 1 km
Approximate scale

is not recommended). From Bealach Cumhann, continue north-westwards up a steep shoulder – an unrelenting ascent of around 300m – reaching easier ground above 870m. The shoulder has sections of exposed rock and a maze of patches of slab and small cliffs, but grassy leads are easily followed and some sections of path may be found. The grass peters out above 1,000m and is replaced by extensive and tedious boulder fields. The route merges with the one between the Ben and the Carn Mor Dearg arête at gr NN170710, then another 200m of ascent through boulder fields leads to the summit plateau (1344m). An emergency shelter is perched atop the ruins of the former meteorological observatory, which was occupied continuously by scientists from 1883 to 1904 and even offered hotel accommodation. The curious position of the modern shelter is designed to keep it above the snow surface in midwinter. There is also a large cairn and an OS triangulation pillar. Keep clear of the edge of the precipitous, 600m-high, north-facing cliffs, which may be corniced with snow, even in summer.

Looking north-west, Loch Eil and the Corpach pulp mill can be seen, but most of Fort William is out of sight. Eastwards there are the Aonachs and the Grey Corries, while to the

south the Mamores and the Glen Coe hills are visible. On a completely clear day (unfortunately, a rare occurrence due to three hundred days of hill fog per year), the Cuillin of Skye and the Antrim hills in Ulster may be seen.

Return south-eastwards, descending to the 1150m level where there is a level section of ridge at the start of the Carn Mor Dearg arête (from here, descend to Coire Giubhsachan by the outward route if wishing to avoid the arête). Another 100m of descent leads to the lowest point on this ridge (1058m), which is narrow and very steep-sided. Sections of path below the ridge crest, mainly on the right (east), assist progress; otherwise, there are lots of granite blocks and plenty of easy scrambling on the crest itself. There are great views of the Ben's cliffs from the cairn on the tiny summit of Carn Mor Dearg (1223m) and, to the north, the pinnacle ridge of Carn Dearg Meadhonach is prominent. Continue eastwards, down a scree-covered ridge with slabby patches, to the col below Aonach Mor (830m, NN187723), then turn right and descend easily southwards into Coire Giubhsachan. Follow the burn all the way to the Old Steall ruins and return to the car park through the Nevis gorge.

27

THE AONACHS

An exhilarating circuit of two lofty Munros

Parking: Head of Glen Nevis road, gr NN168691

Distance: 15km

Height Gain: 1230m

Time: 7½–8½ hours

Terrain: Good path in Glen Nevis, then grassy or stony hillsides, very steep in places

Standard: Strenuous, difficult

OS Maps: Ben Nevis, Fort William & Glen Coe (1:50,000 Landranger sheet 41), Ben Nevis (1:25,000 Explorer sheet 392)

Collectively known as the Aonachs, Aonach Mor and Aonach Beag certainly appear impressive from Glen Spean, but their wild character is

much more apparent when seen from upper Glen Nevis. Although there is a ski-and-snowboard centre on the northern flanks of Aonach Mor (these flanks appropriately named Leac an t-Sneachda, meaning snowy slope), the route to the Aonachs from the car park in upper Glen Nevis avoids the skiing paraphernalia.

From the aforementioned car park, take the well-made footpath eastwards for about 1km, passing through extensive native woodland to reach Steall Meadows, Scotland's Shangri-La and a photographer's paradise. The path goes up and down somewhat as it contours the face of Meall Cumhann and enters the spectacular Nevis gorge; there are some small burn crossings, a section of boardwalk and a couple of easy bits of scrambling. Once on the grassy meadows, there are some very boggy sections but to compensate there are great views of the 100m-high An Steall waterfall and the impressive An Gearanach (982m) rising behind. Where the path meets River Nevis near the cable bridge and Lochaber Mountaineering Club's Steall Cottage, keep left along the river bank, then cross the upper section of the meadows to the bridge over Allt Coire Giubhsachan.

Leave the path on the far side of this bridge (by the desolate ruins of Old Steall) and follow easy, grassy slopes upwards, beside Allt Coire Giubhsachan, into the corrie of the same name.

Aonach Beag and Aonach Mor seen from Roy Bridge

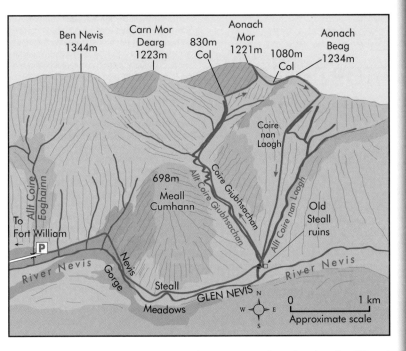

Ben Nevis 1344m
Carn Mor Dearg 1223m
830m Col
Aonach Mor 1221m
1080m Col
Aonach Beag 1234m

Coire nan Laogh

698m Meall Cumhann

Allt Coire Eoghainn

Coire Giubhsachan

Allt Coire Giubhsachan

Allt Coire nan Laogh

Old Steall ruins

To Fort William
P

River Nevis

Nevis Gorge

Steall

GLEN NEVIS

River Nevis

Steall Meadows

0   1 km
Approximate scale

N
W   E
S

Straightforward and mainly grassy walking leads across extensive grassy flats at 500m then there is a steady rise to the top of the corrie, with a final steep pull of around 100m leading to the 830m col and dry-stone-wall shelter between Carn Mor Dearg and Aonach Mor.

Look for a steep spur leading through the steep, craggy face of Aonach Mor, located east and slightly south of the col. It is possible to ascend a slippery path here for 250m, but the route is not easy to find from above so it is inadvisable for descent. There is also some loose rock so it shouldn't be attempted in poor weather or soft snow; an ice axe and crampons will be required in hard winter conditions. Once above the steep ground, at 1100m, the odd elevated southern flank of Aonach Mor suddenly provides better walking and a path leads northwards across grassy turf to the 1221m summit cairn, which sits on a broad plateau that resembles a football field more than a mountain top. Ben Nevis rises behind the graceful curves of Carn Mor Dearg to the west; southwards, Aonach Beag's dome provides foreground to the Mamores; and the scree-covered flanks of the Grey Corries extend to the east. In winter, beware of cornices on the eastern side of the summit plateau.

Return easily southwards to the 1080m col between Aonach Mor and Aonach Beag. Continue by walking south-east, initially up a steep slope with a stony path (often icy in winter), the gradient easing on the approach to the diminutive cairn on Aonach Beag's tundra-like summit at 1234m. The summit, perched near the edge of the impressive eastern cliffs and spectacular north-east ridge, provides exceptionally fine views of Ben Nevis.

Return to Steall by descending easy slopes southwards, keeping the An Aghaidh Gharbh cliffs close on the left until reaching a tiny shoulder at 1100m (gr NN200711). Avoid the potentially dangerous cliff descent eastwards to the 731m col (gr NN211706) between Aonach Beag and Sgurr Choinnich Beag. Turn west from the 1100m shoulder, then south-west along the descending Allt Coire nan Laogh, which follows an easy diagonal shelf, to reach a wet area with ponds at 800m (Coire nan Laogh, gr NN193704). Avoid the gully on the southern side of the shelf. Continue south-south-west through patches of exposed rock with good grassy leads, aiming directly for the Old Steall ruins. Return to the car park through the Nevis gorge via the main Glen Nevis footpath.

28

STOB CHOIRE CLAURIGH

The high point on the wild and rugged Grey Corries ridge

Parking: The Lairig, gr NN256788
Distance: 13km
Height Gain: 1020m
Time: 6–7 hours
Terrain: Track, grassy or stony hillsides, rough stony ridges
Standard: Moderate to difficult
OS Maps: Ben Nevis, Fort William & Glen Coe (1:50,000 Landranger sheet 41), Ben Nevis & Fort William (1:25,000 Explorer sheet 392)

The Grey Corries ridge extends eastwards for over 6km from Aonach Beag, its crest covered with boulders and broken slabs. Vast amounts of quartzite scree give the hills and their corries a grey appearance, hence the name. Great views from the ridge's highest point, Stob Choire Claurigh, include the fine peak Stob Coire na Ceannain.

From Spean Bridge on the A82, take the minor road signposted Corriechoille. Where the public road ends (gr NN252808), turn right (south) onto a rough un-surfaced track that ascends through woodland to Coire Choille Farm. The track is negotiable with care for two-wheel-drive vehicles as far as a parking area at a former railway crossing (gr NN256788). The railway, which ran across the foot of the Grey Corries and formerly serviced the Loch Treig–Ben Nevis tunnel, was removed in the 1980s.

Follow the Lairig Leacach track uphill to a gate with a pedestrian swing gate and enter an area of forestry that was clear-felled in 2006. The track goes uphill fairly steeply, crossing (at 260m) the former shoreline of a glacially dammed loch that disappeared suddenly at the end of the last glacial period, around 10,000 years ago. Continue to a level section and another gate with a swing gate (gr NN262776), immediately followed by a wooden bridge over a burn. Leave the track by turning right and

Stob Coire na Ceannain from Stob Choire Claurigh

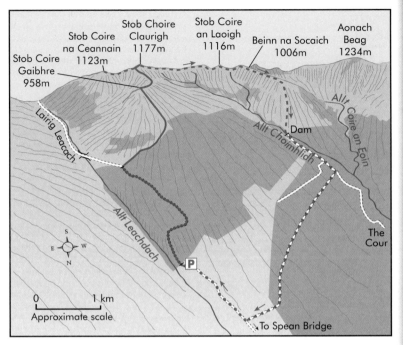

Stob Coire Gaibhre 958m
Stob Coire na Ceannain 1123m
Stob Choire Claurigh 1177m
Stob Coire an Laoigh 1116m
Beinn na Socaich 1006m
Aonach Beag 1234m
Allt Coire an Eoin
Allt Choimhlidh
Dam
Lairig Leacach
Allt Leachdach
P
The Cour
0   1 km
Approximate scale
To Spean Bridge

follow the edge of the uncut section of larch forest on good, short grass with occasional bog. Step over a fence and ascend steep grass with occasional bracken; look out for an indistinct path near the fence that defines the forest's edge. The ground is mainly dry with occasional wet sections. Follow a small burn steeply but easily upwards for about 30m then bear right for the forest edge and follow that upwards to soft, wet ground near 600m.

On reaching the corner of the fence (gr NN257769), head south-south-east, directly uphill on moderately steep, mossy grass and heather, soggy after wet weather but getting drier higher up. An earthen deer path that approaches from the left (east) and slants up to the right across grass and scattered rocks leads to a less steep grassy area. A good but occasionally wet path then bears slightly left for Stob Coire Gaibhre, becoming steep and heading more to the right higher up. Leave this path and head more left (south-east), directly ascending a fairly steep, dry, mossy, turf slope with scattered quartzite boulders, which is very pleasant for walking. Stob Coire Gaibhre's top (958m) is marked with a half-metre-high cairn and fine views include the circular lochan in Coire na Ceannain.

Continue southwards on a well-defined grassy ridge with some outcrops to Bealach Coire na Ceannain (924m) then ascend a broad ridge, steep and stony from 940m to 960m then grassy with stony areas. Above 1050m the ridge is covered in boulders but it levels out above 1100m. Keep left to avoid a rocky hillock then continue up a rough but well-defined ridge with boulders and occasional grassy patches to reach Stob Choire Claurigh's large boulder-strewn summit (1177m), where there is a well-built 2m-high cairn. Views are fine all around, including the Grey Corries ridge and the Mamores, but Stob Coire na Ceannain's tilted rock layers are most impressive.

Return by the upward route, possibly including the narrow, rocky, ridge scramble to Stob Coire na Ceannain (1123m). Alternatively, a longer way down heads westwards along the main Grey Corries ridge but there is rough going over sections of quartzite boulders and the ascent of Stob Coire Cath na Sine is exposed. Straightforward walking then leads to the Munro Stob Coire an Laoigh (1116m, stone-ring shelter); from there, continue to Stob Coire Easain then descend easily via Beinn na Socaich's grassy northern flanks. Pick up the track at the Allt Choimhlidh dam (gr NN240765), heading north then north-east to reach the Corriechoille track 600m north of the parking area.

29

CREAG MEAGAIDH

Soaring cliffs, deep gullies and dark lochans

Parking: Aberarder, gr NN483873
Distance: 16km
Height Gain: 1020m
Time: 6–8 hours
Terrain: Varied paths, gravel to rough and boggy; grassy and stony hillsides, broad ridges
Standard: Moderate to difficult
OS Maps: Fort Augustus (1:50,000 Landranger sheet 34), Loch Laggan & Creag Meagaidh (1:25,000 Explorer sheet 401)

The impressive 12km-long Creag Meagaidh massif, a 4,000-hecatre nature reserve on the northern side of Glen Spean, gives exceptionally fine walking and great views. Although it is possible to traverse the entire range in one day, it is best to split the route into two more manageable portions.

Off-road parking is available by the A86 Spean Bridge–Newtonmore road at Aberarder. Follow a well-graded and pleasant gravel footpath running parallel to the track leading to Aberarder farm, past fields and natural willow, oak and alder woodland. The Coire Ardair and Creag Meagaidh footpath passes just right of the farm, with displays, leaflets and maps in an outbuilding. Pass through bracken, heather, grassland and native woodland including silver birch and rowan, to reach a wooden footbridge. The path then rises more steeply to a gap in a stone wall and continues onto a bracken-and-heather-covered hillside. Above 410m, on easier slopes, pass through a belt of silver birch (a small cairn on the right indicates the rough path to Carn Liath).

Continue on the main Coire Ardair path, leaving the woods and following a bed of former railway sleepers, which are dangerously slippery when wet or icy. Sections of sleepers interspersed with mainly rough, bouldery and boggy path gradually lead up the corrie, through another belt of silver birch. It is quite hard going

The Coire Ardair cliffs of Creag Meagaidh

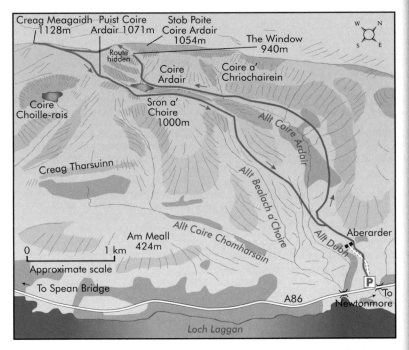

Creag Meagaidh — Puist Coire Ardair 1071m — Stob Poite Coire Ardair 1128m — 1054m — The Window 940m
Route hidden
Coire Ardair
Coire a' Chriochairein
Coire Choille-rais
Sron a' Choire 1000m
Allt Coire Ardair
Creag Tharsuinn
Allt Bealach a'Choire
Allt Coire Chomharsain
Am Meall 424m
Allt Dubh
Aberarder
0 — 1 km
Approximate scale
To Spean Bridge
A86
P
To Newtonmore
Loch Laggan

and particularly tedious as a decent route. Beyond a 20m downhill section, the path fords the burn from Coire a' Chriochairein, no problem given normal water levels. Between here and the lochan in Coire Ardair, contractors 'working' on path improvements have left boggy sections between pleasant pieces of gravel or compacted earth footpath and short sections of sleepers; small burns are crossed easily using stepping stones. Ahead, impressive 400m-high broken cliffs, a playground for ice climbers in hard winters, rise above the lochan (615m). The path keeps right of the lochan, crosses two small burns then rises steeply on grass slopes to steep loose slopes strewn with rocks. Keeping slightly right of centre, a steep, stony and steadily deteriorating path goes straight upwards. Once above the steepest ground, keep left and pass between boulder fields, through a slot. The path rises to the right then traverses left, across an old fence line, passing through the Window (940m); continue by traversing grassy slopes for 150m westwards to reach the path between Stob Poite Coire Ardair and Creag Meagaidh.

Turn left for Creag Meagaidh and ascend a steep flank of mossy grass and bands of stones on a gravel path that becomes indistinct on reaching easier slopes above 1050m. Above

1050m, trend right onto a gently inclined, grassy area and look for a clear path traversing the north side of the 1110m top, passing just north of the curious 4½m-high Mad Meg's cairn. Beyond a dip, a path rises 30m on grass to reach the bald area around the 1½m-high summit cairn (1128m). The fine views include Ben Nevis, Glen Coe, the Mamores, the Cairngorms and the west Highlands.

Return over the 1110m top and descend eastwards on good grass (no path), rising 40m to Puist Coire Ardair (1071m, small cairn). Continue eastwards along a path on a ridge of mixed grass and rocks that narrows dramatically to a promontory thrust out 450m above Coire Ardair's lochan. A fairly steep and stony descent path leads to a level col, then there is a 25m pathless rise to the stony top Sron a' Choire (1000m, small cairn). From there, descend north-eastwards, keeping right of the boulder fields, to gain a relatively boggy flat area at 830m. Continue eastwards, down a steep slope of boulders, grass and heather, becoming easier but wetter lower down. A boggy, four-wheel-drive track leads part of the way to Allt Dubh, best crossed around 600m upstream from Aberarder farm (possibly difficult in wet weather). A short walk leads to the Coire Ardair path and onwards to the car park.

30

CARN LIATH and STOB POITE COIRE ARDAIR

Outstanding views of Coire Ardair

Parking: Aberarder, gr NN483873

Distance: 17km

Height Gain: 1000m

Time: 6–8 hours

Terrain: Varied paths, gravel to rough and boggy; grassy and stony hillsides, broad ridges

Standard: Moderate to difficult

OS Maps: Fort Augustus (1:50,000 Landranger sheet 34), Loch Laggan & Creag Meagaidh (1:25,000 Explorer sheet 401)

The north-eastern part of the Creag Meagaidh group, consisting of the Munros Carn Liath and Stob Poite Coire Ardair, with numerous tops in-between, features broad ridges giving phenomenal views of Coire Ardair. A fine day in these hills ranks amongst the best the Highlands can offer.

From the SNH car park at Aberarder (gr NN483873), follow the Coire Ardair path past Aberarder farm as described for the Creag Meagaidh route. Pass through the stone wall and rise up the heather-and-bracken-covered hillside to a band of silver-birch woodland. About 100m into the woods, a tiny cairn on the path's right-hand side (gr NN472884) marks a rough hill path that slants more steeply uphill in a northerly direction, on the western flank of Na Cnapanan. Follow this path along a line of iron fence posts, through the trees and onto a steep hillside of grass and heather. It is a bit rough but mainly dry with occasional boulders and a mixture of grass, heather roots and earth. Higher up, the gradient eases, with some boggy sections, then it becomes steeper again while ascending the line of a felsite (geological) dyke. Keeping left of the fence, the path improves somewhat, passing over grass and scattered rocks while keeping left of some rough boulder fields. In late summer and autumn this slope is noted for bearberries. A tiny cairn marks the path's sudden end; bear right

On the east ridge of Carn Liath

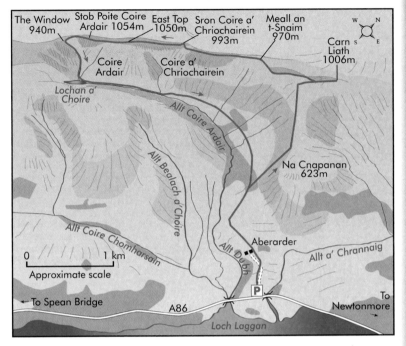

(north-east) across stony or bouldery areas, sometimes level but otherwise rising steadily to the 1½m-high cairn on the summit of Carn Liath (1006m). The expansive views extend from Knoydart's Sgurr na Ciche to the Cairngorms, with Creag Meagaidh's impressive Coire Ardair close by to the south-west.

Return south-west over quartz-feldspar-granulite boulders then continue west on a broad flank with mixed stony, mossy and grassy ground. Indistinct paths gradually descend on mossy grass to the 917m col (Uinneag Coire a' Chaorainn), a strange notch with some tiny ponds that should be crossed using a path at its southern end. From this 'window', a path rises steadily past boulder fields to Meall an t-Snaim's mossy summit (970m, tiny cairn). Further west, a broad, mossy ridge with scattered granite rocks descends 20m then there is a grassy rise to the stony but cairn-less 963m top. An intermittent line of iron fence posts follows the ridge with a fairly clear path all the way. Continue down the ridge to the western end of the next notch, the impressive and bouldery Uinneag Min Choire (935m). A stony cum gravel path zigzags up steep slopes beyond this 'window', then a broad ridge leads to the small cairn on Sron Coire a' Chriochairean (993m), with fine

views of Coire Ardair. A pleasant, steep-sided, well-defined ridge with an indistinct path heads westwards to a dip (960m). More regular fence posts lead the way onwards along a grassy ridge (distinct path), then the ridge bears left, rising on more stony ground towards Stob Poite Coire Ardair. An indistinct path peters out near the stony, 1050m-high eastern top, where there is a small cairn. Continue gradually downhill on stony ground to a dip (1035m), where there are magnificent views of Creag Meagaidh and Coire Ardair. A path is beaten into the mossy grass near the fence line as it rises to the stony, 1054m-high summit and 1m-high cairn. The dramatic views are unforgettable.

Continue westwards to a small cairn then follow the fence posts for a while; where the fence trends leftwards down steep ground, stay on a path of stone and gravel straight ahead to reach the extreme western end of the Window (Uinneag Coire Ardair). Once at the lowest point on this path, turn left on another path for 150m and ascend around 8m to reach the Window at 940m.

From the Window, follow the upward route through Coire Ardair, as described for Creag Meagaidh (in reverse), to reach Aberarder.

31

BEN ALDER and BEINN BHEOIL

Remote and mysterious Ben Alder

Parking: Dalwhinnie railway station, gr NN634846

Distance: 25/48km with/without bicycle

Height Gain: 1260m

Time: 10/14 hours with/without bicycle

Terrain: Gravel track, rough gravel or boggy paths, grassy and rocky slopes, broad ridges

Standard: Moderate to difficult

OS Maps: Glen Garry & Loch Rannoch (1:50,000 Landranger sheet 42), Ben Alder, Loch Ericht & Loch Laggan (1:25,000 Explorer sheet 393)

The Ben Alder and Beinn Bheoil circuit is a fine walk through remote wilderness that takes most people several days, but it can be completed in one very hard day with the assistance of a bicycle on the estate tracks.

In Dalwhinnie, turn off the main road towards the railway station then turn left onto Ben Alder Road to reach a parking area by a level crossing. Cross the railway and continue along a gravel track, with a mixed plantation of spruce and larch on the right and fine views down Loch Ericht. About 500m south-west of the dam's northern end, there is an ostentatious, mock-baronial gatehouse with a three-storey turret, cobbled driveways and stained-glass windows (the gate is normally open). Beyond lots of broom and another mock-baronial building with a turret, the track enters the mostly spruce plantation and continues to a junction 8km from Dalwhinnie. Keep right, since the left fork goes through the gatehouse to Ben Alder Lodge.

From this gatehouse, rise gradually uphill onto open moorland beyond a gate; keep right then left and continue uphill, following the edge of a plantation to a shed at gr NN548787. Turn left onto a path (used by four-wheel-drive vehicles and often very wet) leading across the boggy moor to Allt a' Chaoil-reidhe. About 1km beyond Culra Lodge (on the other side of the river), the path leaves the left bank of the burn

Beinn Bheoil and Loch a' Bhealaich Bheithe

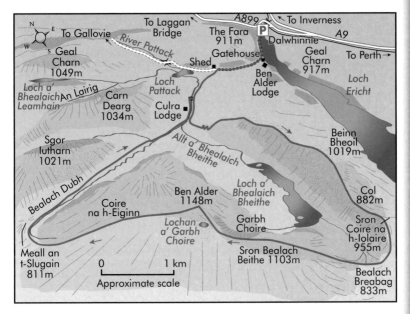

and heads south onto drier ground, ascending steadily. At around 640m (gr NN517743), where the path veers south-west, leave the path and head south-east up a mixed-grass-and-heather flank with scattered rocks, towards the broad, northern ridge of Beinn Bheoil. From the flat area at this ridge's northern end (835m), follow it southwards, with good dry ground consisting of mixed grass and stones rising over a flat area at 900m. Beyond a slight dip, the ridge becomes better defined and steeper for around 80m, ascending to the dome-like summit of Beinn Bheoil, where there is a 1m-high cairn at the southern end (1019m). Continue south-south-west over stony and grassy areas to the 882m col then a short, steep rise of 60m leads towards Sron Coire na h-Iolaire (good views of Loch Ericht and Loch a' Bhealaich Bheithe). From Sron Coire na h-Iolaire, descend south-westwards across grass, heather and scattered boulders to reach the 833m col Bealach Breabag (the apparently more direct descent from the 882m col is steep and is not recommended).

Ben Alder presents a long, steep shoulder to Bealach Breabag; ascend near the burn (Allt a' Bhealaich Bheithe) for the easiest ground, with some loose rock and wet areas for about 200m. The views are great but become even better on reaching the Garbh Choire's lip at around 1080m, where snow often lingers well into summer. Easier-angled ground, a mixture of grass and stones, leads over Sron Bealach Beithe (1103m). Follow the edge of the corrie to a dip (1080m) then rise 50m to a particularly stony area with a creepy, hanging lochan, Lochan a' Garbh Choire, which has no outlet. Near here, in June 1996, the body of 26-year-old Frenchman Emmanuel Caillet was found, dressed in town clothes and shoes and shot dead by a replica revolver. Veer north-north-east and rise gradually to Ben Alder's summit (1148m; partial ring cairn around a concrete triangulation pillar) for marvellous views all around.

Continue west-north-west across grass and stones to reach a flat, grassy area then descend long, grassy slopes via Coire na h-Eiginn, aiming for the craggy hillock Meall an t-Slugain (811m). Cross this bump and descend steep ground to reach the Bealach Dubh pass (722m); turn right onto a good gravel path that descends steeply at first then gradually for 5km to reach the four-wheel-drive track at Culra Lodge. Follow the track for 500m, cross the river using the wood-slat suspension footbridge and return to Dalwhinnie by the outward route.

32

BEINN MHEADHONACH

Beautiful Glen Tilt's native woodland and secretive peaks

Parking: Old Bridge of Tilt, gr NN874663

Distance: 21km

Height Gain: 870m

Time: 6–7 hours

Terrain: Gravel tracks and footpaths, grassy footpaths, grassy and mossy hillsides

Standard: Moderate

OS Maps: Braemar & Blair Atholl (1:50,000 Landranger sheet 43), Atholl (1:25,000 Explorer sheet 394, doesn't show first 700m of the walk), Pitlochry & Loch Tummel (1:25,000 Explorer sheet 386, shows first 700m of the walk)

Beinn Mheadhonach is a shapely but secretive hill, hidden between larger mountains in the Forest of Atholl. Avoid the hill during deer stalking (12 August to 20 October).

From Blair Atholl, follow the minor road to Old Bridge of Tilt and continue on the left fork, sign posted 'Old Blair'. Pass under a curious, stone-arched footbridge then turn left into the car park at gr NN874663 (small sign post reading 'P Glen Tilt').

Follow the Glen Tilt track opposite the car park (unauthorised vehicular access prohibited) past fields, passing through varied natural woodland and plantation forestry. It is a pleasant, easy hike, keeping fairly level until dropping down to the Cumhann-leum stone-arch bridge, after about 5km. There are good views of the dark, peaty waters of the River Tilt slipping quietly below the bridge. Across the bridge, the track rises past some impressive trees. Continue through pleasant mixed woodland and look out for a waterfall just to the right of the track. Immediately beyond a cattle grid, follow a track on the left and cross the stone-arch Gilbert's Bridge. Continue to the warning sign for the firing range then cross the stile on the right (the warning sign is not relevant to the route described here). A forestry track goes uphill into the plantation; follow this, then continue downhill, looking out for a wooden post directing walkers

Beinn Mheadhonach from Glen Tilt

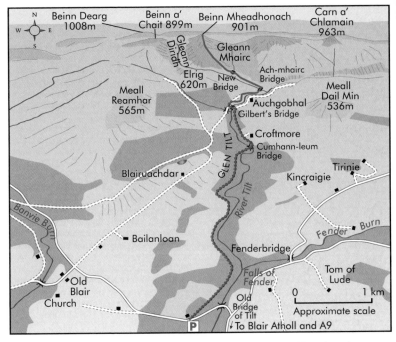

right onto a grassy and somewhat boggy foot-path. This path heads across flat ground and meets the forestry track again at a gate almost opposite Auchgobhal House (on the other side of the River Tilt). Pass through the gate and continue on the track through the scattered trees of Sean-bhaile Wood. There is a steep rise as the track climbs to a terrace about 12m above the Tilt, then the now grassy track continues through scattered silver birch to the impressive Achmhairc Bridge, a slim and delicate-looking stone arch over a narrow chasm and waterfall. The exposed rock (quartz-feldspar-granulite) consists of a mass of blocks and the river has cut through an obvious fault.

Beyond the bridge, the track rises past the ruins of the ancient village at Ach Mhairc Mhor then a grassy path leads to a gate at an electric fence. Keep right up a slope, then a path, grassy at first but becoming gravel, leads through scattered silver birch and former grassy fields into Gleann Mhairc. Beyond a promontory, the path contours along steep slopes with some landslips, then descends to the excellent stone-spanned 'New Bridge', at 330m. This bridge was probably built to assist the villagers drive cattle between the homesteads and summer pastures in the hills above.

A steep rather muddy path on the western side of the Allt Mhairc rises through thick heather then peters out on easier grassy and short heather slopes above. Follow a central line up the prominent southern flanks of Beinn Mheadhonach, with excellent dry walking and occasional paths. Just beyond an odd 1½m-high cairn, there is some steeper ground at around 650m. Higher up, the gradient decreases on cropped heather and patchy gravel; beyond a broken-down stone wall, continue on short grass and granite gravel to a more stony section followed by a 5m dip (gr NN879750). Gradual slopes then lead across odd, humpy terrain to a 1m-high cairn on the rather flat summit (901m). The Ordnance Survey recognises a point 400m to the north, beyond a 5m dip, as the summit, but others disagree; two small piles of stones mark high points on the ridge, which is an interesting walk on mossy grass. There are good views of Beinn Dearg, the deep glens on either side of Beinn Mheadhonach, the steep south face of Carn a' Chlamain, and the mighty tops of bulky Beinn a' Ghlo peeking above intervening ridges.

Most hill walkers return by the outward route since it is shorter and considerably easier than any of the alternatives.

33

BEINN A' GHLO

Graceful curves and great ridge-walking

Parking: Loch Moraig, gr NN906671

Distance: 16km

Height Gain: 980m

Time: 6–8 hours

Terrain: Gravel or boggy tracks, boggy/gravel paths; scree, grass or heather hillsides and ridges

Standard: Moderate to difficult

OS Maps: Braemar & Blair Atholl (1:50,000 Landranger sheet 43), Atholl (1:25,000 Explorer sheet 394)

Beinn a' Ghlo (hill of mist), a prominent group of three well-rounded Munros, gives great ridge walking between the two southern peaks but the highest point, the bouldery and far-flung Carn nan Gabhar, is a more serious proposition requiring around two hours more on an already long day. Only the shorter round of Carn Liath and Braigh Coire Chruinn-bhalgain is described here.

From Blair Atholl, take the minor road to Old Bridge of Tilt and continue to its end at Loch Moraig (gr NN906671); park just beyond a cattle grid. Take the surfaced road for 100m towards Monzie farm, then turn right (gate marked 'Shinagag') and follow a reasonable gravel track steadily uphill past grassy fields. The first Munro, Carn Liath, is a prominent cone slightly to the left. The track levels out shortly before a dismal wooden hut at gr NN923679; just beyond the hut, turn left onto a grassy track, cross a fence (stile) and pass another hut. Turn left on another path for 70m then turn right, descend 5m on a grassy path and cross a flat area. Keeping a broken stone wall immediately to the left, a reasonable path rises towards the hill. Parts of the wall have been converted into grouse butts.

At 470m, the wall heads left but the path continues directly uphill, becoming drier and stonier as well as steeper on reaching the heather-covered, south-west flank of Carn Liath.

Braigh Coire Chruinn-bhalgain

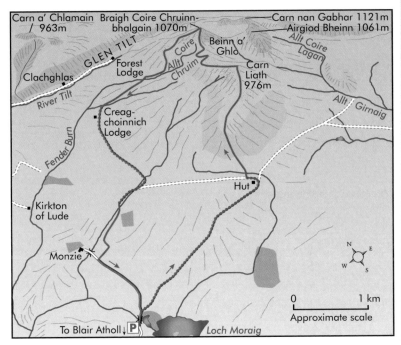

The gradient eases a little then the path becomes steeper, stony and badly eroded, where it is up to 4m wide. Zigzags ease progress upwards to less steep but more stony ground with several cairns; there is a 2m-high cairn at 930m. Rather featureless level areas with intermittent paths alternate with mixed mossy-grass and stone slopes. The summit has a square-section, concrete triangulation pillar (975m) inside a 1m-high stone ring; the large but damaged 1½m-high cairn 10m north offers better shelter and fine views over the other tops of Beinn a' Ghlo.

A broad, stone-strewn ridge with mossy-grass flanks provides fine, dry walking northwards, with an indistinct path to the right (east) of the crest. Beyond a bend to the north-east, pleasant short grass, moss and heather alternate with gravel and boulder patches. The ridge becomes better defined with a path that keeps left then descends fairly steeply to the 760m col between Carn Liath and Braigh Coire Chruinn-bhalgain. A stony path then rises steeply upwards across heather slopes and boulder fields to gain the hill's southern flank, where it becomes intermittent on mixed grassy and stony ground. Beyond a small cairn, an almost level walk leads to Braigh Coire Chruinn-bhalgain's 1m-high summit cairn (1070m). Fine views include the other Beinn a' Ghlo tops, Glen Tilt's deep trench, and the Cairngorms far to the north.

Descend from Braigh Coire Chruinn-bhalgain westwards on rather extraordinary, thick, green moss until reaching quartzite boulders on a level area at 1010m. Continue south-west on boulders (hard going), improving to mixed rocks with grass and moss or short heather, and descend to a pleasantly dry, level area at 890m (small cairn). Lovely short heather leads south-west into a narrow corrie with thicker heather. Keep left of this corrie's burn until reaching a very rough path (gr NN931712), turn right on this, cross the corrie's burn and continue for about 250m. Descend to the main burn on the left (Allt Choire Chruim), cross easily, climb up the southern bank and continue through thick heather over a flat area. Straightforward slopes descend to the derelict Creag-choinnich Lodge and its scattered conifers. A rough, wet, argocat trail heading south from the lodge improves and descends to Monzie, with several burn crossings (one un-bridged). The trail fades out in a field. Keep left, follow a stone wall with an electric fence to a gate, pass through the gate then turn right down to the surfaced road leading from Monzie back to the parking area.

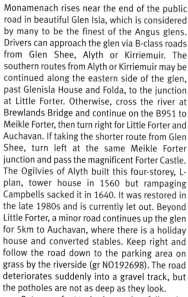

34

MONAMENACH

Easy walking on a rounded hill with excellent panoramas

Parking: Auchavan, Glen Isla, gr NO192698

Distance: 6km

Height Gain: 450m

Time: 2½ hours

Terrain: Tracks and paths

Standard: Easy to moderate

OS Maps: Braemar & Blair Atholl (1:50,000 Landranger sheet 43), Lochnagar, Glen Muick & Glen Clova (1:25,000 Explorer sheet 388)

Monamenach rises near the end of the public road in beautiful Glen Isla, which is considered by many to be the finest of the Angus glens. Drivers can approach the glen via B-class roads from Glen Shee, Alyth or Kirriemuir. The southern routes from Alyth or Kirriemuir may be continued along the eastern side of the glen, past Glenisla House and Folda, to the junction at Little Forter. Otherwise, cross the river at Brewlands Bridge and continue on the B951 to Meikle Forter, then turn right for Little Forter and Auchavan. If taking the shorter route from Glen Shee, turn left at the same Meikle Forter junction and pass the magnificent Forter Castle. The Ogilvies of Alyth built this four-storey, L-plan, tower house in 1560 but rampaging Campbells sacked it in 1640. It was restored in the late 1980s and is currently let out. Beyond Little Forter, a minor road continues up the glen for 5km to Auchavan, where there is a holiday house and converted stables. Keep right and follow the road down to the parking area on grass by the riverside (gr NO192698). The road deteriorates suddenly into a gravel track, but the potholes are not as deep as they look.

Return on foot to Auchavan then follow the private gravel road up the glen (heading for Tulchan Lodge). Immediately beyond the second cattle grid (only 200m along the road), turn left across a field then follow a mainly dry, four-

Caenlochan Glen from Monamenach

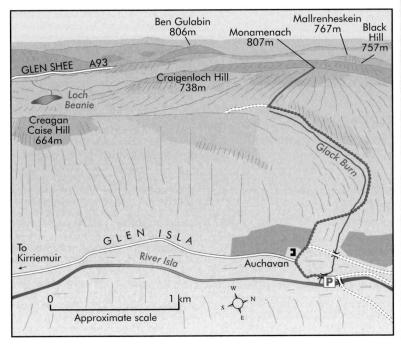

wheel-drive track of mixed grass and gravel through the obvious gap in the dry-stone wall, steeply up the hillside and slanting right. The track crosses the small Glack Burn and the gradient decreases on approaching a col at 620m. When the track levels out, turn right onto a relatively dry argocat track that strikes directly for the summit. It is mostly a grassy path and pleasant to follow. During the rut, large groups of hinds gathered by noisy stags may congregate on the western slopes of the col; an impressive sight. On continuing uphill, an old fence line approaches from the right and follows the path all the way to the top. The slope becomes less steep, with the track crossing very short, cropped heather, and soon the small summit cairn is reached at the junction of two old fences.

The excellent views from the summit (807m) – so easily reached in only 1¼ hours from the car park – include dome-like Driesh and Mayar's cone to the east, with the deep chasm of Caenlochan Glen dominated by Broad Cairn, Lochnagar and White Mounth to the north-east. Cairn of Claise, grassy Glas Maol and the oddly scree-covered Creag Leacach lie to the north and north-west and, beyond a host of heathery ridges to the west, there is Beinn a'Ghlo, Glas Tulaichean and Beinn Iutharn Mhor. Ben Vrackie can be seen through a gap in the hills to the west-south-west. Mount Blair and the transmitter on its summit are prominent to the south.

Return to the car park via the same route. However, to extend the day, take the aforementioned gravel road from Auchavan for 3km to Tulchan Lodge (keep your distance from the lodge) and onwards into the spectacular Caenlochan Glen (7km), which is a national nature reserve. It is also possible to extend the hill walk from Monamenach over the tops of Black Hill (757m), the rocky Creag Leacach (987m), Glas Maol (1068m) and Little Glas Maol (973m), descending to Glen Isla via the Monega Track, a former drove road used by cattlemen and travelling pedlars. The walking is generally good on cropped grass or heather, with only a few peat banks (and the rocks of Creag Leacach) to contend with. It is a fairly long route (20km) with 1150m of ascent and decent so allow at least eight hours for the return trip.

35

BROAD CAIRN

A splendid walk through spectacular upper Glen Clova

Parking: Acharn, Glen Doll, gr NO284761

Distance: 19km

Height Gain: 750m

Time: 6–7 hours

Terrain: Track, path, boulder slopes

Standard: Moderate

OS Maps: Ballater & Glen Clova (1:50,000 Landranger sheet 44), Lochnagar, Glen Muick & Glen Clova (1:25,000 Explorer sheet 388)

The upper reaches of Glen Clova, in the Cairngorms National Park, are considered by many aficionados to be the most spectacular part of the Angus glens. The straightforward hike to Broad Cairn, a Munro, leads through the glen and onto the high plateaux south of Lochnagar.

From Kirriemuir, follow the B955 northwards into Glen Clova and keep to the western side of the glen at the road junction. Beyond the Clova Hotel, a single-track road continues for a further 5km to the Forest Enterprise car park at the foot of Glen Doll. Views of the boulder fields and ridges of Driesh are particularly fine from here.

Re-cross the road bridge over the River South Esk and turn immediately left, through a gate, onto the private gravel road to Moulzie farm. The road passes through mature larch-and-sitka-spruce forest, which was clear-felled in spring 2006. Just beyond the wooden bridge over the Cald Burn, the Capel Mounth path branches off to the right. Continue on the main track, go through a gate and leave the forest. Once out in the open glen, there are great views of the immense boulder fields below the crags of Cairn Broadlands, on the left. Beyond the wooden bridge over the Moulzie Burn, take the track on the right to respect the farmer's privacy. Leave the track at gr NO282781 (continue straight on, since the track goes to the left) and follow a path that keeps left of a plantation. A section of boardwalk

Broad Cairn's Creag an Dubh Loch

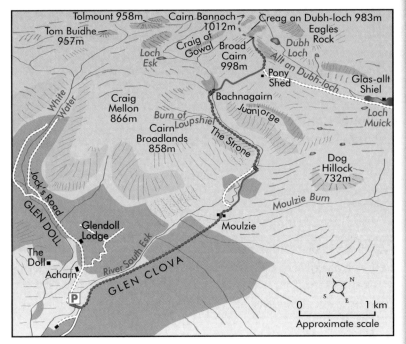

Tolmount 958m — Cairn Bannoch ⌐ Creag an Dubh-loch 983m
1012m ⌐ Eagles
Tom Buidhe — Craig of Dubh Rock
957m Gowal Broad Loch
Loch Cairn
Esk 998m Pony Glas-allt
Shed Shiel
White Water Bachnagairn Alt an Dubh-loch Loch
Craig Juanjorge Muick
Mellon Burn of
866m Loupshiel The Strone
Cairn
Broadlands Dog
858m Hillock
732m
Jock's Road Moulzie Burn
GLEN DOLL Moulzie
Glendoll
Lodge
The River South Esk
Doll GLEN CLOVA
Acharn
P W N
S E
0 1 km
Approximate scale

is followed by a pleasant, mainly earthen, path that heads across grassy swards then crosses a boulder-strewn part of the glen floor (beyond the plantation) to reach the river bank. The river, which flows over rocks and slabs, is crossed using a wooden-slat footbridge.

Turn right onto a four-wheel-drive track keeping reasonably near the river, which swings to the west, with splendid views of the Juanjorge crag and the scattered birch woods below. There is a substantial ford over the Burn of Loupshiel then a very rough and bouldery track ascends steadily through an impressive boulder field towards the larches, firs and Scots pine at Bachnagairn. The river rushes down slabs near the track but in the Bachnagairn woods there is a series of waterfalls between 6m and 8m high and a narrow gorge around 6m deep, well worth a short detour. A fairly steep path rises through the woods to the Roy Tait Memorial Bridge (1981), immediately above the fine 8m-high Bachnagairn Falls.

Across the bridge, the path climbs very steeply with zigzags, paving and stone stairs. The gradient eases at 640m and a good narrow path continues across a heather moor with scattered boulders to the miniature valley of the Style Burn. Turn left 100m before the unin-

habitable pony shed situated at the col. A gravel path (varying between bouldery, sandy and peaty) joins a four-wheel-drive track from the shed; this track ascends heather-clad slopes towards Little Craig (860m), the eastern and rather flat shoulder of Broad Cairn. Little Craig gives fine views of Lochnagar's bulky southern flank, the steep walls and slabs of Creag an Dubh-loch and Loch Muick far below.

On Broad Cairn's boulder-covered summit cone, the pink granite appears greenish due to lichen. These slopes are home to ptarmigan, usually seen in pairs but sometimes in substantial flocks. Clamber over or meander between the blocks to reach easier ground and the final straightforward walk to the 1m-high summit cairn sitting on top of a 5m-high tor of weathered granite plates. Views of Creag an Dubh-loch are particularly good from the summit.

Return by the upward route or continue on a path to the stony top of Cairn of Gowal (991m) and the rocky cone of Cairn Bannoch (1012m), adding 4km and 160m of ascent. From Cairn Bannoch, it is best to return via Broad Cairn's summit – the glens west of Bachnagairn are extremely rough and are not recommended.

36

LOCHNAGAR

Hike around the lip of Lochnagar's stunning corrie

Parking: Spittal of Glenmuick, gr NO310851

Distance: 16km

Height Gain: 860m

Time: 5–6 hours

Terrain: Tracks, gravel or rocky paths

Standard: Moderate

OS Maps: Ballater & Glen Clova (1:50,000 Landranger sheet 44), Lochnagar, Glen Muick & Glen Clova (1:25,000 Explorer sheet 388)

Impressive Lochnagar on the royal Balmoral estate – with near-vertical granite crags looming above a dark corrie lochan of the same name – was immortalised in the poem 'Dark Lochnagar', by Lord Byron. The hill is one of the finest in north-east Scotland and justifiably popular with hill walkers.

From Ballater, take the B976 South Deeside road westbound to Bridge of Muick then continue along the single-track Glen Muick road to its end. Unfortunately, local powers-that-be apply an access charge by imposing parking fees, which is a sad reflection on the growing commercialisation of the countryside. Follow the track across the bridge to the buildings at Spittal of Glenmuick, then turn right and cross the grassy, flat-floored glen to Allt-na-giubhsaich. Keep right to avoid walking in front of the houses. Pick up the track again in the forest above the house and continue beyond the woods to the Allt na Giubhsaich ford. The track then rises across heather moorland to just above the 678m col between Lochnagar and the neighbouring Corbett, Conachcraig.

Turn left and follow the footpath downwards for 10m, then easily uphill across heather slopes dotted with boulders to reach the intrusive Bill Stuart memorial at the Fox Cairn Well. Beyond the well, the path trends leftwards up steep ground, but take a slight detour straight ahead to reach the

The corrie of Lochnagar

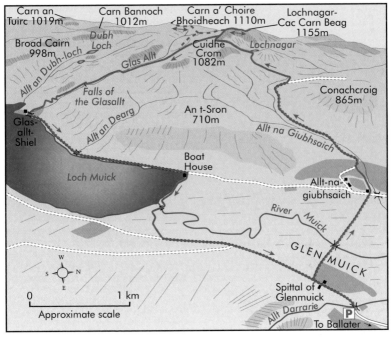

Carn an Tuirc 1019m

Carn Bannoch 1012m

Carn a' Choire Bhoidheach 1110m

Lochnagar-Cac Carn Beag 1155m

Broad Cairn 998m

Dubh Loch

Glas Allt

Lochnagar

Allt an Dubh-loch

Cuidhe Crom 1082m

Falls of the Glasallt

An t-Sron 710m

Conachcraig 865m

Glas-allt-Shiel

Allt an Dearg

Allt na Giubhsaich

Loch Muick

Boat House

Allt-na-giubhsaich

River Muick

GLEN MUICK

W N S E

0   1 km

Approximate scale

Spittal of Glenmuick

Allt Darrarie

P

To Ballater

917m col between Lochnagar and Meikle Pap, an excellent viewpoint for the cliffs and lochan. From the col, continue southwards and upwards through a boulder field to rejoin the path on the shoulder of the top Cuidhe Crom, with great views all the way. Beyond the 1078m spot height, the path follows the cliff edge, often with dangerous, droopy cornices in winter, spring and early summer. Descend 33m to the top of the Red Spout gully, pass over an intervening top and descend to 1049m, then rise past Central Buttress and Eagle Ridge to reach the small granite tor Cac Carn Mor (1150m, curiously translating as 'big pile of shit'). From there, the path heads northwards, gradually descending to 1140m (where the ground may be rather boggy), then rising again to the substantial summit tor, Cac Carn Beag (1155m, 'small pile of shit'). To reach the top – where there is a stone-built, triangulation pillar and a viewpoint indicator – scramble easily through an obvious passage between the granite blocks and descend the same way. Given the height of Lochnagar, the extensive views are no surprise. Beyond Deeside's forests lie Ben Avon's tors, while in the other direction the southern plateau extends as far as Glen Clova and Glen Shee.

Although return to the car park is shortest by retracing the outward route, it is more inter-esting to take the Glas-allt-Shiel path, which descends steadily south-eastwards from near the aforementioned 1049m spot height (gr NO251854).

Munro baggers may wish to include White Mounth's Carn a' Choire Bhoidheach in their tally, adding another 2km to the day. To get there, follow the path south-westwards from Cac Carn Mor around the grassy edge of the Stuic cliffs, with Loch nan Eun 180m below. Walk 300m south from the path on good grass to reach the summit at 1110m. Return to the lowest point on the plateau (1040m, gr NO241852), then descend south-eastwards on grass and scattered rocks into Coire an Daimh Mhoile to pick up the Glas-allt-Shiel path.

The Glas-allt-Shiel path, of mixed gravel and stone, drops steeply in tight zigzags past the impressive Falls of the Glasallt, to reach the royal hunting lodge at Glas-allt-Shiel, a large and rather grand Victorian building constructed from granite blocks. A 2½km hike along Loch Muick's western gravel road leads to a boathouse at the loch's northern end; leave the track here and follow the beach eastwards to the wooden footbridge over the loch's outlet. A good gravel path continues further east to Loch Muick's eastern gravel road, then it is only 1km to the car park.

BEINN A' BHUIRD
and BEN AVON

A circuit of two exceptional Cairngorms Munros

Parking: Linn of Quoich, gr NO119912
Distance: 34km
Height Gain: 1130m
Time: 12–14 hours
Terrain: Track, paths; boulder, gravel and grass slopes
Standard: Difficult
OS Maps: Grantown & Aviemore (1:50,000 Landranger sheet 36), Braemar, Tomintoul & Glen Avon (1:25,000 Explorer sheet 404)

Although the magnificent Beinn a' Bhuird–Ben Avon circuit is an arduous day trip for most walkers, cycling into Glen Quoich (or camping) reduces the distance and height gain to 22km and 1010m, respectively. Flocks of ptarmigan may be seen on these hills.

From Braemar, drive westwards to Linn of Quoich via Linn of Dee, both well worth exploring. Around 100m west of the end of the public road, a track rises steeply to join the main four-wheel-drive track on the western side of Glen Quoich, a pleasant and generally level route through native Scots pine forest. Look out for large anthills by the track. After 6km (at gr NO080947), camping is possible by the Allt an Dubh-ghlinne, which is difficult to ford dry-shod in wet weather or during snow melt. Across the river, keep left (north) and cross a grassy plain where deer may congregate. The track ends in pine woods at gr NO079955; the upper section, constructed for a failed skiing project in the 1960s, was later removed by an innovative conservation project. A new, well-drained, gravel path now slants gradually uphill, crossing the former track at 680m, then heads through gravel, grass and heather towards An Diollaid (750m). Above 750m, the path follows the former track, continuing northwards up a broad ridge and passing a tiny, roofless, stone shelter. The gradient eases as the path crosses a shoulder

Beinn a' Bhuird's Coire an Dubh-lochain, with Ben Avon beyond

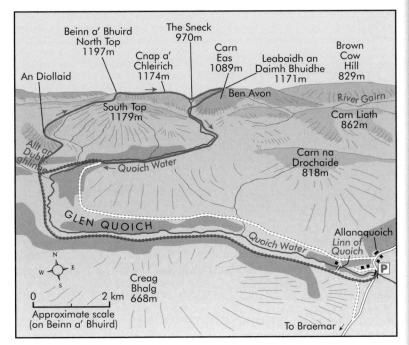

of sand and gravel but then it rises more steeply before ending at 1080m. Turn right (south-east) for the col between Beinn a' Bhuird's tops, with great views eastwards over Coire an Dubhlochain to Ben Avon and westwards to Beinn Mheadhoin and Beinn MacDuibh.

Continue northwards up a gradual slope, cross a subsidiary top, with more great views eastwards. Another gradual rise leads to the north top of Beinn a' Bhuird, a flat, featureless area of sand, gravel, patchy grass and scattered stones with a 1m-high cairn (1197m). From the cairn, head east across similar ground to a 3m-high granite tor (gr NJ105011), then cross the top Cnap a' Chleirich or bypass it easily on its northern flank. East of Cnap a' Chleirich, beyond an area of moss and boulders, steady descent is followed by a steep and loose 30m drop, with patchy, gravel-covered slab lower down. The Sneck (970m), between Beinn a' Bhuird and Ben Avon, is a curious spot with some large wind-sculpted granite boulders. Cross a boulder-strewn hummock in the col, then follow a steep gravel path upwards to Ben Avon's west top (1138m), with impressive views of Beinn a' Bhuird's Garbh Choire and the forbidding Mitre Ridge. Continue over easy rocks and gravel to Ben Avon's summit tor, Leabaidh an Daimh Bhuidhe (1171m). Scramble easily to the central notch in the tor, then continue (straightforward, apart from one slightly awkward move low down) rightwards to reach the unmarked and rather exposed summit. The slightly lower southern peak of the tor is trickier to ascend.

Return over the west top, head south to gr NJ122003 then bear right (west) down steep but easy slopes of short grass and heather. Keep right of a narrow gully, then cross its burn where it reaches the Glas Allt Mor, the main burn flowing south from the Sneck. Cross the burn and pick up a rough path which improves enormously after passing the 1m-high boulder, Clach a' Chleirich; zigzag down to cross the burn, then continue (tediously) to the path junction at gr NO117961, which may be hard to find. Turn right (west) and follow a rough, boggy and rather poor path towards and through the pinewoods of Glen Quoich. There is also a path on the north side of the river. Continue to the ford at gr NO093952; cross the river and follow the north-side track back to the aforementioned camping area, or take the other track southwards to Linn of Quoich.

38

CAIRN GORM and BEINN MACDUIBH

Exceptional vistas on the arctic Cairngorms plateau

Parking: Coire Cas car park, gr NH989061

Distance: 18km

Height Gain: 1080m

Time: 6–7 hours

Terrain: Gravel tracks, mountain paths, some boulder fields, desolate plateaux

Standard: Moderate

OS Maps: Grantown & Aviemore (1:50,000 Landranger sheet 36), Cairn Gorm & Aviemore (1:25,000 Explorer sheet 403)

Beinn MacDuibh, the second-highest mountain in Britain, is centrally located on the Cairngorm plateau. The approach from the north, via Cairn Gorm, provides fine views of sheer rock faces, wild corries and desolate plateaux.

Leave cars in the Coire Cas ski-area car park at the end of the Cairn Gorm ski road. Keep right of the funicular-railway ticket office, pass between the station and the exhibition building then follow a good gravel track, passing left underneath the railway. Ascend fairly steeply initially then easily past various ski-company buildings. Go under the railway again, pass several ski tows; continue straight on, then zigzag to the left, uphill, right, uphill then left. Continue uphill, then right onto a fenceless, fairly steep ski-tow route. Bear left for 20m then right, uphill and between two snow fences. Beyond where the fence on the left ends, a steep gravel or sand track ascends then turns sharply left onto an easier gradient (with a snow fence on the left). A steep ascent past a ski tow and railway tunnel leads to the Ptarmigan restaurant and upper railway station, where a sign indicates the walkers' entrance (railway passengers are not allowed out of the building or off the veranda).

Turn right onto the paved path, oddly delineated by blue rope up to 1210m then excessively cairned every 10m to Cairn Gorm's

Einich Cairn and Braeriach from Beinn MacDuibh

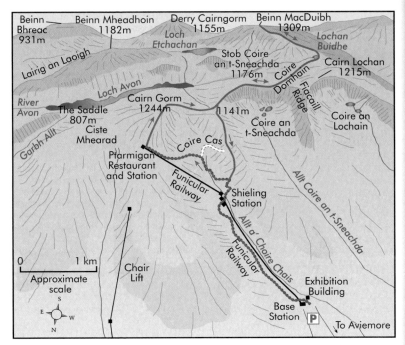

summit. The upper section, an easy sandy path between large granite boulders, leads to the 1½m-high summit cairn (1244m). The concrete-block structure 50m south houses the Heriot-Watt University automatic weather station and sports a 6m-high mast. Views from the summit include Bynack More's and Beinn Mheadhoin's tors, and the spectacular cliffs of the Northern Corries.

Continue towards Beinn MacDuibh by heading westwards from Cairn Gorm's summit (there is no obvious path). Meander downhill on gravel between boulders, aiming for gr NH999038, just south of the 1141m top, Fiacaill a' Choire Chais. Pick up the path heading south to the grassy 1099m col, followed by a level section of broken slabs, then a stony rise to the next top, Stob Coire an t-Sneachda (1176m, cairn). A mostly good, gravel path traverses this top's southern flanks but it eventually disappears so it may be faster to pass directly over the summit. From Stob Coire an t-Sneachda, head west-south-west on a steadily descending path through grass, gravel and scattered rocks towards Cairn Lochan, with great views of the vicious-looking Fiacaill Ridge on the right.

Beyond the 1111m col at the head of Coire Domhain, bear left (south) on an easy path that traverses grassy slopes below the steep flanks of Cairn Lochan for 2km, as far as Lochan Buidhe. The path keeps right (west) of the lochan, the highest body of water of its size in Britain (1125m). A stonier path continues southwards and uphill, with a few large cairns. Look out for fine examples of moss campion while the cairned, but pathless, route passes through a boulder field. The route levels out on more grassy ground south-west of the 1186m top with a gravel/stony path. A sudden, steep, bouldery ascent of 50m leads to an easier traverse of the western flanks of Beinn MacDuibh's north top, with cairns marking the way across a desolation of boulders and gravel. A steady 30m rise across gravel and boulders leads past several stone-ring shelters to the flat boulder-strewn summit, where there is a 2m-high cairn (1309m), oddly topped with a concrete trian-gulation pillar. There is also a circular, Cairngorm Club view indicator dating from 1925 and a stone-wall shelter. Fine views include Braeriach and Cairn Toul to the west.

Return via Stob Coire an t-Sneachda as far as the cairn on Fiacaill a' Choire Chais. A boulder-and-gravel path descends north-north-west, with some stone stairs and paved sections, trending right into Coire Cas to pick up the track down to the car park.

39

BEINN MHEADHOIN

Scale a remote and amazing summit tor

Parking: Coire Cas car park, gr NH989061

Distance: 15km

Height Gain: 1400m

Time: 7–9 hours

Terrain: Tracks, pathless hillsides, bouldery or stony in places, scramble on summit tor

Standard: Moderate to difficult

OS Maps: Grantown & Aviemore (1:50,000 Landranger sheet 36), Cairn Gorm & Aviemore (1:25,000 Explorer sheet 403)

One of the finest hills in the Cairngorms, the centrally located Beinn Mheadhoin (meaning 'middle hill') is remote from any public road but well worth the effort to gain its remarkable summit. The shortest route is the approach from Cairn Gorm; the alternative route from Linn of Dee via Derry Lodge is more than twice the distance. Keep a look out for hardy residents of the sub-arctic Cairngorm plateaux, especially ptarmigan.

Follow the Cairn Gorm ski road to its terminus at the Coire Cas ski area; cars can be left in the large parking area there. A gravel track meanders through the ski area and ascends steeply to the Ptarmigan restaurant (for details, see the Cairn Gorm and Beinn MacDuibh walk). From the Ptarmigan, continue south-east on a path slanting across Cairn Gorm's slopes to reach the upper end of the highest ski tow at 1150m. Where the path trends southwards just before the ski tow, leave the path and follow the 1150m contour across a boulder-strewn area called Ciste Mhearad (Margaret's Coffin). A romantic tale from centuries ago relates how young Margaret died of despair here when a despotic Mackintosh chieftain condemned her sweetheart to death for a misdemeanour.

Continuing in a south-easterly direction, descend steeply for around 60m to a small burn at gr NJ012042. Descend less steep, grassy slopes with scattered rocks and occasional outcrops,

Beinn Mheadhoin and Loch Avon from Beinn MacDuibh

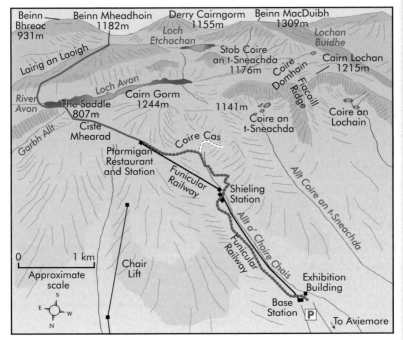

keeping left (north) of the northern end of an area of unpleasant broken slabs at gr NJ015038. Continue the descending traverse below the slabs, slanting downwards on steeper ground to reach the Saddle (807m), the col between Strath Nethy and Glen Avon. The Saddle is a wonderful place to enjoy views across beautiful Loch Avon, its western end hemmed in by beetling crags. The northern flanks of Beinn Mheadhoin rise across the eastern end of the loch.

Cross the Strath Nethy–Loch Avon path at the Saddle and descend southwards on grass and scattered rocks for 80m to reach the path along the shore of Loch Avon. Turn left (east), taking the path to the loch's outlet, which may be difficult to cross during a thaw or after heavy rain. In full winter conditions, the river is often covered with snow, making the crossing fairly dangerous, so adequate care should be taken. Once across the river, ascend steep slopes (grass with scattered rocks and some stony patches, with a faint zigzag path) in a direction just south of south-east, to reach the 950m contour above Sron Ghorm (gr NJ028027). Change to a more south-westerly direction and head up less steep but stonier slopes, trending in a more southerly direction to reach the summit tor.

There are several tors near the top of the hill, known collectively as the 'Barns of Beinn Mheadhoin': the largest of these is the summit (1182m), a spectacular 12m-high, vertical-sided, granite monolith, with a scrambling route up its northern end. Just below the top, the lack of holds creates one quite exposed move, with a 10m drop down an exposed slab on the eastern side. In icy conditions, this may deter some walkers; it is particularly difficult in descent and an ice axe may be of little use. The top of the tor has some curious potholes in the granite rock surface; there normally is not a cairn.

Return to the Coire Cas car park by the outward route. Alternatively, continue south-west past the smaller of Beinn Mheadhoin's tors then descend steeper ground to reach the path between Loch Etchachan and Loch Avon. Turn right, descend towards Loch Avon, pass the huge Shelter Stone (sleeping space for ten people) and ford the potentially hazardous Feith Buidhe. Continue along the north-western shore of Loch Avon for 0.6km then ascend the steep path on the eastern side of Allt Coire Raibeirt. Connect with the Beinn MacDuibh to Coire Cas path at the 1099m col at the head of Coire Raibeirt (gr NH999035) and follow it northwards to the car park.

40

BYNACK MORE

Ancient pine forests and desolate heathery moors

Parking: Glenmore Lodge, gr NH988095

Distance: 19km

Height Gain: 790m

Time: 5½–6½ hours

Terrain: Mainly good paths and tracks, some steep grassy and bouldery slopes

Standard: Moderate

OS Maps: Grantown & Aviemore (1:50,000 Landranger sheet 36), Cairn Gorm & Aviemore (1:25,000 Explorer sheet 403)

Isolated from the central Cairngorms by the deep trench of Strath Nethy, Bynack More proudly overlooks the moors of deepest Moray.

Take the Cairn Gorm ski road as far as Glen More then turn left onto the single track road leading to Glenmore Lodge and park just before the locked gate located 200m beyond the lodge. Signs erected by the Scottish Rights of Way and Access Society direct walkers to various destinations; the route to Bynack More follows the Lairig an Laoigh track to the base of the hill. Ignoring the track on the left – signposted 'cyclists/walkers' – follow the level gravel track going straight ahead into the Scots pine forest. Look out for red squirrels, which are not uncommon in this area. Cross a concrete bridge, pass a Forest Enterprise sign – which has information on the 'Glenmore Caledonian Forest Reserve' – and keep straight on at a junction where there is another sign with details on the Glenmore Forest Park. Continue gradually uphill to an area with more open views of the pudding-shaped Creag nan Gall ahead, with its attractive slopes of scattered pines and scree. The track remains level, passing through the deeply-incised Ryvoan Pass, with a lovely mix of steep heather slopes, pines and scree. A short detour on the right leads to the Green Lochan, a wonderful spot with submerged logs and splendid gravel beaches backed by scree slopes.

Loch Avon and Bynack More from Beinn Mheadhoin

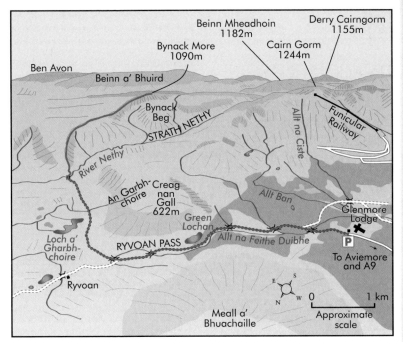

The trees thin out to be replaced by thick heather. At the junction near Ryvoan, keep right (signposted Braemar) on a rougher four-wheel-drive track that rises gradually onto a heather moor with occasional pines, some dwarf willow and juniper. Beyond the sign for the RSPB Abernethy nature reserve, the track continues past the scenic An Garbh-choire then heads slightly downhill and crosses the corrie's small burn (stepping stone). The track continues across more heather moorland then a slight descent leads to a wooden footbridge over the River Nethy. On the right, before the bridge, there remains only the foundation of the former Bynack Stable.

Cross the bridge and follow a well-maintained gravel path through thick heather, bearing left and rising steadily towards the northern shoulder of Bynack More. The path becomes quite peaty then stonier on steep ground, more gradual above 750m with short grass and heather predominating. The main path levels out above 780m; look out for the sandy/gravelly right fork that gradually bears right to traverse the 818m top on its eastern side. There are pleasant views across to Beinn a' Bhuird and Ben Avon on the left, with Creag Mhor's summit tor visible just left of Bynack More's green, tundra-like summit cone. Bynack Beg's tor is visible just to the right of Bynack More.

Descend easily on a pleasant path to the 810m col then follow the scarred gravelly path that goes steeply up to the right of an outcrop, keeping closer to the centre of the summit cone then slightly left (east) of centre at a bouldery section. Above this, bear right and ascend steeply to cross the outcrop-covered ridge, then keep right (west) on a path through boulders. There are fine views behind, towards Meall a' Bhuachaille. The path becomes steeper again, regaining the ridge then keeping right of a section that is covered in huge granite boulders. Beyond a level area of grass and scattered rocks, keep right of another bouldery ridge then gradually ascend 5m to the 2m-high summit cairn (1090m), with great views across the Little Barns of Bynack to Beinn a' Chaorainn. The tors on Beinn Mheadhoin are visible to the south-south-west, followed by Beinn MacDuibh and Cairn Gorm further right.

Return via Bynack Beg (a path descends from just below the aforementioned section of ridge covered in huge granite boulders) and the wet Strath Nethy, or return by the upward route. Keep right of point 818m on descent – the path to the left (west) is initially wider but it eventually peters out.

41

BEN RINNES

Expansive views from an isolated peak

Parking: Glack Harnes pass, gr NJ285359

Distance: 7km

Height Gain: 540m

Time: 3 hours

Terrain: Stony track, then gravel footpath with steep sections including stone stairs

Standard: Moderate

OS Maps: Elgin & Dufftown (1:50,000 Landranger sheet 28), Buckie & Keith (1:25,000 Explorer sheet 424)

Shapely and isolated Ben Rinnes attracts walkers from far and wide to experience the magnificent view from the summit. The hill is also popular with whisky enthusiasts, since there are no less than three distilleries on its flanks: Glenfarclas (with the largest stills on Speyside) to the north-west, and the two Diageo distilleries, Benrinnes and Dailuaine, both to the north.

There are several possible routes up the hill, including a direct ascent from the Benrinnes distillery. However, the recommended approach is from the minor road between Glen Rinnes and Milltown of Edinvillie via the Beatshach, where there is a car park at the south-east end of the Glack Harnes pass (gr NJ285359).

From Glack Harnes, a steep, four-wheel-drive track (closed to vehicular traffic) zigzags steeply up the heather-covered slopes of Round Hill. Salmon-pink granite, gravel and rocks will be seen on the way, but towards the summit of Ben Rinnes look out for an area of considerably paler granite (caused by chemical alteration of the pink feldspar). The track meanders across the flat, heathery top of Round Hill and passes through a gate, where pedestrians use a curious little stile that opens in the middle and counts each person passing through. Another fairly steep climb follows, with the rocky track passing the occasional stunted pine looking lost in the heather. Shortly before the summit of Roy's Hill

Ben Rinnes from Glenlivet

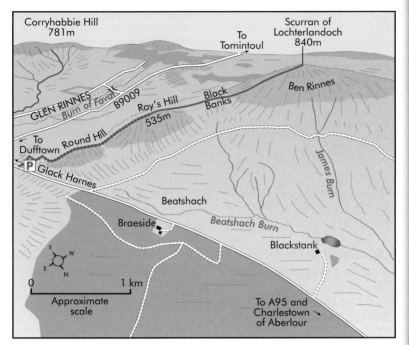

Corryhabbie Hill 781m
Scurran of Lochterlandoch 840m
To Tomintoul
GLEN RINNES
Burn of Favart
B9009
Roy's Hill 535m
Black Banks
Ben Rinnes
To Dufftown
Round Hill
P
Glack Harnes
James Burn
Beatshach
Braeside
Beatshach Burn
Blackstank
0   1 km
Approximate scale
To A95 and Charlestown of Aberlour

(535m), the track becomes a well-constructed footpath; the path passes over this subsidiary top then gradually descends about 10m on the other side before continuing through the peat-covered area called the Black Banks.

The final section of the route leading up the hill's summit cone is mostly very steep with occasional sections of stone stairs. It is a fine example of modern footpath engineering. It was constructed with the assistance of machinery and helicoptered-in rocks during 2004 and 2005, with the costs being met by public bodies and the Scottish Mountaineering Trust. Bizarrely, a report reached a local newspaper that 'dead sheep were being taken by helicopter off the hill'! The original route, a scar up to 20m wide, was an environmental disaster but it is gradually recovering and re-vegetation will continue if walkers keep to the new footpath.

The gradient decreases just below the summit tor, which boasts the peculiar name 'Scurran of Lochterlandoch'. It is a natural granite structure, much broken down and easily ascended on its northern side, but the eastern side is a cliff around 6m high that offers some shelter from inclement weather. The top of the tor sports little more than a damaged triangulation pillar (840m) but there is a panoramic view of rolling hills extending to distant horizons, including patchwork fields, forests and an unsightly wind farm. On a clear day, look for the narrow entrance to the Cromarty Firth, the lonely peaks of Caithness far beyond the wide expanse of the Moray Firth and the prominent tors of Ben Avon to the south (looking like a sow on her back). Nearer to hand, the communities of Dufftown and Charlestown of Aberlour, with their attendant distilleries, can be seen nestling in sheltered glens below the hill.

Unless transport has been arranged from an alternative pick-up spot, return by the outward route.

Friends of Ben Rinnes, a registered charity, looks for volunteer help with footpath maintenance on the hill. To offer assistance, check out the organisation's webpage.

42

STOB COIRE A' CHEARCAILL

A distinctive hill with vertical cliffs and broad ridges

Parking: Stronchreggan, gr NN071725

Distance: 11km

Height Gain: 780m

Time: 4–5 hours

Terrain: Track, grassy hillsides and ridges

Standard: Easy

OS Maps: Ben Nevis, Fort William & Glen Coe (1:50,000 Landranger sheet 41), Ardgour & Strontian (1:25,000 Explorer sheet 391)

Although rarely climbed, Stob Coire a' Chearcaill is a fine hill with near-vertical summit cliffs and magnificent views of Ben Nevis. It is a rather shy Corbett, only visible from main roads in a few places, including the string of roadside bed-and-breakfasts in Achintore, about 2km south-west of Fort William's town centre.

While it is possible to cross Loch Linnhe by the Fort William to Camusnagaul foot-passenger ferry, this adds about 7km of road walking to the day. It is quicker and easier to drive around Loch Eil, taking the pleasant, single-track road from Kinlocheil to Ardgour as far as Stronchreggan. About 200m beyond the houses at Stronchreggan, look out for the large lay-by on the right and park there.

The gravel track into Gleann Sron a' Chreagain, which starts at a gate just north of the road bridge over the river, penetrates much further into this wild glen than shown on current maps. Use the stile and follow the track through scattered, natural, deciduous woodland and gorse, past some partly broken down and ancient-looking walled enclosures. The river flows over rock steps of pink granite and the attractively varied landscape includes grassy areas and heather slopes with bracken. About 150m beyond another gate, there is a bridge over a fair-sized burn then the track ascends steeply to where a small burn is piped underneath.

Stob Coire a' Chearcaill seen across Loch Linnhe

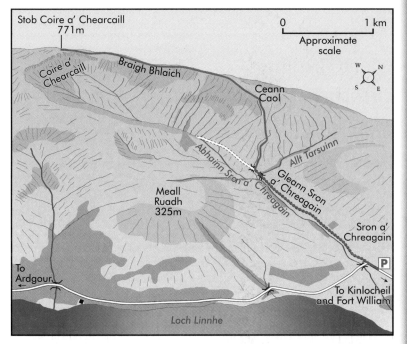

Turn right 3m before this burn and follow a path uphill by its right (east) bank. The pleasant watercourse is lined with occasional trees. The path soon peters out so continue along the east bank, through long grass mixed with areas of shorter grass and short heather. Cross the burn at gr NN054734. A steady, grass-covered slope leads to a barbed-wire fence (cross with care). Steep slopes beyond the fence lead to a series of small burns; cross the first and continue to the second, which should be followed to easier slopes higher up. Cross the second burn and continue to a third, slightly larger, burn (marked on OS maps); it is fairly steep for around 80m and has a small waterfall (gr NN048739).

Above the waterfall, the gradient decreases considerably. Keep left (due west) and cross a fairly level, grassy area with some boggy sections. On reaching the broad ridge of Ceann Caol at the 500m contour (gr NN045739), the walking becomes quite pleasant with short grass and heather and only a few unavoidable peat hags, boggy sections or tussocks. The route meets an old fence line, with only some main posts left standing. A steady rise leads past a small cairn at 600m, across stony and grassy areas, to a 609m top. The following section gives great walking, mainly on short grass and heather; dip

to 594m then rise to the grey-and-white rocks of quartz-feldspar-granulite on the 700m top, where there is a junction of three ancient fence lines and a cairn about half-a-metre high. Don't follow the old fence lines, but continue south-west to a steep-sided, grassy notch (easy to circumvent on the right) and rise up the grassy ridge towards the summit. The ground becomes stony above 740m. Beware of steep cliffs and gullies to the left (east) which may be corniced in winter. A square-plan triangulation pillar (770m) and a 2m-high, partly damaged cairn (771m) 25m to the west identify the summit. On a clear day, the fantastic views include Ben Nevis, the Mamores, the Glen Coe hills, the Glen Finnan and Gulvain groups, and the inhospitable Ardgour hinterland to the south-west.

Temptation may lead some walkers to complete the circuit of Gleann Sron a' Chreagain, but the descent into the head of the glen (around gr NN032720) involves very steep heather and the option of keeping high above Braigh an Fhraoich is tedious. There are also deer fences without stiles, bogs, precipitous slopes and very difficult ground in other places. It is advisable to return to the road by following the outward route.

SGORR CRAOBH A' CHAORAINN and SGURR GHIUBHSACHAIN

Climb spectacular Sgurr Ghiubhsachain and its neighbour

Parking: Callop, NM924792
Distance: 15km
Height Gain: 1040m
Time: 6½–7½ hours
Terrain: Rough paths, mainly grassy slopes and ridges
Standard: Moderate to difficult
OS Maps: Mallaig & Glenfinnan (1:50,000 Landranger sheet 40), Ardgour & Strontian (1:25,000 Explorer sheet 391)

The Corbetts of Ardgour are known and respected for their difficulty, with long grass, tussocks, deep heather, cliffs and bogs commonplace. However, the ascent of Sgurr Ghiubhsachain, the fine peak seen to the left of Loch Shiel from the Glenfinnan monument, is straightforward.

Turn off the A830 Fort William–Mallaig road 400m west of the railway bridge at gr NM924794. Follow the unsurfaced road southwards towards Callop, cross the bridge over the river, turn right then right again into the car park. Return on foot to the junction just south of the river bridge (sign: Ardgour 18 miles), then follow the unsurfaced road past riverside brambles to the house at Callop. The road bears right to the house but keep to the river bank (faint path), where there is pleasant natural woodland with Scots pines further along. Pass through a gap in the wall on the right into a field; the river has washed the former bank away. The path remains poor to the Allt an Fhaing ford; beyond this crossing, pass through a deer fence by means of a swing gate. The variably rocky and swampy path rises steadily to the crossing of Allt Coire na Leacaich, which may be impossible in wet weather. Continue uphill more steeply, go through another gate in a deer fence and rise to gr NM915765, where the path levels out.

Strike up the steep bank on the right and gain the eastern ridge of Meall na Cuartaige,

Sgurr Ghiubhsachain and the Glenfinnan Monument

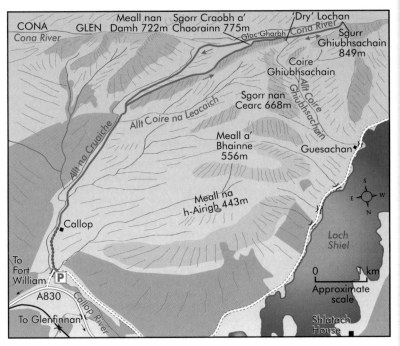

passing a large block of rock, neatly split in two. The going is mostly good; dry and grassy with patchy rock slab and a faint path in places. The ridge levels out at 480m then rises gradually to 510m; avoid steep slopes ahead by following a wide and level grassy ledge just south (left) of Meall na Cuartaige, about 50m below the top. Regain the ridge beyond Meall na Cuartaige at gr NM904763, keeping right of a hillock. Cross easy ground to the foot of the Corbett Sgorr Craobh a' Chaorainn, then ascend the 'peak' by keeping left of the centre, taking a shallow gully with occasional rock and boulders. Unfortunately, the 'top' proves to be a false summit. A wide ridge continues easily for 400m horizontally, but there are some rocky patches. There is a well-built, 1½m-high cairn on the summit (775m) where there are great views of Sgurr Ghiubhsachain, Streap, Gulvain and Ben Nevis.

Continuing south-westwards from the summit, a descent of 25m leads to a 25m-high cliff with overhangs; this can be avoided easily on broken rocks on the south (left). Do not attempt to descend the cliff directly. From the foot of the cliff, walk easily south-westwards down a broad, grassy ridge with scattered rocks as far as a wide col. Rise 10m over a hillock and descend to a 'lochan' (gr NM885750) that is normally just a peaty area with impressive peat hags up to 1½m high. Although a descent can be made northwards via Coire Ghiubhsachain, this is not recommended due to long grass and extremely bad tussocks.

From the col, keep right of the main ridge on good grass then ascend steep grass to the left of slabs to reach a little col just north of Sgurr Ghiubhsachain's summit (815m, gr NM 876753). Turn left (south) on a broad ridge, where there is a rocky section requiring hands for balance. The summit (849m), at the southern end of a level area, has a fine 1½m-high cairn. Views in all directions, particularly northwards along Glen Finnan, are magnificent.

Return to the little col (gr NM876753) and descend to the lochan (gr NM885750) by retracing steps. From the lochan, head east and slightly south, traversing Glac Garbh's grassy south-facing slopes; it is generally not too steep, but there are two steep-sided grassy gullies to cross. Pick up the usually wet path back to Callop from the col at gr NM900748.

44

STREAP

A magnificent, multi-topped mountain with narrow ridges

Parking: Drochaid Sgainnir, gr NM931799
Distance: 17km
Height Gain: 1170m
Time: 8–9 hours
Terrain: Forest tracks, steep, grassy slopes, narrow ridges with a little basic scrambling, wet argocat trail
Standard: Moderate to difficult
OS Maps: Mallaig & Glenfinnan (1:50,000 Landranger sheet 40), Loch Morar & Mallaig (1:25,000 Explorer sheet 398)

The Streap circuit is a very fine hill walk but is not easy under snow, when elementary winter climbing skills may be required. Stalking information (mid-August to mid-February) should be checked locally.

Turn off the A830 Fort William–Mallaig road at Drochaid Sgainnir (gr NM931799) and park just before the latched gate. Follow the generally level track into Gleann Dubh Lighe, the river with little waterfalls and natural woodland on its banks. Keep right at a junction. Beyond a short, steep section, 200m of level track leads to another junction; turn right and head downhill, descending 10m to a wooden bridge over a narrow gorge. Continue past mature forestry and open areas with views of Streap then rise past young trees to the Gleann Dubh Lighe cottage.

The track continues up the glen, with some ups-and-downs, to reach a latched gate, where there are great views of wild-looking hills ahead. A rougher and occasionally boggy track continues across open ground past some small burns and a walled enclosure to reach a bridge over the Dubh Lighe river (gr NM948838). Cross both the bridge and Allt Caol (easy), pass another walled enclosure and head north-north-west over initially boggy ground. Head towards a curious, grassy cone (gr NM946843) then follow the burn to its left; it goes to Bealach Coire nan Cearc. Steep but good ground leads to a pleasant, grassy corrie

The ridge north-east of Streap Comhlaidh

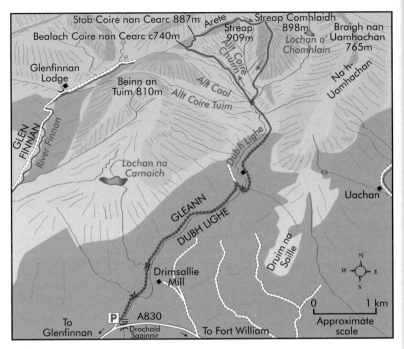

(560m) noted for large rocks and mountain flowers, including butterwort. Ascend grass and scattered rocks to the right of some scree to reach the bealach, with views of Loch Beoraid and Eigg beyond, Sgurr nan Coireachan and Sgurr na Ciche to the right.

At the bealach, turn right onto the steep, craggy flank of Stob Coire nan Cearc; keep right on grassy ramps with faint paths, keep central in the mid-section on short, dry grass between outcrops and pass a tiny pond. Follow a faint path bearing right then ascend directly to the summit (887m, no cairn). The magnificent views include Streap's knife-edge ridge to the north-east.

Descend a faint path on the broad but fairly steep north-east ridge (grass with small outcrops); pass over a bump to reach a col (790m) then follow a level ridge with many small outcrops that becomes grassy over a minor top (840m). The shattered rock scenery down on the right includes a 10m-high spire and a deep hole with a small pond in it. The ridge continues to a dip, narrowing to an exposed knife-edge with a path on the crest; use hands for balance through craggy sections. To get through a difficult-looking rock band about three-quarters of the way up Streap, scramble easily for 2m just left of the crest then traverse a short slab on the right. A narrow grassy ridge with

occasional slab leads to the 1m-high cairn on the grassy summit (909m).

Descend steeply eastwards for 15m then continue more gradually downhill. The path fades out but there are occasional iron fence posts. A faint path keeps right then descends a broad ridge to a grassy col (818m). The interesting ascent of Streap Comhlaidh is extremely steep on grass between outcrops, with an exposed 1m-high broken rock step. Easier, mossy grass leads to the top (898m, no cairn), with more fine views. Continue towards the 859m-high south top, descend 50m (no path) to a narrow col then rise on a faint path to the top (no cairn). Descend the easy mossy/grass south ridge, very steep below 700m but less so around 550m. Keep right (west) to avoid a crag and descend a steep grass ramp followed by less-steep grass leading to Allt Coire Chuirn. Avoid boggy ground with unpleasant tussocks by keeping right; once across the burn, bear left and follow a wet argocat trail for around 300m to reach the bridge over the Dubh Lighe at gr NM948838, then return as per the outward route.

45

ROIS-BHEINN and SGURR NA BA GLAISE

Impressive peaks and ridges with wonderful seaboard views

Parking: Lochailort Inn, NM768824
Distance: 17km
Height Gain: 1200m
Time: 7–8 hours
Terrain: Track, argocat trail, grassy hillsides and ridges (sometimes very steep)
Standard: Moderate to difficult
OS Maps: Mallaig & Glenfinnan (1:50,000 Landranger sheet 40), Ardnamurchan (1:25,000 Explorer sheet 390)

Moidart's Rois-bheinn group, located just south of Lochailort, consists of three Corbetts and several tops relatively close together. Steep, rocky hills with grassy leads between quartz-feldspar-granulite outcrops add up to a paradise for walkers and the views of the peaks, connecting ridges and the western seaboard are magnificent. Corbett-baggers usually include the steep-sided An Stac in their tally, but this adds 255m to an already hard day.

Park at Lochailort Inn, by the A830 Fort William–Mallaig road; walk 150m east along the roadside (direction Glenfinnan), then turn right onto a track that descends left of a house and deteriorates towards the River Ailort. Cross a wooden bridge then turn left onto a surfaced road leading to Glenshian Lodge. Pass a modern house, keep left at the junctions and follow the river bank. The stone-built lodge and its tennis courts are passed on the left; continue on a gravel track between a cottage and a boat shed. Beyond some old stone buildings, mixed woodland and rhododendrons, the pleasant gravel track heads southwards between Allt an t-Sagairt and interesting glaciated slabs. Avoid a track bearing left; continue through an open gateway, with Scots pine on the left and an ancient deer fence on the right.

On reaching two decrepit, brick buildings, turn left off the track (where the track turns right).

Sgurr na Ba Glaise and An Stac

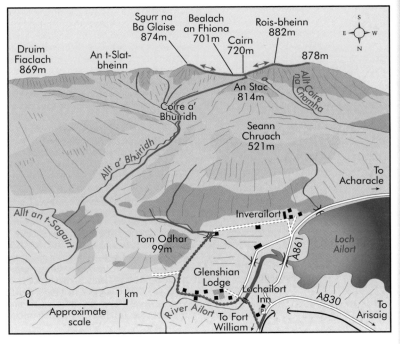

A faint grass path crosses wet ground and passes between some rhododendrons and trees, crosses a small burn then becomes a clear gravel path, rising steeply to another small ford in an attractive, secluded, partly wooded glen. The path rises to a ridge south-east of Tom Odhar, where it crosses a four-wheel-drive track twice, keeping about 100m west of the Allt a' Bhuiridh on an open, grassy hillside until merging with the aforementioned boggy and stony four-wheel-drive track. Rise steadily to a junction (keep right) then continue into Coire a' Bhuiridh, parallel to the burn, with good views of An Stac and Sgurr na Ba Glaise ahead. The track gets nearer the burn, remaining easy but boggy and becoming indistinct above 300m, where there is a 5m-high boulder. Continue into the corrie, keeping just right of the burn. Keep right (west) of the slabby crag at gr NM772787 where steeper, grassy slopes with outcrops lead west-south-west to easier ground, with two flat areas and a short steep rise to the 559m col due south of An Stac. From the col, ascend steep slopes south-west to a flat area at 600m and walk alongside the wall that rises steeply to the south-east. Keep left of a crag for the final 50m haul up steep grass to a shoulder (720m) above Bealach an Fhiona, where there is a cairn. The bealach is reputedly haunted and more than one person has reported hearing voices here – in full daylight.

To reach Rois-bheinn, follow the wall westwards across a flat area then uphill to a well-defined ridge followed by a broad flank of mixed grass and scattered stones. The triangulation pillar at the summit (882m) vanished many years ago but bits of it may be found in the 1m-high cairn. The best views are from the larger well-built cairn on the west top (878m), which lies beside the wall 0.7km to the west and beyond a dip at 830m. The islands of Rum and Eigg look magnificent from this lofty perch.

Return to Bealach an Fhiona (701m) and continue easily eastwards over grass and occasional stones to a shoulder (730m). Very steep ground continues with grass and scattered rock for 140m up to Sgurr na Ba Glaise, where there is a cairn (874m) at the northern end of the rounded summit. Hikers on a mission may wish to continue eastwards over the craggy ridges of An t-Slat-bheinn and Druim Fiaclach, but it is hard work and descent routes are not easy. It is best to return to the wall just west of Bealach an Fhiona then descend via the upward route.

46

FRAOCH BHEINN

An easy ridge-walk of pleasant and varied character

Parking: Head of Loch Arkaig, NM988916

Distance: 7km

Height Gain: 820m

Time: 4½–5½ hours

Terrain: Steep grassy hillsides, some tracks, faint paths

Standard: Moderate

OS Maps: Loch Alsh, Glen Shiel & Loch Hourn (1:50,000 Landranger sheet 33), Loch Morar & Mallaig (1:25,000 Explorer sheet 398)

The head of Loch Arkaig is a wild, remote and beautiful place, steeped in the history of long-dead clansmen and the redcoat soldiers who pursued them following the 1745 Jacobite rebellion. Of the numerous mountains around the head of the loch, Fraoch Bheinn is one of the easiest, with fine views all the way to the top. The route is mostly very pleasant with short grass on the upper slopes making for enjoyable walking.

From the commando memorial just north of Spean Bridge on the A82, take the B8004 to Gairlochy; continue on the B8005 to the eastern end of Loch Arkaig via the curious 'Dark Mile' then follow the winding minor loch-side road to its end, 2½km west of Murlaggan.

Parking possibilities at the end of the public road are, unfortunately, somewhat limited. From the gate at the turning area, head back towards Murlaggan for about 200m then turn left (west-north-west) onto the pathless hillside. The steep grass, with some bracken, is boggy in places but the ground improves as height is gained and the grass gets shorter. Aim for the little col north of the 246m hillock at gr NM983919 and, once on the level ground there, turn around for fine views of Streap and the beaches at the head of Loch Arkaig.

From the col, continue north-west contouring horizontally for about 100m to pick up an old

Braigh nan Uamhachan and Streap from Fraoch Bheinn

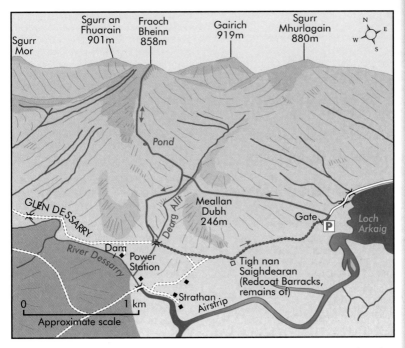

Sgurr an Fhuarain 901m
Fraoch Bheinn 858m
Gairich 919m
Sgurr Mhurlagain 880m
Sgurr Mor
Pond
GLEN DESSARRY
Meallan Dubh 246m
Gate
Loch Arkaig
Dearg Allt
River Dessarry
Dam
Power Station
Tigh nan Saighdearan (Redcoat Barracks, remains of)
Strathan Airstrip

0   1 km
Approximate scale

path that heads for a pass between Glen Dessarry and Glen Kingie. Follow this path for a short way then descend slightly to the left and easily cross the Dearg Allt at a flat area just above a tree-lined gully (gr NM983921). Ascend the grass slope on the north-west side of the burn to reach an argocat track; follow this steeply uphill to the north then north-west, gaining about 80m to reach a gently sloping area at 310m (gr NM982923).

Where the track heads off horizontally to the right (east), keep left (north-west) onto the open hillside, pass some outcrops and cross a fence. Ascend northwards on steep, grassy slopes with some outcrops; the gradient eases towards a small, flat area with a pond at 410m. Above the pond, there is a craggy flank with slabs, outcrops and grassy leads but it is a lot easier than it looks and actually very pleasant. At 510m, there is a slight dip of 4m but otherwise the slope is steadily and steeply uphill, with a faint path on good, short grass. Continue past outcrops to a level area at 710m, with a tiny pond on the right. The route passes some interesting slabs with fine examples of granite-gneiss foliation. Steep short grass between small crags and an indistinct path lead upwards to easier slopes but still with some outcrops. The

spacious, undulating, grassy summit (858m) is marked by a 1m-high cairn between scattered outcrops of the granite-gneiss bedrock.

There are good views all around, including Gairich to the north-east, the shapely Sgurr an Fhuarain behind Fraoch Bheinn's north top, and the tent-shaped Sgurr Mor. Westwards, there are impressive schist slabs on the eastern flank of Druim a' Chuirn while to the south lie Streap and Gulvain, with Loch Arkaig's beaches below.

Return to the argocat track by following the upward route. As an alternative to the direct line back to the end of the public road, follow the argocat track to Glen Dessarry. The track is steep and boggy but it is easier and quicker than following the line taken on ascent; the track takes a strange route, keeping well right (west) of the Dearg Allt between 200m and 170m. On reaching Glen Dessarry, turn to the left and follow the gravel four-wheel-drive track easily to the end of the public road. The track passes Tigh nan Saighdearan, the remains of the redcoat barracks, where government troops were stationed in 1746 while suppressing the clans and fruitlessly searching for the fugitive Bonnie Prince Charlie.

47

SGURR NA CICHE GROUP

Three thrilling Munros and ridges in the Rough Bounds

Parking: Head of Loch Arkaig, NM988916

Distance: 27km

Height Gain: 1530m

Time: 9–11 hours

Terrain: Track, rough boggy paths, steep rough hillsides and ridges

Standard: Moderate to difficult

OS Maps: Mallaig & Glenfinnan (1:50,000 Landranger sheet 40), Loch Morar & Mallaig (1:25,000 Explorer sheet 398)

The distinctive peak Sgurr na Ciche, at the western end of a 10km-long ridge, overlooks spectacular Loch Nevis but is best approached from the head of Loch Arkaig, via Glen Dessarry. The ridge between Sgurr na Ciche and Sgurr nan Coireachan is typical of the Rough Bounds (as this area is sometimes called), with complex Moine Thrust geology, plenty of exposed rock, occasional scrambling and magnificent views.

Leave cars near the locked gate (gr NM988916) at the western end of Loch Arkaig and continue on a gravel track 1km westwards to Strathan, passing a former barracks used by government troops during the post-1746 suppression of the clans. Rumours persist that a vast amount of Spanish gold destined for Bonnie Prince Charlie's war effort was buried near here following news of the prince's catastrophic defeat at Culloden. Despite comprehensive searches, only a few gold pieces have been found.

At the junction, bear left and downhill to Strathan, where the farmer keeps an airstrip for his microlight. Beyond a rusty, corrugated-iron building, keep straight ahead, cross a wooden bridge and continue to a locked gate. Cross the stile and follow the track into the plantation for 300m, then turn right onto the track for Glen Dessarry, initially steeply uphill then fairly level. Look out for wild boars in a fenced-off area – they delight in escaping and digging up the

On the ridge to Garbh Chioch Mhor

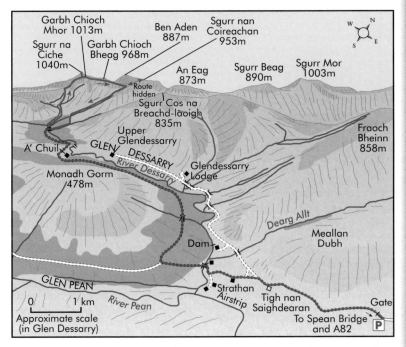

aforementioned airstrip. Beyond the forest edge (gr NM943923), the track descends 30m, crosses grassland then enters a younger plantation. Continue for 1½km to a bridge (gr NM930934), cross this and keep left on a swampy four-wheel-drive trail running close to the river bank. A steep ascent above 150m keeps right (east) of Allt a' Giubhais, leading to a gap in the upper fence. A gradual ascent leads to the junction with the path from Upper Glendessarry. The path and adjacent four-wheel-drive trail continue rising gradually, with boulder-hopping across boggy sections or detours around the worst parts.

At gr NM914949, just 0.2km before the Bealach an Lagain Duibh col at the top of the glen, turn right onto a steep often boggy four-wheel-drive trail that zigzags steeply uphill on grass between outcrops for around 300m. At 590m, where the trail bears left, head northwards, following an easy hill-walkers path on a broad grassy shelf that gradually slopes upwards to the north. On reaching the burn flowing from the col Feadan na Ciche, turn right (north-east) into a steep narrow gully with lots of boulders, easier for the final 50m. From the col, turn left onto a path and scramble up a steep, baldy, craggy slope, keeping left higher up and steeply gaining the ridge just east of

Sgurr na Ciche's summit (1040m), where there is a 1m-high cairn but no triangulation pillar.

Return to Feadan na Ciche and follow a steep path to Garbh Chioch Mhor, following a stone wall up to and across a shelf, weaving between extensive quartz-feldspar-granulite outcrops. Keep right of a crag to gain the western top of Garbh Chioch Mhor (1000m) then cross a dip to the main summit (1010m, cairn). Continue eastwards into an area of mica-schist, with a steep, stony descent of 40m followed by a rocky but level ridge, further descent then a level or gradually rising and grassier ridge over Garbh Chioch Bheag (968m). The stone wall follows the well-defined rocky ridge eastwards, taking the easiest line to Bealach Coire nan Gall (733m).

A steep path rises on grass and scattered rocks alongside an old fence line to reach the cairn on top of Sgurr nan Coireachan (953m), with more great views. It is best to return to Glen Dessarry via Bealach Coire nan Gall then descend mainly grassy slopes southwards to reach the path running south-east along the edge of the plantation. On reaching Allt Coire nan Uth, follow the path by this burn to reach the bridge at gr NM930934 then return to Loch Arkaig on the forest track.

48

BEINN BHUIDHE

A superb viewpoint for Loch Nevis and Knoydart

Parking: Mallaig, gr NM674969, then ferry required
Distance: 21km
Height Gain: 1020m
Time: 6½–7½ hours
Terrain: Tracks, gravel footpaths, grassy hillsides and ridges
Standard: Moderate to difficult
OS Maps: Loch Alsh, Glen Shiel & Loch Hourn (1:50,000 Landranger sheet 33), Loch Morar & Mallaig (1:25,000 Explorer sheet 398)

The fine mountains on the Knoydart peninsula include the shapely Beinn Bhuidhe, which presents its finest aspect towards Sourlies at the inner end of Loch Nevis. Beinn Bhuidhe is less rough and more pleasant for walking than some of the Knoydart Munros. Views of Loch Nevis from the summit are magnificent and upper parts of the hill have good alpine flowers. Distance, time and height gain are given from the pier at Inverie.

Most people take the Mallaig–Inverie ferry and stay several days in or near Inverie; book accommodation well in advance. Follow the track eastwards from Inverie towards Loch an Dubh-lochain as described for the route to Sgurr Coire Choinnichean. Turn left at the junction beyond the monument (gr NM797991) and follow the Mam Meadail (Sourlies) track towards Inverie River. Cross the wooden-slat footbridge then keep left on a mainly good, gravel, argocat track heading east into Gleann Meadail. Beyond some natural woodland, the track passes Kilchoan estate's Druim Bothy (locked).

Continue on an earthen or gravel path through more pleasant beech and silver-birch woodland near Allt Gleann Meadail towards an impressive, narrow, craggy section of glen, with some huge boulders across the river. A short descent leads to a wooden-slat bridge across the river. The well-drained path rises steadily, with a steeper section followed by easier ground rising into the upper glen. Descend slightly towards the

Beinn Bhuidhe's east ridge and Sgurr na Ciche, photo by Richard Webb

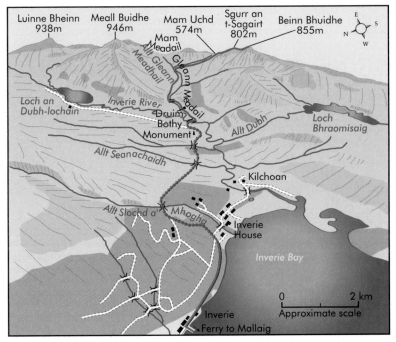

river and cross it at gr NM833980, easy under normal conditions. From the river, head southeast towards the col Mam Uchd; initially, avoid a slabby knoll (300m) by keeping left on rather rough, pathless ground, with a mixture of boulders, grass and bog. Pass a 5m-high boulder with a pointed top. Easier, fairly level, boggy grassland leads to steeper grass above 330m. Avoid a rock gully (gr NM835971) by ascending a grassy slope 70m to the right (west). Fairly steep grass and scattered boulders rise for around 50m to reach easier-angled slopes leading towards Mam Uchd (574m).

Beyond an easy section of peat hags, turn right (west) at the col and ascend steep, grassy slopes (avoiding areas of boulders) to reach a fairly level area of grass and scattered rocks. There are great views eastwards across the exceptionally rough and craggy Meall Bhasiter to Sgurr na Ciche and Garbh Chioch Mhor. Keep left of more boulders and ascend a steep grass ramp to reach short grass of moderate gradient just left (south) of the main ridge. Continue through broken crags and outcrops above 700m, keeping right on grass. The impressive rock tower looming ahead, Sgurr an t-Sagairt (802m), is not as dangerous as it looks, but it is steep. Follow a ledge to the left below a rock band then ascend a steeper section of ridge, meandering easily between quartz-feldspar-granulite outcrops on short grass. At 750m, a faint path goes left across the base of the tower then zigzags upwards to take a more central line, continuing upwards to the top on very steep grass (use hands for balance) between outcrops. The views just get better and better.

A descent of about 10m on a grassy ridge with many outcrops leads to a broad col then a faint easy path ascends steadily on a broad grassy ridge to the summit of Beinn Bhuidhe, Sgurr Coir' an Fhir-eoin (855m), where there is a small cairn near a damaged cylindrical stone-chip triangulation pillar and mossy grass between schist boulders and outcrops. Impressive views from the top include Rum, Skye, Loch Nevis, Loch Morar and the Knoydart peaks from Sgurr na h-Aide to Ladhar Bheinn.

It is best to descend by the outward route. The alternatives are not particularly pleasant; the apparently direct route from the power house (via Allt Dubh) should be avoided due to tussocks and very rough ground. Likewise, the descent northwards from Bealach Buidhe involves some steep ground and exceptionally nasty boggy tussocks.

49

SGURR COIRE CHOINNICHEAN

A finely shaped peak overlooking the west coast and islands

Parking: Mallaig, gr NM674969, then ferry required

Distance: 12km

Height Gain: 900m

Time: 5–6 hours

Terrain: Track, steep grassy hillsides and ridges

Standard: Moderate

OS Maps: Loch Alsh, Glen Shiel & Loch Hourn (1:50,000 Landranger sheet 33), Knoydart, Loch Hourn & Loch Duich (1:25,000 Explorer sheet 413)

The impressive schist peak Sgurr Coire Choinnichean soars above Knoydart's remote village of Inverie, its summit beckoning travellers on board the ferry from Mallaig. While it is possible to ascend the hill directly from the village, it is extremely steep. Alternatively, a pleasant walk along the track by the Inverie River leads to the easier southern flanks of the hill.

There are daily ferries from Mallaig to Inverie except on Sunday. Otherwise access Inverie by private boat or on foot by two-day-long trails from Loch Arkaig or Kinloch Hourn; the village is not connected to the national road network. There is not time to climb the hill and return to Mallaig the same day and, aside from camping, accommodation should be arranged well in advance.

On arriving at Inverie's pier, turn right onto the surfaced road that heads for Inverie House and Loch an Dubh-lochain. Pass through pleasant mixed woodland, with a Knoydart Forest Trust sign on the left and good views of Rum across the beach on the right. Keep left then keep left again, where Scottish Rights of Way and Access Society signs point uphill (the right fork leads to Inverie House, Kilchoan and the Knoydart Foundation bunkhouse). Follow the gravel track uphill through broadleaf forest and rhododendrons. Avoid the private track on the left signposted for Torrie Cottage and Shieling. Go

Inverie and Sgurr Coire Choinnichean

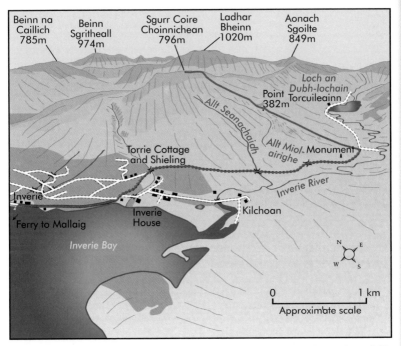

Beinn na Caillich 785m
Beinn Sgritheall 974m
Sgurr Coire Choinnichean 796m
Ladhar Bheinn 1020m
Aonach Sgoilte 849m

Loch an Dubh-lochain
Point 382m
Torcuileainn

Allt Seanachaidh

Allt Miol-airighe
Monument

Torrie Cottage and Shieling

Inverie

Inverie River

Kilchoan

Inverie House

Ferry to Mallaig

Inverie Bay

0   1 km

Approximate scale

through the gate on the main track, cross Allt Slochd a' Mhogha (bridge) then follow the walled forest edge, uphill at first then level. On the left rise the very steep, bracken-and-thick-grass-covered slopes of Sgurr Coire Choinnichean; they should be avoided. Beyond the forest, the track descends past a broadleaf shelter belt and a trackside wall then passes through a mature plantation. The track then stays fairly level above the Inverie River, passing below the curious monument on Torr a' Bhalbhain to reach the junction at gr NM797991 (turn right here for Sourlies and Beinn Bhuidhe). The monument commemorates Nazi sympathiser Lord Brocket, who owned Inverie House and the accompanying estate in the 1930s and 40s, and features a large cross atop a large dome.

Turn left, off the track, then ascend grass-and-bog-myrtle slopes due northwards, with some boulders and outcrops above 70m. Tedious long grass is a nuisance on a flat area at around 120m. Keep right of a slabby crag (140m to 170m), ascending a steep ramp where short grass and heather alternates with longer grass and occasional bracken patches. An unpleasant section of waist-deep grass and tussocks on a steep slope leads to a flat area at 280m. Keep left up an easier, grassy ramp to a small, flat area at 320m; keep left of the crag beyond this area by slanting up yet another grassy ramp. A large, flat area with outcrops (382m) leads to a dip. Avoid the steep outcrops ahead by keeping left on easy grass with small outcrops, but keep right of the small waterfall. Ascend steep but easy (and mercifully short) grass to the right, weaving between small crags to reach a flat area with some exposed peat (650m). A very steep, 50m-high, grass slope leads upwards; keep left of a small crag to reach easier ground with a mossier surface. Continue northwards to reach the broad grass ridge 300m east of Sgurr Coire Choinnichean's summit. Once on the ridge, turn left (west) and then follow a faint path, steeply at first then fairly level, followed by various grassy and mossy bumps to reach the half-metre-high summit cairn (796m). The cairn sits on a broad area that is very steep sided so there is quite an airy feeling with expansive views all around. The steep flanks of Ladhar Bheinn dominate to the north-east, but eyes are irresistibly drawn to the west where Rum and Eigg float like ships on the Hebridean sea.

Due to the steep slopes to the west, it is advisable to return by the outward route.

50

LADHAR BHEINN

Sensational ridges, cliffs and corries in the heart of Knoydart

Parking: Kinloch Hourn, gr NG949066
Distance: 32km
Height Gain: 1940m
Time: 13–15 hours (best split into two or three days)
Terrain: Varied paths and tracks, steep grassy slopes and narrow ridges
Standard: Difficult
OS Maps: Loch Alsh, Glen Shiel & Loch Hourn (1:50,000 Landranger sheet 33), Knoydart, Loch Hourn & Loch Duich (1:25,000 Explorer sheet 413)

Complex and impressive Ladhar Bheinn dominates the wild Knoydart peninsula with its impressive cliffs and narrow ridges. The finest route to the mountain includes both the surprisingly hard Kinloch Hourn–Barrisdale coastal path and an ascent via the wild and remote Coire Dhorrcail (the Inverie approach is easier but relatively uninteresting). There are no access restrictions since Ladhar Bheinn is owned by the John Muir Trust. Boat transport between Arnisdale and Barrisdale may be arranged in Arnisdale.

The single-track road to Kinloch Hourn is an adventure in itself; park off-road just beyond the farm buildings (gr NG949066). Walk along the road to the turning area then follow the footpath along the southern shore of Loch Hourn. In places, the narrow path is perched precariously between broken cliffs and slabs that drop about 2m into the water; rowans, rhododendrons and huge boulders add interest. Beyond the first hut at Skiary, the cliffs pull back from the coast and the path rises 40m to reach the substantial Allt Coire Mhicrail (footbridge). Continue downhill then rise steeply past an old fence to a shoulder and descend steeply with zigzags to reach several burn crossings at Camas Ban (normally hop-skip-and-jump, but possibly challenging in wet weather). A fairly steep and eroded rise through some thick bracken leads to a wide col at 110m behind Creag Raonabhal, then a steep

Stob a' Choire Odhair and Loch Hourn

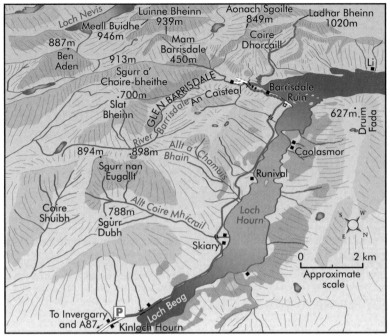

descent leads to a straightforward burn crossing, with Runival house below on the right. The path then keeps near the shore, with a beautiful built-up section passing through wonderful natural woodland (including Scots pine) and some thick heather. Beyond some burn crossings and easier ground, the path rises and falls several times near the shoreline. Ascend gradually to the footbridge over Allt a' Chaolas Bhig then a steeper ascent of 60m leads to gradual rises or traverses, with a final steep descent to the ruined church at Barrisdale Bay.

A track follows the shore for 1km south to the tree-sheltered Barrisdale House, then onwards for 600m to the farm buildings and rather basic hostel; camp for a very modest payment across the track to avoid the noisy generator at 7am!

From the hostel, continue southwards for 100m, cross the bridge then turn immediately right onto a path heading across grassy flats. Beyond a burn crossing, keep left and ascend steep slopes, with an easy rock step and lots of tight zigzags (some thick bracken), followed by a rising traverse above 180m. Views over Barrisdale Bay are exceptionally fine from here, especially at high water. The path skirts some trees, passes below a small cliff then traverses into Coire Dhorrcail, with Ladhar Bheinn's mica-

schist cliffs and Stob Dhorrcail's steep spur straight ahead. Continue into the corrie to a level area at 250m, cross the Allt Coire Dhorrcail (gr NG845041) then ascend fairly steep, grass slopes with scattered rocks in a west-north-west direction to reach Druim a' Choire Odhair at around 700m. Turn leftwards (south-west) and follow the ridge path; although steep and eroded in places with some easy scrambling, it is a magnificent route with wonderful views. Above 870m, a steep, narrow, grassy ridge, precipitous on both sides, leads to Stob a' Choire Odhair (960m, small cairn).

The narrow, exposed ridge continues to a dip (920m) then the path rises steeply to a level section; 40m of further ascent leads to a tiny cairn on the summit ridge. Continue about 200m to the right (west) for Ladhar Bheinn's highest point (1020m, small cairn). The badly-damaged cylindrical triangulation pillar (1010m) is 300m further west-north-west. Views from the ridge, including Skye and Loch Hourn, Stob a' Chearcaill's ribbed flanks, Sgurr na Ciche and Ben Nevis, are amongst the best in the Highlands.

It's best to return to Barrisdale the same way since Ladhar Bheinn's south-east ridge is tedious, with serious scrambling in places. Return to Kinloch Hourn by the outward route.

51

GLEOURAICH and SPIDEAN MIALACH

Spectacular peaks and ridges overlooking Loch Quoich

Parking: Loch Quoich (Allt Coire Peitireach), gr NH029030

Distance: 11km

Height Gain: 1190m

Time: 7–8 hours

Terrain: Good stalker's paths, rough hill paths, ridges, bouldery and grassy hillsides

Standard: Moderate to difficult

OS Maps: Loch Alsh, Glen Shiel & Loch Hourn (1:50,000 Landranger sheet 33), Glen Shiel & Kintail Forest (1:25,000 Explorer sheet 414)

The shapely hills north-east of Loch Quoich, Gleouraich and Spidean Mialach, are connected by a high-level ridge and the circuit of both is a fine walk with excellent views. Loch Quoich was artificially enlarged for the Glen Garry hydro-electric project when Scotland's largest rock-fill dam (320m long, 38m high) was completed in 1962. Despite the fact that the area is amongst the wettest in Europe, with annual rainfall up to 5500mm per year in some places, the loch often has artificial shoreline scars.

Drive along the single-track road towards Kinloch Hourn that leaves the A87 at Loch Garry; pass the Loch Quoich dam and park just beyond Allt Coire Peitireach at gr NH029030. Beyond an estate sign, a stony or gravel path ascends through rhododendrons, gorse and silver birch to reach open, grassy hillside. Pass under the electricity cables then steep zigzags lead the path up to the left. There are some small outcrops above 400m and great views across Loch Quoich as far as Ben Aden and Sgurr na Ciche. Tight zigzags up a steep section are followed by some muddy areas on easier ground. The path zigzags up a steep, craggy flank by following a grassy lead, with a good view of Sgurr a' Mhaoraich on reaching an easier ridge at 640m. Follow the grass or gravel path northwards up this ridge (Druim Seileach), gradually rising on grass with outcrops and passing a curious stone

Cloud sea lapping Spidean Mialach, photo by Niall Sclater

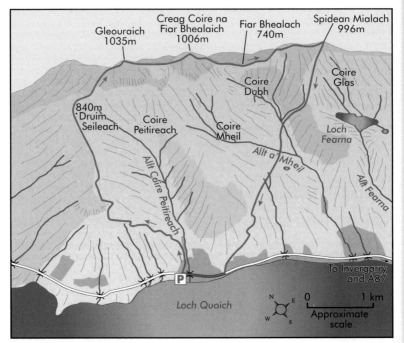

wall at 780m. There are great views of Loch Quoich and the bridge over its northern arm. The ridge levels out at 840m with the path traversing its grassy left-hand (western) side, rejoining the ridge north of the highest point then descending to a col (814m).

Avoid a gravel path that trends right from the col towards a stone-wall shelter by taking a hill-walkers path going east-north-east, directly up a steep grassy flank with scattered rocks and some bouldery areas. On meeting Gleouraich's northern ridge, bear right (east), descend 5m then rise steadily on a patchy path through grass, rocks and outcrops, with some broken quartz-feldspar-granulite slab. A final, mainly grassy, rise leads to the well-built 1¾m-high cairn (1034m), where there is no triangulation pillar or shelter. Views are outstanding in all directions.

Continue south-eastwards then eastwards on a narrow, bouldery ridge, with a 2m downwards rock step avoidable on the right. An easy earthen or gravel path then leads through grass and stones to the 947m col. From there, a stony or gravel path rises through outcrops, broken slab and boulder fields past cliffs on the left to reach the summit of Creag Coire na Fiar Bhealaich (1006m, no cairn). The path then descends to

the right (east) and easy zigzags head left to reconnect with the ridge at 940m (great views of Spidean Mialach all the way). A steep, stony ridge with zigzags descends to a grassy section (790m), with a 4m rise followed by a final slabby and bouldery descent to the 740m Fiar Bhealach.

From the bealach, a path rises south-eastwards up a bouldery slope then steep grass, with a stony approach to a flat, grassy area (920m) then an easier path rises over grass and stones to a minor top. Bear right, descend 3m then a gradual stony rise leads to a 1m-high cairn (977m). Descend gradually over stones and grass with slabby, schist cliffs on the left then ascend steadily on a faint path over grey stones to reach Spidean Mialach's fairly small summit (996m), with a well-built, 1½m-high, stone ring shelter.

A path descends south-west from the summit, crossing stony areas but fairly grassy below 900m with some slippery boggy or indistinct sections. From the 580m col above Loch Fearna, descend rough boggy slopes westwards, pass a 4m-high boulder, cross the burn then pick up a mainly good gravel stalkers path leading back to the road 400m east of the starting point.

52

BEINN NAN CAORACH and BEINN NA H-EAGLAISE

Unparalleled coastal and mountain views

Parking: Corran, Arnisdale, gr NG849094

Distance: 12km

Height Gain: 1055m

Time: 5½–6½ hours

Terrain: Tracks, then pathless grassy and stony slopes and ridges

Standard: Mostly moderate, with one very steep section

OS Maps: Loch Alsh, Glen Shiel & Loch Hourn (1:50,000 Landranger sheet 33), Knoydart, Loch Hourn & Loch Duich (1:25,000 Explorer sheet 413)

The Beinn nan Caorach and Beinn na h-Eaglaise circuit is one of the finest hill walks in the western Highlands, giving magnificent views of surrounding peaks and sections of the western seaboard. Some routes on these hills are very steep and are not advisable for casual walkers, but alternatives are available and are described here.

Leave vehicles in the Corran car park, at the end of the Shiel Bridge–Arnisdale single-track road. Follow the road back northwards for 400m, then turn right and take the four-wheel-drive track into Glen Arnisdale for 1½km. The track passes some buildings then follows the pleasant, tree-lined river bank. On reaching the bridge at gr NG861098, leave the track, turn left and cross a grassy field to locate the narrow footbridge over the Allt Utha, just upstream from the locked estate cottage Achadh a' Ghlinne. Beyond the bridge a rough, four-wheel-drive track ascends the eastern side of the Allt Utha ravine in a series of very steep zigzags. Above the zigzags, the gradient eases and pleasant walking leads to a junction at gr NG865107. Turn right and follow another steep zigzag track, gaining height rapidly then reaching easier ground near the top of Eas na Cuingid, an impressive 30m-high waterfall plunging into a narrow gully. The track enters Coire Chorsalain; above the falls, leave the track, cross the burn

Beinn na h-Eaglaise and Beinn Sgritheall

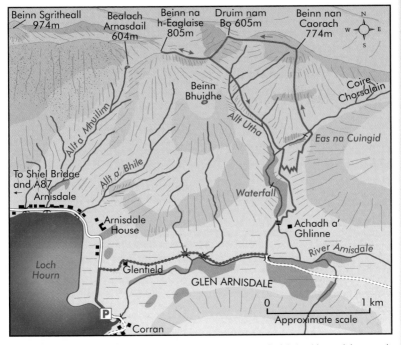

Beinn Sgritheall 974m · Bealach Arnasdail 604m · Beinn na h-Eaglaise 805m · Druim nam Bo 605m · Beinn nan Caorach 774m · Coire Chorsalain · Beinn Bhuidhe · Allt a' Mhuilinn · Allt Utha · Eas na Cuingid · To Shiel Bridge and A87 · Arnisdale · Allt a' Bhile · Waterfall · Arnisdale House · Achadh a' Ghlinne · River Amisdale · Loch Hourn · Glenfield · GLEN ARNISDALE · 0 · 1 km · Approximate scale · P · Corran

and strike due north on pathless ground towards Beinn nan Caorach. Easy, grass slopes, although somewhat wet, give way to steeper, broken ground with patchy grass, outcrops and occasional scree. There are three steep sections with easier gradients in-between, at 150m, 300m and 390m above the falls. Beyond the final 30m-high steep section, trend right on easier ground (mixed grass and loose stones) towards the small summit cairn (774m), a great place to relax and take in the scenery. On approaching the summit, the views improve dramatically; Ladhar Bheinn and a mass of other Knoydart hills beckon beyond Loch Hourn, while the Saddle dominates to the east. The impressive, alpine-looking peaks, Beinn na h-Eaglaise and Beinn Sgritheall, soar into the sky to the west.

From Beinn nan Caorach, follow old fence posts easily north then north-west over mixed stones and grass, descending to the sward named Bealach Dhruim nam Bo (580m). Ascend slightly to the broad ridge Druim nam Bo (605m, probably a former cattle pasture), then descend south-west to a dip at 547m. The route to the top of the impressive spire of appropriately named Beinn na h-Eaglaise (hill of the church) looks suitably imposing, but a path leads easily upwards through the steepest ground at around

670m to a wonderful airy ridge and the summit cairn at 805m, another spot with great views.

The descent to Bealach Arnasdail and its curious little lochan is possible in dry conditions but this route becomes incredibly steep with much loose rock and precarious grassy ledges. It is not recommended except for mountain goats. Part of the descent (which follows the dilapidated old fence line) cannot be seen from above; dangerous crags and gullies lie to the left and should be avoided. The path from Bealach Arnasdail to Arnisdale village is poor, wet and muddy; the author slipped hereabouts and ended up covered in mud from head to foot. It is also possible to descend the south-south-east ridge of Beinn na h-Eaglaise via Beinn Bhuidhe (639m), with steep grass slopes leading down to Achadh a' Ghlinne. However, it is much easier to return carefully north-eastwards to the 547m dip then follow the old fence line descending south-east on easy grass into Coire Dhruim nam Bo. Continue by dropping steeply down to the Allt Utha and, at gr NG865112, pick up a path which connects with the track to Achadh a' Ghlinne. Return easily to the car park along the Glen Arnisdale four-wheel-drive track.

53

THE SADDLE and SGURR NA SGINE

Impressively steep and rugged peaks dominating Glen Shiel

Parking: Malagan, Glen Shiel, gr NG973138

Distance: 13km

Height Gain: 1410m

Time: 6–8 hours

Terrain: Steep grassy or stony slopes or ridges, paths in places

Standard: Moderate to difficult

OS Maps: Loch Alsh, Glen Shiel & Loch Hourn (1:50,000 Landranger sheet 33), Glen Shiel & Kintail Forest (1:25,000 Explorer sheet 436)

The highly recommended Saddle and Sgurr na Sgine circuit provides some of the best views in the north-west Highlands. For a shorter walk, the Saddle can be climbed on its own, using the descent route suggested here for ascent. Walkers without scrambling experience may prefer the 'easy' route described here since the exciting Forcan Ridge alternative includes a short but tricky section between Sgurr na Forcan and the Saddle's east top. Check deerstalking information 11 August to 20 October.

Leave cars by the northbound A87 Invermoriston–Kyle of Lochalsh road in Glen Shiel's Malagan lay-by, gr NG973138. From the lay-by, walk 100m north, turn left and pass through a gate with signs for Kinloch Hourn, Loch Quoich and Tomdoun. Follow an argocat track that becomes a grassy footpath for a while, rising behind a former gravel quarry. The track becomes very boggy on bearing left to reach the wooden footbridge over the tree-lined Allt Mhalagain (gr NG971135). Beyond the bridge, keep right on another path, passing through grass and bog myrtle to reach a deer fence (gate). Go through the gate into a young plantation and continue uphill on Faochag's craggy north-east ridge, with a steep path easing off above 200m. Cross the fence using a dilapidated stile at 280m then follow the path directly up the steep ridge, with little crags and outcrops between

The Saddle and Sgurr na Forcan from Glen Shiel

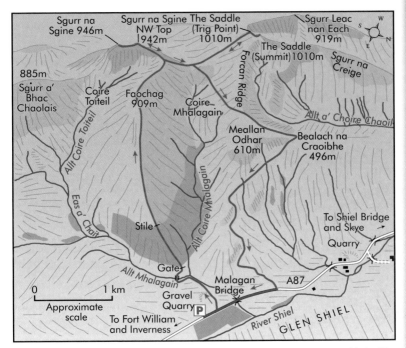

400 and 550m. Above these crags the gradient eases off a couple of times then there is a steep pull up the grassy summit cone, with scattered rocks near the top. The final easy 20m leads to Faochag's summit half-metre-high cairn (909m), a magnificent viewpoint for Glen Shiel.

An almost level, well-defined ridge (grassy with scattered rocks) descends westwards to a dip, passes over a top (880m), then curves south-west to another dip (850m) with some tiny ponds. A rougher ridge with outcrops and looser rock rises fairly steeply southwards to reach Sgurr na Sgine's north-west top (942m, small cairn). Continue over a 921m dip then rise gradually to the main summit (946m). The 1½m-high summit cairn overlooks the steep eastern face and gives great views of the South Glen Shiel Ridge.

Return to the 880m top (gr NG946122) then descend north-west towards the ponds at Bealach Coire Mhalagain (699m), a straight-forward, moderately steep slope of grass and scattered rocks. From the bealach, head slightly north-of-west on a rising traverse into a grassy corrie for around 0.6km. Keep left and below scree to meet a steep flank that leads north-wards to easier-angled ground above 930m. Keep right of the ponds at 965m and 995m but keep left of the direct ascent to the triangulation

pillar, following a grassy ramp to avoid a boulder field. Once on the grassy ridge, turn right to reach the Saddle's cylindrical, concrete triangulation pillar (1010m), surprisingly not the highest point on the hill. Continue eastwards, descending by path to a dip (995m) then rise upwards on a narrow rocky ridge (steep slabby quartz-feldspar-granulite cliffs on the right) to reach the cairn on the well-formed, conical, rocky summit, about 40cm higher than the triangulation pillar top (1010.4m). The view eastward, down the spectacular cliff-girt Forcan Ridge and along Glen Shiel below, is awe-inspiring.

The easiest way down is to return to the triangulation pillar and descend to Bealach Coire Mhalagain by following the upward route. From the bealach, descend north-east into the rather rough Coire Mhalagain, traversing steep slopes beneath the Forcan Ridge. A dry-stone dyke may be followed through boulder fields but the ground is much less rough around 80m lower down. A path from the foot of the Forcan Ridge goes across the 601m col (gr NG950133) and the rough but flat Meallan Odhar (610m) to connect with a well-drained gravel stalker's path descending from Bealach na Craoibhe (496m) to Malagan in Glen Shiel, meeting the A87 600m north-west of the lay-by.

54

SOUTH GLEN SHIEL RIDGE

Superlative, multi-topped ridge-walking

Parking: Glen Shiel, gr NH044115

Distance: 17km (including 3km on the A87)

Height Gain: 1180m

Time: 6–7 hours

Terrain: Paths, grassy and rocky ridges with occasional paths, some scrambling

Standard: Moderate to difficult

OS Maps: Loch Alsh, Glen Shiel & Loch Hourn (1:50,000 Landranger sheet 33), Glen Shiel & Kintail Forest (1:25,000 Explorer sheet 414)

The entire South Glen Shiel Ridge traverse, from Creag a' Mhaim to Creag nan Damh, is a magnificent expedition requiring a high level of fitness and competent route-finding abilities. It is advisable to split the ridge into two halves, utilising a good path from central Glen Shiel for ascent or descent. The eastern half, which includes the interesting ridge of Aonach air Chrith, is described here.

Leave cars in the eastbound A87 lay-by at gr NH044115, about 3km west of Cluanie Inn. Across the road, a path descends to Allt Coire a' Chuil Droma Bhig, where there are enormous stepping stones. Ascent of the Druim Coire nan Eirecheanach spur is assisted by a recently renovated stalkers path, initially avoiding the steep Meall na Doire by trending left, then zigzagging upwards to 570m. The path ends abruptly where the gradient conveniently eases. Continue up the easy-angled and well-defined ridge, with pleasant walking on short turf. At 700m, the ridge becomes steeper, becoming narrow above 750m, with an odd, narrow lochan on the left at 900m. From Maol Chinn-dearg's rounded grassy summit (981m, cairn), there are fine views along the ridge (both east and west), with the Five Sisters, the Three Brothers and A' Chralaig to the north. Looking south, there is the narrow Glen Quoich arm of Loch Quoich, wedged between Sgurr a' Mhaoraich and Gleouraich.

The ridge between Aonach air Chrith and Maol Chinn-dearg

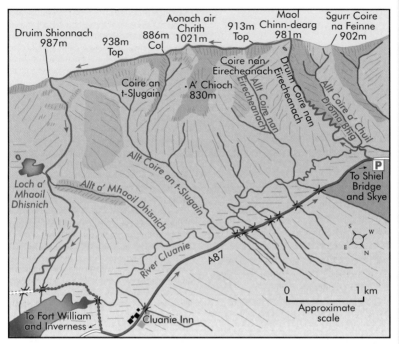

Although it is only 2km eastwards to the next Munro, Aonach air Chrith, it takes most walkers about an hour. An easy, grassy descent leads to a col at 890m. The ridge then narrows dramatically and becomes progressively more exciting. When heading east, hill walkers may find themselves on an odd section of ridge with near vertical drops all around, with easy ground lying just a few metres to the right (south). Return a considerable distance westwards until a way is found to the easier ground. There are numerous ups-and-downs on the ridge beyond and, past the 855m dip at gr NH043082, it becomes alpine in character (in winter, cornices may be encountered) with some easy scrambling on a shattered crest of quartz-feldspar-granulite. The summit of Aonach air Chrith (1021m), supported by three fine ridges, has a large cairn and is a good place to stop and admire the views. The north ridge of the mountain is particularly attractive for photography.

An easy descent on mixed grass and stones leads south-east to a col at 886m. From this col, a mainly grassy ridge rises over a 923m top then the ridge undulates, rising to 938m then becoming a little narrower and stonier for a while after a 900m dip at gr NH065082. Continue to the 987m-high Munro, Druim Shionnach, easily reached by ascending its wide western flank (with one narrow section near the top).

Munro baggers may want to add Creag a' Mhaim to their tally; it is an easy walk out and back, adding about an hour to the day. It is also possible to descend Creag a' Mhaim's south-east ridge and return to Cluanie Inn via the old Tomdoun–Cluanie road, but it is a long way around. The descent from Druim Shionnach to Cluanie Inn is advised.

From Druim Shionnach's cairn, descend northwards on a ridge with scattered rocks that becomes barred by a steep cliff at gr NH073090. There is an easy way down a 20m-high gully on the left but it is steep and rather loose. Below the crag, the ridge has some rough patches of boulder fields and scree alternating with grass. The ground becomes more heathery and grassy as the route nears Loch a' Mhaoil Dhisnich. Pick up the rough stalkers path near the loch's outlet (if it can be found) and descend to the Tomdoun–Cluanie track, for the final 1km to the inn and a welcome drink in the bar. Then the fittest member of the party can volunteer to walk 3km westwards along the road to pick up the car.

55

MULLACH FRAOCH-CHOIRE and A' CHRALAIG

Exciting narrow ridges and phenomenal views

Parking: Loch Cluanie (An Caorann Mor), gr NH087121

Distance: 17km

Height Gain: 1120m

Time: 7–8 hours

Terrain: Partly on tracks and boggy path, grassy hillsides, narrow grassy or rocky ridges

Standard: Moderate to difficult

OS Maps: Loch Alsh, Glen Shiel & Loch Hourn (1:50,000 Landranger sheet 33), Fort Augustus, Glen Albyn & Glen Roy (1:50,000 Landranger sheet 34), Glen Shiel & Kintail Forest (1:25,000 Explorer sheet 414)

Although a circuit of the fine peaks Mullach Fraoch-choire and A' Chralaig is best achieved by using ridges and corries from Glen Affric, very long access routes put off most people. The alternative, approaching from Loch Cluanie, involves ascending steep, grassy slopes.

From the A87 roadside car park at gr NH087121, or the smaller parking area by the bridge at gr NH091121, follow the roadside eastwards to the beginning of the four-wheel-drive track and path to upper Glen Affric. The rocky and often wet track makes for rather rough walking up the glen, An Caorann Mor. Beyond the end of the track at gr NH081148, boggy paths lead through the 404m pass between Stob Coire na Cralaig and Ciste Dhubh. In wet weather, this section may be extremely unpleasant, but the higher-level path may be somewhat drier. Both paths ford the substantial burn, Allt Coire a' Ghlas-thuill. Shortly after the paths rejoin, there is another burn crossing (gr NH078166). Leave the path beyond this ford and slant north-eastwards across the foot of Coire Odhar, crossing the first of its two burns below 470m because, above this level, both burns run through difficult-to-cross ravines. On the northern flank of the corrie, zigzag up steep, grassy slopes for 400m of vertical ascent to gain a level section on Mullach Fraoch-choire's north-western ridge (gr NH089177). Turn right for the summit, which

A' Chralaig from Stob Coire na Cralaig

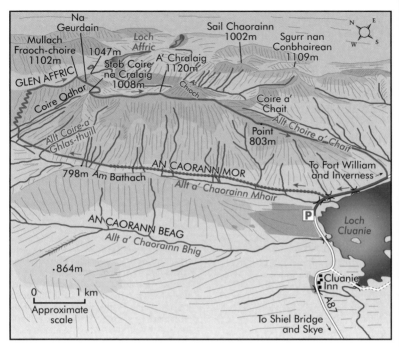

lies around 1km to the south-east. After about 50m of ascent on steep ground, the slope eases then another 30m of ascent leads to a small grassy top (983m). From there, a grassy then more rocky ridge passes a dip (970m) then remains fairly level before rising (now mostly grassy with scattered stones) to the 1102m summit, the apex of a fine cone supported by three ridges. The summit sports a moderately sized cairn and is a great place to enjoy the panorama. Ciste Dhubh, the North Cluanie Ridge and the Five Sisters of Kintail lie to the west, Sgurr nan Conbhairean lies to the east, while the next section of the route, the ridge to Stob Coire na Cralaig and A' Chralaig, lies to the south (with Ben Nevis just to the left of A' Chralaig).

The ridge path leading towards Stob Coire na Cralaig descends easily southwards towards the imposing and rather crumbly Na Geurdain pinnacles. The path avoids these by traversing steep slopes on the eastern (left) side, with only one or two sections of easy scrambling. Where the ridge twists to the south-west, the path rejoins the narrow crest then there is easy walking to a dip at 949m. A moderately steep ascent leads to the small cairn on Stob Coire na Cralaig (1008m), an exposed location with cropped turf and no shelter. Continue south-south-east to a

dip at 952m, then follow A' Chralaig's twisting but delightful northern ridge. There is straightforward walking at first but the path disappears on the stony upper section, where the ridge – a heap of blocks of rock – offers a little scrambling. A' Chralaig's huge summit cairn at 1120m can be seen for miles and is a good place for a rest, with fine views.

From the summit, descend the south-east ridge to a top at 1051m, which lies above the north-east ridge to A' Chioch. The ridge levels out and widens to form a shoulder (1037m), with the steep and rough eastern ridge descending eastwards to the col with Sgurr nan Conbhairean. The easiest way down descends the easier-angled and well-defined south ridge, which drops for 1km to a shoulder at 803m; it is mostly short grass but there is patchy scree in places. Below 803m, the ridge swings south-east and becomes indistinct, with slabby outcrops on the way down to Allt Choire a' Chait (gr NH106122). Fairly steep slopes with long grass, rocks, bracken and heather lead down to the A87, then a roadside walk leads back to the car parks.

AM BATHACH

A majestic, grassy peak in a rugged mountain wilderness

Parking: Loch Cluanie (An Caorann Mor), gr NH087121
Distance: 9km
Height Gain: 610m
Time: 4–5 hours
Terrain: Path, grassy ridges, trackless grassy glens, track
Standard: Easy
OS Maps: Loch Alsh, Glen Shiel & Loch Hourn (1:50,000 Landranger sheet 33), Glen Shiel & Kintail Forest (1:25,000 Explorer sheet 414).

Like many other hills in Glen Shiel the spectacular, apparently conical-shaped peak, Am Bathach, at the extreme eastern end of the North Cluanie Ridge, is actually part of a long, fairly narrow ridge with steep sides. Ascent or descent is not recommended anywhere except at the ends of the ridge.

There is ample parking in a large lay-by off the eastbound A87 (gr NH087121). Parking for two or three cars is also available by the westbound A87 Invermoriston–Kyle of Lochalsh road, just east of the bridge over Allt a' Chaorainn Mhoir (gr NH091121). From the main car park, follow the road 100m eastwards and pass through a double gate in a decrepit deer fence on the left. A gravel, and sometimes boggy, stalkers path, which is not shown on maps, goes straight uphill and reaches the eastern fence of the pine-wood plantation (on the left). It is quite steep on passing through a wide gap between the main forest and a smaller stand of trees. The gradient eases near the upper edge of the woods, the path becoming indistinct after crossing the remains of another deer fence. From there, enjoy a good view over the plantation and the dire bogs at the foot of An Caorann Beag to Cluanie Inn and the switch-back South Glen Shiel Ridge.

A faint hill-walkers path continues straight up the broad grassy ridge ahead, easy going at

Ciste Dhubh and Sgurr nan Ceathreamhnan from Am Bathach

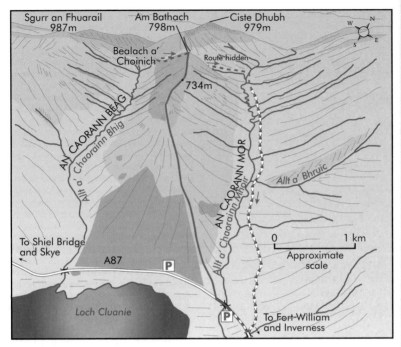

Sgurr an Fhuarail 987m — Am Bathach 798m — Ciste Dhubh 979m

Bealach a' Choinich — Route hidden

734m

AN CAORANN BEAG

Allt a' Chaorainn Bhig

AN CAORANN MOR

Allt a' Chaorainn Mhoir

Allt a' Bhruic

To Shiel Bridge and Skye

A87 P

0 — 1 km

Approximate scale

Loch Cluanie

P To Fort-William and Inverness

first but it gets steeper. On the steep ground, there is excellent walking on short grass and heather, and the path becomes clearer. Most walkers ascend rapidly to a very steep section between rocky outcrops at 600m. Take great care here in wet, windy or snowy conditions. The gradient now eases considerably, with a path up the centre of a wonderful wide and dry grassy 'rooftop'. The path passes a small, 660m top (tiny cairn, gr NH079132), descends around 5m to a dip, then rises along another fine ridge around 10m wide. Steep slopes plunge precipitously to the boggy glens on either side, giving almost 'aerial' views of Loch Cluanie and A' Chralaig. The ridge narrows to around 5m wide and reaches a small top at 700m. Another 5m drop is followed by a steady rise to the 734m top then a pleasant stroll leads to a dip at 705m, with great views of the summit cone straight ahead. The path ascends steadily across mossy grass to the summit (798m), where there is a half-metre-high cairn and a fantastic view of the alpine-looking Ciste Dhubh and Sgurr nan Ceathreamhnan. To the west lie the Five Sisters of Kintail, with the great spire of Sgurr Fhuaran soaring skywards behind the north-east ridge of Sgurr a' Bhealaich Dheirg. Look out for the curiously shaped Dun Caan (on the Isle of Raasay),

just to the right of Sgurr nan Saighead, the penultimate peak of the Five Sisters.

The driest way down is to return via the upward route. Otherwise, descend the broad, easy, moss-and-grass ridge north-west to Bealach a' Choinich; there is a faint path with only one steep section low down. The bealach has several rocky knolls and a tiny lochan; look out for an interesting 20m-long mica-schist slab featuring fine deformation patterns. Keep right, avoiding crags north of the lochan, and descend into the wet-floored Coire Fhearchair; it is drier on the north side of the burn. Keep high above the burn below 450m since precipitous flanks plunging into the water are best avoided. It is also possible to cross to the southern side of the burn at around 450m (gr NH070151). Easy but boggy grass slopes lead to the upper part of the glen, An Caorann Mor, a notoriously swampy area with a burn that may be difficult to cross dry-shod. On the eastern side of the glen, follow the tedious, gravel, four-wheel-drive track from gr NH080148 for 3km back to the A87, just east of the car parks.

125

57

NORTH CLUANIE RIDGE

An exceptionally fine ridge traverse

Parking: Glen Shiel, below Bealach an Lapain, gr NH009135

Distance: 12km

Height Gain: 1220m

Time: 6–8 hours

Terrain: Steep grassy or stony slopes or ridges, paths in places

Standard: Moderate

OS Maps: Loch Alsh, Glen Shiel & Loch Hourn (1:50,000 Landranger sheet 33), Glen Shiel & Kintail Forest (1:25,000 Explorer sheet 436)

The North Cluanie Ridge (also known as the Three Brothers) is an easier option than other ridge walks in Glen Shiel and it is a particularly fine three-Munro winter expedition.

Leave cars in the off-road parking area by the A87 Invermoriston–Kyle of Lochalsh road at gr NH009135. A badly eroded path that is often very wet, muddy and slippery goes straight uphill in a gap between forestry plantations, towards Bealach an Lapain. Traverse right above the upper edge of the eastern plantation for about 100m then turn left and ascend an eroded muddy path on a very steep spur. This path slants leftwards to avoid some small crags (c600m) then zigzags up steep grass slopes, easier near the bealach, where there is a small cairn (725m). Turn right on a fairly steep, yet easy, earthen and gravel path, easier on grass for a while, then steeper on a broad, well-defined ridge, becoming gravelly with scattered rocks then grassy for the final 40m to Saileag's 956m-high summit. Relax by the half-metre-high cairn and enjoy views including the Five Sisters and large numbers of other peaks from Glen Affric to Ben Nevis.

A broad, well-defined ridge heads eastwards over a minor top, descends to a dip then rises 4m over another top. Descend steadily by gravelly/stony path on a narrow ridge; this broadens into a flank and becomes steeper low

Aonach Meadhoin and Am Bathach from A' Chralaig

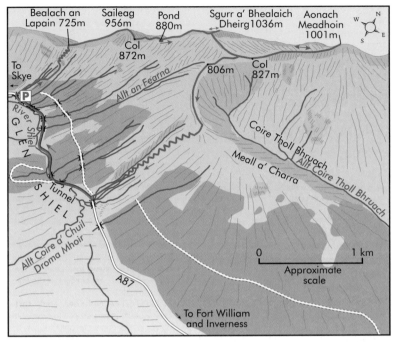

down. From the 872m col, continue eastwards over the narrow 889m top (there is a bypass path on the southern side), descend to a dip then rise to the 911m top, which has a precipitous craggy northern side but the ridge is a pleasant mixture of grass and boulders with a path near the crest or on the easier southern flank. Descend to the 880m col, mainly grassy with one narrow section including a short easy scramble; there is a bypass ledge on the left (north). A curious pond lies beneath a cliff on the southern side of the ridge.

Now ascend Sgurr a' Bhealaich Dheirg, keeping right of a rocky ridge on a path. Grassy slopes higher up are followed by scattered rocks, boulders on the right and finally 10m of scree leads to a broad grassy ridge with a half-metre-high cairn on the western end at 1014m. Follow a path sparkling with mica flakes, rising gradually to a 1m-high cairn at the eastern end (1030m). To reach the highest point, follow the north-eastern spur; a path on grass leads to a stone wall then it rises through boulders on a narrow crest. Cross the wall on the crest to gain the ridge's eastern side then rise 5m to the well-built, 1½m-high, summit cairn (1036m), which entirely blocks the ridge.

Return to the wall's southern end, then take a path on the left, descending easily mainly on grass (some scattered rocks) to the next col at 827m. Avoid the path on the right; it descends to Meall a' Charra. From the col, rise steeply on a broad, grassy ridge with a good path to a level section, a steep ascent then a little grassy top. Beyond a 4m dip, rise 6m to a very narrow, level ridge, then dip 6m on an entertaining rocky ridge (or bypass on the right). A steep rocky rise leads to an easier path on grass and the 1m-high cairn on the flat grassy summit of Aonach Meadhoin (1001m), with great views of Ciste Dhubh and Sgurr an Fhuarail nearer at hand.

Return to the 827m col, rise 5m then take a good traverse path on the left leading to a minor bump (806m) and a mossy/grassy descent to Meall a' Charra, the path becoming indistinct. Turn right (at around 620m) and descend steep grass to an old fence with another fence lower down. Zigzag down steep pathless but easy grass and bracken slopes to reach the A87 then walk along the road back to the car park.

58

FIVE SISTERS OF KINTAIL

Unsurpassable walking on exciting peaks and ridges

Parking: Glen Shiel, below Bealach an Lapain, gr NH009135

Distance: 12km

Height Gain: 1610m

Time: 8–11 hours

Terrain: Steep grassy or stony slopes or ridges, paths in places

Standard: Moderate to difficult

OS Maps: Loch Alsh, Glen Shiel & Loch Hourn (1:50,000 Landranger sheet 33), Glen Shiel & Kintail Forest (1:25,000 Explorer sheet 436)

The Five Sisters of Kintail are an impressive sight from Loch Duich or Shiel Bridge. The high-level ridge walk between the peaks is a wonderful but rather long expedition, with paths most of the way. Logistical problems arise due to the start and finish being far apart; the easiest solution requires using two cars.

Cars can be parked by the A87 Invermoriston–Kyle of Lochalsh road at gr NH009135. From there, follow the eroded path steeply uphill towards Bealach an Lapain (725m) as described for the North Cluanie Ridge route. At the bealach's small cairn, bear left (west) on fairly level, grassy ground. A well-defined, mainly grassy, ridge rises from the eastern end of the bealach towards Beinn Odhar, which has a virtually level but quite narrow summit ridge with scattered rocks and outcrops. There is a slight rise over the central top at 895m (small cairn). Beyond the steeper western top (893m), a steep flank of grass and scattered rocks leads upwards for 50m to the western end of Sgurr nan Spainteach (named after a small Spanish force which was defeated by government troops at the Battle of Glenshiel in 1719). After a dip, the steep-sided ridge rises to the cairn on the 990m-high summit, with wonderful views of the peaks and ridges ahead. Continue westwards, over the minor 978m top, then down a sharp ridge to a dip (925m) just north of an odd hollow. The ridge

Five Sisters of Kintail from Bealach Ratagain

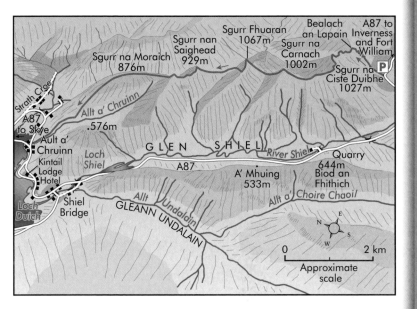

has lots of loose boulders, some exposed rock and downward scrambling, and steep drops down cliffs and gullies on the northern side. A path bypasses the hollow then keeps left (south) to avoid a steep craggy face ahead; on reaching the rough south-east ridge of Sgurr na Ciste Duibhe, bear right and follow the steep path uphill to the well-built, 1½m-high summit cairn (1027m), on the eastern end of a small plateau with many quartz-feldspar-granulite outcrops.

Continue across Sgurr na Ciste Duibhe's summit area to the western top then follow a broad, gradually descending, rocky ridge (with some bouldery areas and intermittent path) in a westerly direction. Bear north-west over a minor top (964m) and walk down to Bealach na Craoibhe (850m). From the bealach, a broad stony ridge with some outcrops and a short level area at 920m rises to Sgurr na Carnach (1002m, half-metre-high cairn). The blocky and much rougher northern ridge of Sgurr na Carnach initially drops steeply for around 40m but it eases off before another drop that leads to a wide col, Bealach na Carnach (865m). The path then ascends the very steep and loose southern ridge of Sgurr Fhuaran (1067m), the highest of the Five Sisters, with a 1½m-high cairn and very fine views of the western seaboard and Skye.

From Sgurr Fhuaran, descend 90m on the steady west-north-west ridge to a short level section then a descending traverse path heads

to the right (east) for 150m, losing around 20m vertically. On reaching the north flank, observe that a steep, loose section below the summit has been avoided. Continue by descending the north flank to reach a reasonably grassy, well-defined ridge that curves and dips to Bealach Buidhe (820m), with fine views of Sgurr nan Saighead's slabby, east-facing cliffs. Continue steadily uphill on mixed grass and rocks to Sgurr nan Saighead's summit (929m, cairn); descend the interesting narrow western ridge, passing a minor top then the larger cliff-girt Beinn Bhuidhe (869m).

Beyond Beinn Bhuidhe, descend the steep northern ridge to a col (770m) then cross broken, stony ground with outcrops to reach the almost level summit of the last of the Five Sisters, Sgurr na Moraich (876m), and descend a straightforward flank with grass and scattered rocks or outcrops, in a west-north-west direction. This route meets a path high above the Allt a' Chruinn gully at gr NG953197; follow this path steeply downhill to a fence line and Ault a' Chruinn's houses, by the A87.

59

SGURR AN AIRGID

Wonderful views of Loch Duich and Kintail

Parking: St Dubhthach's church and cemetery, gr NG946212

Distance: 9km

Height Gain: 840m

Time: 3½–4 hours

Terrain: Paths

Standard: Moderate

OS Maps: Loch Alsh, Glen Shiel & Loch Hourn (1:50,000 Landranger sheet 33), Glen Shiel & Kintail Forest (1:25,000 Explorer sheet 414)

A bulky hill of unprepossessing appearance, closer inspection reveals Sgurr an Airgid to be a fine viewpoint and it is in consequence one of the most popular 'straightforward' hill walks in the Kintail district.

Leave the A87 Invermoriston–Portree road just north of the Loch Duich causeway, 2½km north of Shiel Bridge, then take the minor road eastwards towards Morvich for 250m and park in the cemetery parking area at gr NG946212. Go through the gate on the northern side of the road, opposite the car park. Follow a narrow, four-wheel-drive track (an argocat route not yet shown on maps) through some silver birch and brambles, then zigzag steeply up the grassy hillside, crossing several small burns, including the same one no less than three times. Continue in a north-easterly direction, slanting gradually up very steep slopes. The track suddenly ends at 270m above sea level but a stalkers footpath continues, gaining another 20m to reach a deer fence and gate. Beyond the gate, the mainly grassy path crosses a fairly level area then steadily climbs through grass, heather and patches of bracken until blocked by the deep gully of the Allt na Ruaraich. On gaining height, there are increasingly impressive views across Loch Duich and Ratagan to Beinn Sgritheall. Look up deep and wild Gleann Lichd to Saileag and Sgurr a' Bhealaich Dheirg at its head. To the

Sgurr an Airgid and Loch Duich

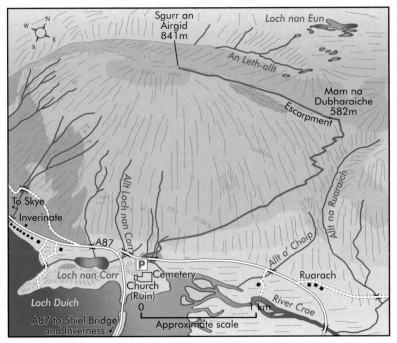

left of Gleann Lichd, there is the serrated western ridge of Beinn Fhada while, to the right, the massive lump of Sgurr na Moraich rears steeply behind Morvich and the Saddle can be seen behind Sgurr an t-Searraich. The lime-green lower parts of Gleann Lichd lie behind the attractive scattering of whitewashed houses in the populated Strath Croe area at the foot of Sgurr an Airgid.

On reaching the Allt na Ruaraich gully, the path turns westwards and climbs in stony zigzags, long at first, then shorter, until easier-angled ground is reached. The well-made stalkers path ends at the edge of a rather wide and somewhat boggy pass called Mam na Dubharaiche (582m), where there is a good-sized cairn. A faint path, which may be a bit wet, heads westwards from here towards the foot of Sgurr an Airgid's eastern ridge. The path becomes considerably more distinct on reaching the upper edge of a curious 10m-high escarpment, which is followed towards Sgurr an Airgid. Further on, it ascends a slope running parallel to the rocky main ridge (on the left). This section may be quite muddy when wet. On the right, look for the Torridon hills and, further right, the prominent spire of Bidein a' Choire Sheasgaich soaring skywards.

The slope becomes increasingly boulder-strewn and the path becomes hard to follow, but it continues upwards and joins the main ridge above its rocky section. The ridge continues for around 600m horizontally towards the summit, now broad and mainly grassy with a more distinct path. Look out for some large boulders, holes and odd depressions. There are several sections with steep drops down into the corrie on the right; beyond the last of these, the path peters out in a level area with higher ground on both right and left. Trend leftwards up a short steep slope with scattered broken rock and grass to find the summit cairn and a damaged cylindrical triangulation pillar (841m).

There are excellent views all around, including the Cuillin Ridge on Skye, the Skye Bridge and Raasay beyond the lower western top, Sgurr na Seamraig (824m). Other points of interest include Rum, Knoydart, the Five Sisters of Kintail and the little cone of Am Bathach to the right of Beinn Fhada. The Glen Affric hills, the Lapaichs, Bidein a' Choire Sheasgaich, Torridon and Beinn Bhan (Applecross) complete a superb 360-degree panorama.

Return to the road by the way of the outward route.

AONACH BUIDHE

An imposing glen, immense waterfalls and natural woodland

Parking: Killilan (River Ling), gr NG940303
Distance: 34km
Height Gain: 1000m
Time: 9–10 hours (5–6 hours if bicycle used)
Terrain: Gravel road and path, grassy slopes
Standard: Moderate
OS Maps: Glen Carron & Glen Affric (1:50,000 Landranger sheet 25), Glen Shiel & Kintail Forest (1:25,000 Explorer sheet 436)

Many people savour the remote hills between Glen Shiel and Glen Carron by backpacking through for several days but it is also possible to experience this magnificent area on a day trip by walking or cycling along beautiful Glen Elchaig and climbing Aonach Buidhe. Cyclists may have time to explore the extraordinary, 113m-high Falls of Glomach, Britain's second highest waterfall, hidden from viewers in the glen but well worth a visit.

From the A87 Invermoriston–Kyle of Lochalsh road 1½km west of Dornie, take the minor road along the shore of attractive Loch Long, towards Killilan and Camas-luinie. Park just beyond the River Ling in the area provided at the start of the Killilan road (gr NG940303). Follow the surfaced, private road eastwards to the stalkers cottage and slightly shabby Killilan lodge. The road continues past a plantation that includes rhododendrons; beyond the house at Faddoch the trees become more scattered, with better views of the glen. Past the junction for the bridge and house at Coille-righ, the road becomes a gravel track, with occasional surfaced sections. There is a locked gate 600m horizontally beyond the Coille-righ junction, with an unlocked pedestrian and bicycle gate adjacent. Beyond a young plantation and the Allt an Daimh bridge, the track rises – with great views of the waterfall Eas Ban on the other side of the glen – then descends past

Aonach Buidhe

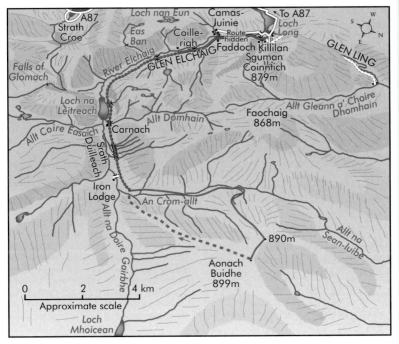

another young plantation to an impressive narrow section of glen at Cragag. A fairly steep ascent takes the track high above the river and past an older plantation to gr NH009271, where a path heads southwards for 1¼km (with 280m of ascent) to the Falls of Glomach. The main track continues past natural woodland, a plantation and Loch na Leitreach, then ascends through natural woodland to reach the buildings, tumbling burn and bridge at Carnoch.

Continue further up the glen past three small plantations to gr NH042294; a rougher four-wheel-drive track heads further up the glen, with the main track descending to a bridge on the right and crossing to the estate's Iron Lodge. Bicycles should be left here. Follow the four-wheel-drive track north-eastwards up the glen for 0.5km, then bear left at the next junction onto a steep, four-wheel-drive track heading for the col between Aonach Buidhe and Faochaig. Cross a stony area below a gully then ascend steeply to a level area and An Crom-allt, normally easy forded. Across the burn, it is generally steep (with a small burn crossing) to a cairn. About 100m further on (gr NH041320), just shy of the col at 470m, a cairn on the right marks a very steep argocat trail that zigzags uphill for 70m, keeping right of the burn's south-east-heading branch. Look for occasional faint paths and cairns on slopes of steep grass

with occasional rocks, becoming easier above 600m.

Bear left (north-east) on reaching a grassy shelf at gr NH045317; pleasant, gradual and easy slopes of short grass and heather, without a path, lead upwards towards the stony western summit. Once Bidean a' Choire Sheasgaich's impressive spire appears to the north, bear right on a mixed grass and stony flank, easy at first then steeper, with great views down to Iron Lodge. Short mossy grass with stony areas gives excellent walking to a dip between the eastern and western summits then similar ground rises past some crags on the left to reach the well-built, 1½m-high summit cairn (899m). The expansive views include Bidean a' Choire Sheasgaich, its neighbour Lurg Mhor, the distant Torridon hills, and the high ridges of both the Lapaichs and the Carn Eighe–Mam Soul group. Northwards, the remote whitewashed Maol-bhuidhe cottage – said to be the birthplace of the mother of a former Moderator of the Church of Scotland – stands out amongst the grass and heather.

The best way back to Killilan is to return the same way, but it is also possible to shorten the route a little by descending steep slopes southwards, directly towards Iron Lodge.

61

THE LAPAICHS

An outstanding ridge traverse with wild peaks, corries and lochans

Parking: Loch Mullardoch dam, gr NH221315
Distance: 21km
Height Gain: 1760m
Time: 10–12 hours
Terrain: Varied grassy or stony slopes or ridges, occasional paths
Standard: Difficult
OS Maps: Glen Carron & Glen Affric (1:50,000 Landranger sheet 25), Loch Monar, Glen Cannich & Glen Strathfarrar (1:25,000 Explorer sheet 430)

The Lapaich's fine ridges overlook Loch Mullardoch's hydroelectric scheme in Glen Cannich. To avoid the dreadful two-hour loch-side walk to An Socach, take the estate's eight-person boat to Socrach (gr NH141311).

From Socrach's triangular-faced chalet (Seldom Inn), follow a reasonable earthen path steadily uphill on the Allt Coire a' Mhaim's heathery northern bank. Where the corrie levels out at around 480m, cross the burn (normally easy) and head slightly south-of-west (no path) to pick up the ridge rising towards Meall a' Chaisg. Beyond some boggy ground with heathery peat hags, ascend a fairly steep, grassy flank and pick up a path through grass and scattered rocks above c700m. The gradient eases off above 800m, becoming steeper again up to Meall a' Chaisg (c1040m), then a delightful, well-defined and fairly level ridge of short grass leads to the summit of the first Munro, An Socach (1069m), where there is a cylindrical, concrete, triangulation pillar but no cairn or ring shelter. There is a fine view over the impressively steep-sided east top (c1050m) towards An Riabhachan.

Continue along the grassy ridge to a dip, rise about 15m to the east top then descend nearly 200m towards Bealach a' Bholla (c860m); a path is worn into a steep, grassy slope with scattered rocks. Cross the wide col and follow a path straight up the middle of a broken crag

Looking south from Sgurr na Lapaich

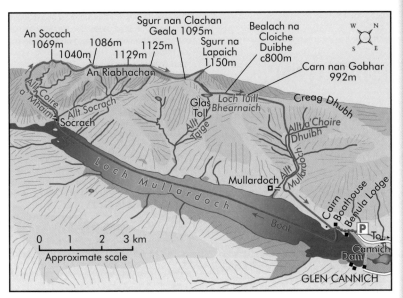

(c25m) to reach a pleasant, grassy ridge leading to An Riabhachan's west top (1040m). Follow the ridge south-east to a dip (c1000m) from where a narrow ridge leads upwards to a 30m-high steep section, with An Riabhachan's south-west top (1086m, cairn) immediately above. From the south-west top, a pleasant, broad ridge with short turf heads north-east; beyond a minor dip, there is An Riabhachan's main summit (1129m), with a three-quarter-metre-high cairn. The path continues eastwards past another dip on the broad ridge to reach the north-east top (1125m). Descend to Bealach Toll an Lochain (c825m) on a fine ridge only 1m wide in places. There are some rocky pinnacles and a steep cliff to the north, but there is no scrambling and the views northwards to the lochans in Toll an Lochain are good.

From the bealach, a steep, unrelenting slope of grass and moss with scattered rocks leads to the summit of Sgurr na Lapaich, becoming stonier near the top. A steep path may be found near the edge of the precipitous slopes above Toll an Lochain (on the left). The summit has a stone-built, square, cross-section, triangulation pillar (1150m) surrounded by a stone ring shelter, which is three-quarters of a metre high. Great views include southwards over Sgurr nan Clachan Geala and westwards to An Riabhachan.

The easiest way off Sgurr na Lapaich begins by descending the southern flank (grassy with scattered rocks and solifluction terraces up to 1m high) to the broad 1030m col below Sgurr

nan Clachan Geala (gr NH161346). From the northern end of the col, descend eastwards towards the northern tip of Loch Tuill Bhearnaich; it is fairly easy but rather steep at first, descending an exposed grassy slope with care, then following a ridge flanked by rock outcrops. Beyond the loch, continue north-west, ascending around 35m to reach Bealach na Cloiche Duibhe, where a huge block of schist offers shelter.

To reach Carn nan Gobhar, follow the broad ridge heading east-south-east, becoming steeper and more bouldery with height gained. The bouldery summit (992m) is marked by a diminutive half-metre-high cairn. The slightly lower southern summit has a well-built, 2m-high cairn. From the northern summit, head east-north-east on good, springy, mossy grass to reach the 850m col with Creag Dhubh then turn right and descend steep, firm turf into the more heathery Coire Dubh; cross Allt a' Choire Dhuibh and pick up the intermittent path to Mullardoch, mostly fairly good but occasionally boggy. Turn left before the footbridge to pick up the poor boggy path heading for the Mullardoch dam. Keep high above the loch's shore and look out for the Clan Chisholm cairn just before the boathouse.

62

FUAR THOLL

Immense sandstone cliffs in a fantastic mountain landscape

Parking: Achnashellach, gr NH005484
Distance: 12km
Height Gain: 900m
Time: 4½–5½ hours
Terrain: Track, good paths, grassy slopes, scree path, un-bridged river crossing
Standard: Moderate
OS Maps: Glen Carron & West Affric (1:50,000 Landranger sheet 25), Glen Carron & West Monar (1:25,000 Explorer sheet 429)

Fuar Tholl's wonderful Coire Mainnrichean, completely hidden from the casual view of motorists, contains a tiny lochan overlooked by the impressive, 170m-high, Torridonian sandstone Mainreachan Buttress. From the large car park on the eastern side of the A890 Auchtertyre–Achnasheen road at Achnashellach's public telephone (gr NH005484), cross the road and follow the track through woodland towards Achnashellach railway station. Walk across the railway line at the level crossing then continue uphill 10m to a gate. About 100m beyond the gate, take a left turn at a track junction; follow a level track through rhododendrons and coniferous forest to another gate then continue through smaller trees, with good views of the steep Leth Chreag cliffs.

Just beyond a small burn, a sign reading 'Public Path to Loch Torridon by Coire Lair' points left. Turn left and walk to a gate, which has a rather curious, circular gate adjacent to it. Beyond the gates, a pleasant gravel path bears right past gorse and riverside trees, with splendid views of Fuar Tholl across the River Lair. The varied coniferous woodland includes some Scots pine. Cross a wooden bridge over a burn and leave the forest for the open, heather-covered hillside. Beyond a sign regarding stalking, the path goes more steeply uphill. Look for a path on the left (gr NG994491) leading in 50m

Fuar Tholl's Mainreachan Buttress

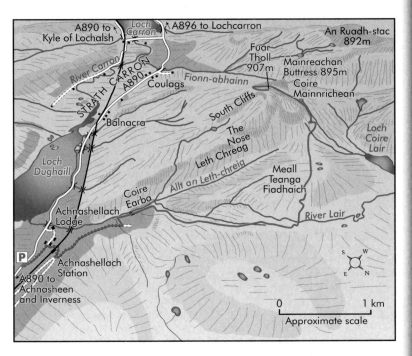

to a good viewpoint of a narrow, vertical-sided gorge with waterfalls, pools and trees perched on impossible-looking ledges. Take care at this viewpoint, it is extremely exposed.

The main path, mostly gravel but with some paved sections, continues steeply uphill. Above 330m, the gradient decreases and the path crosses some sandstone slabs with white veins. Keep a sharp look-out for a junction at a half-metre-high cairn, where a path goes to the left (a 1m-high cairn 130m further along the main path indicates the junction with a path going right for Easan Dorcha and Loch Clair). Take the path on the left and descend to the Lair, difficult to cross in wet weather but in summer it may be forded dry-shod using stepping stones. Pick up the path on the south-west side of the river heading to the right of Fuar Tholl, crossing a wilderness of heather, bog and sandstone boulders called Meall Teanga Fiadhaich. The steep, stony path occasionally crosses slabs then undulates across a fairly level area for nearly 1km, with good views of Sgorr Ruadh on the right.

Above 490m, the path climbs steeply uphill, with excellent views across Loch Coire Lair to Beinn Liath Mhor. Cross a small burn and continue steeply to more level ground above 590m, now with excellent views of Mainreachan Buttress. At 625m, the path crosses Allt Coire Mainnrichean. Leave the path, keep left of the burn and head across grass between rock outcrops, aiming directly for the foot of the buttress, until beyond the corrie lochan (on the right). Now ascend into the upper corrie on grass with scattered rocks, keeping left of the buttress and between scree slopes to the left and right. Ascend steeply between rock outcrops and pick up a steep hill-walkers path; the gradient eases on grass, then steep, loose boulder scree leads 90m up to a col. There are two paths on the scree, the right-hand one zigzags and is heavily used, but the left-hand one is easier.

At the col (855m, gr NG973488) there is a half-metre-high cairn; turn left and follow an easy path over a hump, then cross flat stones, grassy, mossy and scree patches to reach the summit, where there is a triangulation point (907m) in local stone and a circular wall-shelter. The views are wonderful; from south to east, Loch Carron, the Glen Affric hills, and the impressive Sgurr Choinnich. To the west there is the bulky An Ruadh-stac, Maol Chean-dearg and Beinn Damh.

Return to Achnashellach by the same route.

137

BEINN BHAN

Breathtaking cliffs, corries and lochans

Parking: Bealach na Ba road, gr NG763438

Distance: 10km

Height Gain: 470m

Time: 4½–5½ hours

Terrain: Stalkers paths, rough hill paths, boulder fields and slab-covered areas

Standard: Moderate to difficult

OS Maps: Raasay & Applecross, Loch Torridon & Plockton (1:50,000 Landranger sheet 24), Kyle of Lochalsh, Plockton & Applecross (1:25,000 Explorer sheet 428)

Scotland's second-highest and most spectacular mountain road crosses Bealach na Ba (626m) between Kishorn and Applecross. The Corbett, Beinn Bhan, lies only 4km north-east of the pass; although the exceptionally rugged landscape is not easy to cross, a straightforward route follows a mainly gravel path starting near the ruinous shieling just off the road at 450m (gr NG763438, limited parking).

A 1m-high wooden post identifies the path to the shieling, not visible from the road since it is located below a 5m-high slope. Shielings accommodated people who looked after cattle on the mountainsides during summer seasons centuries ago. Keep right of the shieling on a partly boggy path that descends steadily through grass, heather and scattered outcrops. Beyond a dip, there is a 4m rise followed by gradual downhill on a mainly gravel path that passes occasional outcrops and slab to reach an easy crossing of the Allt Coire nan Cuileag.

Continue uphill on a mainly gravel path with some soft or wet areas and pass a small lochan. Easily negotiate the burn at gr NG776440 then ascend more steeply to the east, passing areas of slab. The cairned path turns to the north-west and rises gradually across grass, heather and scattered boulders, then becomes indistinct. Look for the final section of path rising steeply to the east; cross some small burns and pass

Beinn Bhan from Sgurr a' Chaorachain

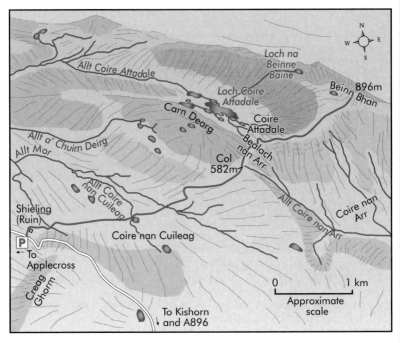

sections of broken slab to find a good gravel path that peters out just before a level area at 580m. Continue eastwards across unpleasant ground with large boulders, dangerous holes and thick heather. Pick up a path across slightly better but still very rough terrain that leads 0.2km to the 582m col between Carn Dearg and Sgurr a' Chaorachain. Cross the col and descend a steep bank of grass and heather to reach a rough area with some small ponds and burn channels. Continue onto a pleasant and obvious 3m to 5m-wide ledge that gradually slopes uphill and north-west for around 0.3km, with a path developing across patchy slab, mossy grass, heather and boulders. Turn a corner (left) beneath the crag above the ledge then descend 3m to a tilted slab with a small cairn that lies about 50m south of the pass Bealach nan Arr (c600m).

From the bealach, head eastwards, keeping right (south) to reach a path that slants upwards to the left (north) to gain a slabby shelf. Ascend steep broken and bouldery ground to the east by keeping left; find a way through broken slab, outcrops, boulders, grass and heather. Rise steadily to the right of the rough 676m top, crossing brown and pink sandstone slab with occasional boulders and little ponds then descend

about 6m to a dip (with a steep, stony gully to the south). Sections of stony path follow a cliff edge, passing rough, broken slab, small crags and scattered boulders. The path ascends steeply, going through a little slot in broken crags then slanting up to the right through a boulder field, where it disappears. Keep left (heading east) and ascend a gradual, boulder-strewn slope with mossy grass and occasional moss campion. Higher up, broken slab and loose rock lead to grassy areas between slabs and large boulders. Cross a relatively flat area of broken slab with some mossy grass then descend 10m over boulders and grass to a dip. The approach to Beinn Bhan's summit is a steep boulder field but once the fairly extensive summit plateau is reached, there is more pleasant walking on a mixture of stones, boulders and mossy grass. The highest point (896m) is marked by a natural-stone triangulation pillar surrounded by a stone-ring shelter, which is 1½m high.

Just east of the triangulation pillar, steep cliffs drop to the lochans in Coire na Poite, with impressive views of rock towers to the right. Further afield, look for the fine outlines of Beinn Alligin, Liathach, Beinn Damh, Raasay and the Cuillin of Skye.

Return to the road by the same route.

(64)

BEINN DAMH

Incomparable views from a fine peak

Parking: A896 near 'The Torridon' hotel, gr NG887541

Distance: 11km

Height Gain: 930m

Time: 4½–5½ hours

Terrain: Stalkers paths, rough paths, rocky slopes and rocky ridges

Standard: Moderate

OS Maps: Raasay & Applecross, Loch Torridon & Plockton (1:50,000 Landranger sheet 24), Kyle of Lochalsh, Plockton & Applecross (1:25,000 Explorer sheet 428)

Beinn Damh, a magnificent Torridonian sandstone and quartzite mountain with sweeping curves and impressive cliffs, provides the hill walker with a straightforward walk to the summit and a vantage point that is hard to beat. Check deerstalking information before setting out.

There is space for several cars by the roadside at gr NG888540, by the westbound A896 Kinlochewe to Shieldaig road and just beyond the Allt Coire Roill bridge. Parking is also available at the nearby Torridon Inn pub, which is associated with 'The Torridon' hotel, a wonderful building where smartly dressed guests can admire the internal decor and views across the lawn. From the Torridon Inn keep left, cross the bridge and follow the path signposted 'Beinn Damh hill track' as far as a stile at the A896 (gr NG887541), about 100m west of the roadside parking at the Allt Coire Roill bridge.

A path leaves the south side of the A896 (gr NG887541) and ascends through rhododendrons and mixed forest with plantation and native Scots pine. A steep 60m climb leads to two small burn crossings then there is further ascent to a ridge between the second burn (Allt Dubh), on the right, and the main Allt Coire Roill on the left, the latter flowing through an impressive gorge with a substantial waterfall. Just beyond the waterfall, the trees thin out and the path forks; keep right on a well-made gravel stalkers

Loch a' Mhadaidh Ruadh and Beinn Damh

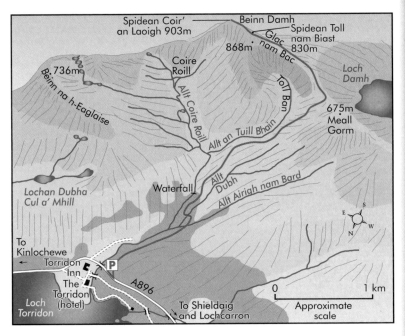

path and ascend easily across heather moorland to gr NG880525. From there, the path deteriorates into a rather peaty and boggy hill-walking route that slants upwards into the corrie Toll Ban, on the eastern slopes of Sgurr na Bana Mhoraire/Meall Gorm, ultimately reaching the northern end of a wide col at gr NG876518. The col is a good place for a break, with fine views across Loch Damh (immediately below precipitous slopes to the west) to the bulky Ben Shieldaig beyond.

From the col, bear left and ascend the broad, north-west ridge of Beinn Damh, with a reasonably clear path on a fairly steep slope of cropped turf. The ridge becomes a little less steep above about 700m and it continues to the north-west top of Beinn Damh (868m), but this top is liberally covered in quartzite boulders so it is best to avoid it by following an obvious and very wide sloping ledge on the south-west flank, named Glac nam Bac. The bypass path is reasonably clear at first but is not easy to find further on. The route is not particularly difficult, being mostly mixed grass and stones, with only a few narrow sections of boulders. Head south-east along Glac nam Bac towards Spidean Toll nam Biast (830m, gr NG888505), another top on the ridge, but the boulder fields on that top cannot be avoided, necessitating wobbling up

and over the summit. Descend to a dip (810m), then a pleasant, bouldery ridge without any scrambling leads upwards and eastwards, ascending the final 90m to the heavily boulder-strewn summit, Spidean Coir' an Laoigh (903m). The ridge may have a well-developed snow cornice on the left (northern) side in winter, but the ridge is not particularly narrow so it is easy to keep right on the final ascent.

The top sports a large cairn and gives an extraordinary view down the eastern ridge of the mountain (Stuc Coir' an Laoigh), with the isolated peaks of Maol Chean-dearg and An Ruadh-stac rising from the moors beyond. There are also great views northwards, across Loch Torridon to curvaceous Beinn Alligin and, further east, there are the impressive peaks Liathach and Beinn Eighe. Just south-west of the summit, the curious 'Stirrup Mark' is a large horseshoe-shaped boulder feature of apparently natural origin. It is easily seen from the A896 Shieldaig–Lochcarron road, but steep scree slopes deter most hikers from above.

Return to the road by following the outward route.

65

BEINN ALLIGIN

A very exciting and airy ridge traverse

Parking: Coire Mhic Nobuill, gr NG869576

Distance: 10km

Height Gain: 1290m

Time: 7–8 hours

Terrain: Rough paths, narrow grassy and rocky ridges, unavoidable prolonged scrambling

Standard: Very difficult; mountaineering skills required in winter conditions (grade II/III)

OS Maps: Raasay & Applecross (1:50,000 Landranger sheet 24), Torridon – Beinn Eighe & Liathach (1:25,000 Explorer sheet 433)

Although Beinn Alligin's two magnificent Munros are easily reached, there is plenty of opportunity for scrambling on the spectacular Horns of Alligin.

From Torridon village, drive towards Lower Diabaig for 4½km (parking area on the left, gr NG869576). A boggy/stony path leads onto the heather-clad hillside from the information sign, rising gradually with some scrambling on smooth pink sandstone rock steps. Above a stile at 180m, a steep ascent with some large stone steps leads to easier ground with boggy areas and patchy slab above 250m.

The path becomes eroded and bouldery towards the burn from Coir' nan Laoigh (Allt an Glas); follow the left bank steeply upwards, past a grassy area with scattered boulders at 560m, with great views of the corrie's headwall crags. Continue steeply upwards, on a persistently rough, stony and eroded path. Cross the burn at 755m then ascend a stony path on grassy flanks to a half-metre-high cairn on a flat, stony area (885m). A grassy slope with scattered rocks leads north-east to the summit, where a natural-stone triangulation pillar (Tom na Gruagaich, 922m) sits on top of a 2m-high outcrop with precipitous 430m-high cliffs on the far side. Exceptional views range from northern Skye to Sgurr Mhor, with its prominent Eag Dhubh gully, and the Horns.

Sgurr Mhor of Beinn Alligin

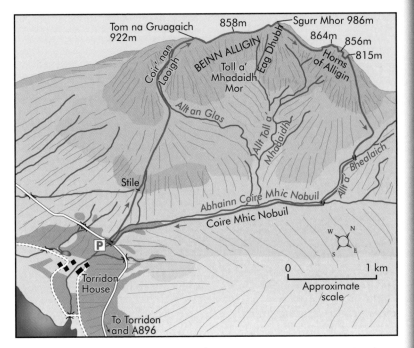

Heading north, a path descends gradually for 50m to a narrow, rocky ridge with big steps, grassy patches and steep drops on both sides. A clear path leads to a 2m-high rock step (moderate scramble, or use a path 10m below the ridge on the western side). Continue easily downwards to the 767m col, with a 1m-high step avoided on the west, some easy block steps, then a 5m rock-step at 780m, avoided on the right (east).

From the col, a path ascends a wide, grassy ridge with outcrops to a half-metre-high cairn on a baldy top (858m), continuing to a dip (833m). Steep, grassy flanks with a loose rocky mid-section lead upwards to the top of the impressive 8m-wide slot, Eag Dhubh. A very steep, stony path rises to Sgurr Mhor's summit ridge, with a 2m-high cairn (986m) and outstanding views. Walkers wishing to avoid the Horns should return from here, via Tom na Gruagaich.

For the Horns, descend eastwards on a stony and grassy path that gets steeper lower down (easy 1m-high step). The fun begins on climbing the first horn, beyond the grassy 757m col; keep left at the path junction following two easy rock steps, each 1m-high. A series of complex rocky outcrops is tackled by using ledges to the right then scrambling steeply up

2m to 3m-high rock steps to regain the ridge on the left. There is a 1m-high cairn (864m) on the summit. Continue east on a fine ridge, as narrow as 2m in places. A steep, easy scramble downwards is followed by walking then an easy 2m-high step. From the col (825m), scramble up horn number two, following an airy ledge to the right. Regain the ridge and cross boulders to the top (856m, half-metre-high cairn). Keep right on descent through a notch in a 2m-high rock step, with moderate scrambling. A steep path leads to the short, narrow, 790m col. The direct ascent of the third horn is hard but an easy traverse path leads to the right; on reaching a narrow ridge, turn left for the top (815m).

A rocky path then descends steeply south-eastwards to more level ground (c600m), with slab, boulders, grass and cairns. Continue south-east to an exceptionally steep, bouldery and craggy drop with intermittent scrambling (some awkward moves) and stone stairs that leads directly to a path junction on easier ground (gr NG882603); keep right towards a wooden bridge, then continue to another junction (keep right) and the wooden bridge over Abhainn Coire Mhic Nobuil. A pleasant path leads past waterfalls, birch and pine trees to the road just east of the car park.

66

LIATHACH

Terrific exposed ridges and pinnacles

Parking: Glen Torridon, gr NH934567

Distance: 7km

Height Gain: 1270m

Time: 6–7 hours

Terrain: Steep hill-walkers paths, narrow rocky ridges with some hard scrambling, exposed by-pass paths

Standard: Very difficult; mountaineering skills required in winter conditions (grade II/III)

OS Maps: Glen Carron & Glen Affric (1:50,000 Landranger sheet 25), Torridon – Beinn Eighe & Liathach (1:25,000 Explorer sheet 433)

Mighty Liathach soars over 1000m from the floor of Glen Torridon. It is a dangerous-looking, brooding giant of sandstone tiers capped with sparkling quartzite. The exciting pinnacle ridge between the two Munros includes some tricky and highly exposed sections and it is no place for bad weather or novices.

Start in Glen Torridon, by the A896 Kinlochewe–Shieldaig road 700m east of Glen Cottage (gr NG936567, parking at gr NH934567). A footpath ascends to Allt an Doire Ghairbh, impressively cascading from hidden corries above. Cross the burn above a little waterfall and follow the path on its eastern side. Very steep gradients begin in earnest above 145m; no real difficulties are encountered on the path but there are rock steps with minor scrambling and some loose surfaces. At 300m, the path keeps to the right on easier slopes of grass and heather, returning to the burn 80m higher up, where the first of the hidden corries is encountered. The OS maps show the path ending at gr NG938575 but in fact it continues uphill on grassy slopes with scattered rocks just to the right of the burn, into Toll a' Mheitheach. Very steep slopes with scattered rocks continue upwards into the precipitous Coire Liath Mhor; at gr NG937579 the path traverses to the right, reaching the upper cliffs at 700m (gr NG938579). The path trends steeply up to the right (hands

Liathach's Spidean a' Choire Leith

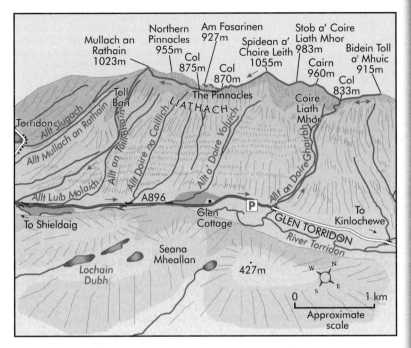

for balance) then zigzags left, then right again, to gain the main ridge at a narrow 833m col. A highly recommended ten-minute detour to the right (east) leads to the 915m top, Bidein Toll a' Mhuic, with fantastic views westwards to the beautiful curves of Spidean a' Choire Leith.

From the 833m col, a fairly exposed, wall-like ridge of mixed grass and rock leads to a steep, stony ascent and a top with a curious, barrel-like cairn (960m). A 15m descent is followed by a steep clamber up a path to the almost flat top of Stob a' Coire Liath Mhor (983m, cairn). Continue south-west to a col at 930m, then ascend steep quartzite blocks to reach the top of Spidean a' Choire Leith (1055m, cairn), with wonderful views in all directions.

Descend a loose path through steep blocks south-westwards to connect with an easier-angled, broad, grassy ridge at 940m. A path follows the crest over two minor tops (c950m and c930m) and descends gradually to a narrow, rocky neck where the scrambling begins, with a bypass path down on the left. Avoid a false ridge with a near-vertical east face that goes out to the right (gr NG926577). A steep descent of around 50m leads west-south-west, with some scrambling on sandstone steps and a particularly scary section on a narrow rock ledge, to

reach a col at 870m (gr NG925576). The extraordinary path traversing the southern flank of the Am Fasarinen pinnacles goes off to the left (south) here; it is very exposed but without the scrambling or climbing necessary on the ridge.

The main ridge continues fairly easily with minor scrambling up to a level section with steep cliffs on both sides then a little further to the conical Am Fasarinen top (927m). The westwards descent from this top is precipitous with smooth sandstone steps for around 50m and it is only advised for climbers with mountaineering experience.

The bypass path and the main ridge reconnect at the col west of Am Fasarinen (875m, gr NG922574) then the path rises easily westwards, traversing grassy slopes south of the 903m top to gain the easy but narrow ridge of Mullach an Rathain (1023m), where there is a triangulation pillar and a 1m-high cairn. After enjoying the views, descend steep slopes south-south-west then south-south-east to reach the loose path on the west bank of the eastern branch of Toll Ban's burn. Easier gradients below 600m take the path further down then southwards, away from the burn, to end at the popular wild campsite in Glen Torridon.

67

BEINN EIGHE

Stupendous rugged peaks, arêtes and corries

Parking: Loch Bharranch, Glen Torridon, gr NG978578

Distance: 14km

Height Gain: 1250m

Time: 7–9 hours

Terrain: Good gravel paths, grassy and rocky hillsides, narrow rocky ridges with some scrambling

Standard: Moderate to difficult; mountaineering skills required in winter conditions

OS Maps: Gairloch & Ullapool, Loch Maree and Glen Carron & Glen Affric (1:50,000 Landranger sheets 19 and 25), Torridon – Beinn Eighe & Liathach (1:25,000 Explorer sheet 433)

Big, bold and beautiful, the multi-topped Beinn Eighe is in a class of its own. The main ridge of shattered quartzite blocks stretches for 6km east–west but the hill's finest feature is the wonderful Coire Mhic Fhearchair, with its loch and the spectacular Triple Buttress rising behind. The complete ridge traverse is a lengthy expedition with some tricky scrambling but the two Munros can be linked by a shorter route that gives excellent views of the entire range.

Start by the A896 Kinlochewe–Shieldaig road in Glen Torridon (gr NG978578). A path rises gradually towards a small block of trees, fording Allt Coire an Laoigh both before and after the plantation. Keeping right of the burn, the path rises steadily uphill across mixed grass and boulders, becoming rather steep between 320m and 470m, with zigzags helping to ease the punishing gradient. There are some impressive waterslides and waterfalls in the burn to the left. Above 470m, less-steep slopes lead into the grassy Coire an Laoigh with the path passing large quartzite-block scree fans above 550m.

The mainly gravel path keeps close to the corrie's small burn, heading west, crossing firstly a tributary at gr NG970594 then the main burn 200m further on. The steep loose headwall of Coire an Laoigh is scaled by a scree path, keeping right of broken crags; it is very hard work. A cairn marks the ridge above the headwall.

Coire Mhic Fhearchair, Beinn Eighe

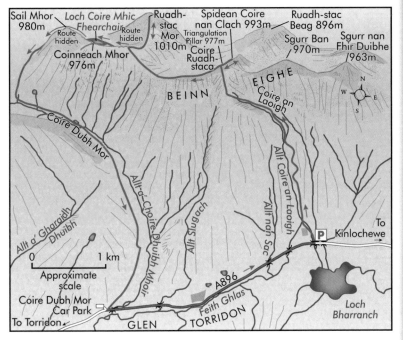

Turn right (north) and ascend 110m on this steep, scree-covered ridge to reach Spidean Coire nan Clach's natural-stone triangulation pillar (972m), oddly located on a broad section of the main ridge, well below the Munro summit. Continue north-east along the main ridge, level at first with a well-defined path, then the route gets steeper over a blocky 977m top. Descend about 10m beyond this top then scale the steep well-defined summit tower on a narrow ridge with some minor scrambling. From the top (993m, small cairn), there are fine views eastwards across Sgurr Ban.

Return via the triangulation pillar and continue westwards along the ridge; there is a steep drop to a fairly level section, hard going on quartzite blocks and slabs with some straightforward scrambling. Continue downwards to a broad col (c820m) then follow a more pleasant ridge uphill to Coinneach Mhor's mainly grassy plateau. It is worthwhile continuing west-wards across the plateau to Coinneach Mhor's highest point (976m, gr NG935601) for spec-tacular views across Sail Mhor and Loch Coire Mhic Fhearchair. The route to Beinn Eighe's highest Munro, Ruadh Stac Mor, continues north-wards from Coinneach Mhor's eastern cairn (950m, gr NG950601). A path descends steeply

to a col (868m) then a well-defined, stony ridge leads to a widening grassy plateau with stony patches that slopes steadily upwards towards Ruadh Stac Mor's odd little summit cone (1010m, cairn). Views are fantastic, with steep mountains and lochs all around.

Return southwards to the 868m col then turn right (west) and descend a steep, loose, scree gully into Coire Mhic Fhearchair; it is much easier to scramble on the solid rock forming the right-hand wall of the gully. Rough, bouldery and craggy ground below 800m leads past a series of lochans, with no obvious path until the head of Loch Coire Mhic Fhearchair is reached. Follow the path along the eastern side of the loch, cross the loch's outlet above the waterfall and stop there to admire wonderful views of the loch, the corrie and Triple Buttress. Slant down to the left to pick up the much improved path to Glen Torridon, with stone stairs and boulders in places (it takes two hours to reach Glen Torridon from Coire Mhic Fhearchair). The path curves around Sail Mhor and connects with the Coire Dubh Mor path, which is mainly easy gravel with some bouldery sections but there is a fairly steep descent to the road. The route ends near the Coire Dubh Mor car park, about 2¼km west of the start.

68

BEN WYVIS

Fine vistas across the Moray Firth

Parking: Garbat, gr NH411672

Distance: 13km

Height Gain: 950m

Time: 5–6 hours

Terrain: Easy approach paths, steep loose mountain path, grass/moss plateau

Standard: Moderate to difficult

OS Maps: Beinn Dearg & Loch Broom (1:50,000 Landranger sheet 20), Ben Wyvis & Strathpeffer (1:25,000 Explorer sheet 437)

Access to Ben Wyvis has been improved dramatically in recent years by the Footpath Trust, including a new car park by the A835 Conon Bridge–Ullapool road and new footpaths. Ben Wyvis overlooks the Black Isle and Inverness, giving commanding views of much of the Moray coast plus the fringes of the north-west Highlands. Be aware that severe weather is not uncommon on the rather exposed summit plateau. During deer stalking (20 September to 20 October), avoid the west face and the descent from Tom a' Choinnich.

Leave cars in the parking area at gr NH411672. A wide gravel path heads north, parallel to the road, with a mature plantation on the right. Cross Allt a' Bhealaich Mhoir on the new wooden bridge then use the swing gate through the deer fence (right). A narrow footpath heads east and rises steadily through bracken, heather and young trees on the north side of the river, with a young plantation to the left and more pleasant natural woodland by the river banks to the right. The path crosses a forest track at 210m then ascends steep stone flags to reach easier ground above. Go through the swing gate in the deer fence at 250m then an easy earthen or gravel path continues through more bracken, heather or young trees, reaching another swing gate on a level area at 350m. A national-nature-reserve sign about Ben Wyvis, erected by SNH, gives details

Glas Leathad Mor from Glas Leathad Beag

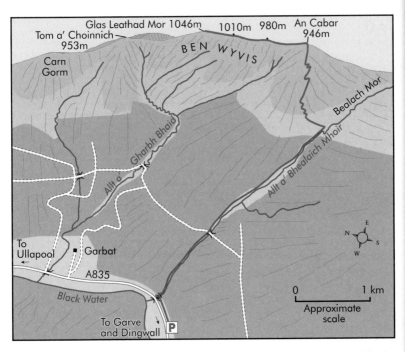

Tom a' Choinnich 953m

Carn Gorm

Glas Leathad Mor 1046m   1010m   980m   An Cabar 946m

BEN WYVIS

Bealach Mor

Allt a' Gharbh Bhaid

Allt a' Bhealaich Mhoir

To Ullapool

Garbat

A835

Black Water

To Garve and Dingwall

P

N E S W

0   1 km
Approximate scale

of the unusual, mossy, summit plateau, the ptarmigan, and dotterel, a rare bird that is known to nest on the hill.

Keep left at a path junction and follow a good gravel path towards An Cabar's base, initially crossing an easy grass-and-heather moor, with stepping stones across a soft area. Very steep sections above include stone steps and zigzags, with great views into Bealach Mor, the chasm between Ben Wyvis and Little Wyvis. The good gravel path gains the western flank of An Cabar (steep grass and heather) on less steep ground but the path's condition deteriorates suddenly on meeting the older rough, bouldery and peaty path at around 570m. Wet, slippery and peaty ground improves above 645m, where there is a 4m-high boulder. Pass through small outcrops onto steep grass and heather then the muddy path becomes stony or gravelly on steep ground, trending right and rising gradually before a sharp left turn and a steep stony and earthen incline through occasional quartz-feldspar-granulite outcrops above 690m. With the rapid gain in height, views improve, Seana Bhraigh becoming prominent to the north-west. A stony path with zigzags leads to an easier grass slope; the path keeps right of the 'ridge' then zigzags very steeply through outcrops on

the left, with a steep drop below. On regaining the ridge, easier grass with an earthen or occasionally stony path rises to the mossy-grass summit of An Cabar (946m, 1m-high cairn), where there are excellent views of the Cromarty, Beauly and Moray Firths.

From An Cabar, head north-north-east across scattered rocks and mossy grass to a broad col (930m). Two parallel paths eroded into the woolly fringe moss easily ascend Glas Leathad Mor's ridge to reach a half-metre-high cairn (980m). Descend 6m to a dip then a fairly steep rise leads to easier ground but with an indistinct path. A tiny cairn sporting a fence post may be seen. Beyond a level area with scattered rocks on the broad ridge (1010m), look out for more isolated fence posts; steep drops appear on the right then a gradual rise on a clearer path leads to the grassy summit (1046m), where a square-section concrete triangulation pillar is surrounded by a circular stone-wall shelter. On a clear day, head eastwards for a short way for the best views into the hill's wild eastern corrie.

Although it is possible to descend via Tom a' Choinnich, the rough low ground and plantation forestry deter most walkers. It is much easier to return by the upward route.

69

A' CHAILLEACH
and SGURR BREAC

Splendid ridge-walking around wild corries

Parking: Lochivraoin track end, gr NH162761

Distance: 16km

Height Gain: 1080m

Time: 6–8 hours

Terrain: Track, gravel footpaths, grassy or stony slopes

Standard: Moderate

OS Maps: Gairloch & Ullapool, Loch Maree and Beinn Dearg & Loch Broom (1:50,000 Landranger sheets 19 and 20), An Teallach & Slioch (1:25,000 Explorer sheet 435)

The ridges, corries and lochans of the Fannichs offer fine views and superb walking opportunities. The range is cut into two unequal parts by a deep pass, with the finest hills, A' Chailleach and Sgurr Breac, lying immediately to the west.

Take the A832 Braemore Junction–Gairloch road to the Lochivraoin track end at gr NH162761, with ample parking 150m towards Gairloch (northwest). Follow the gravel track 1km towards Loch a' Bhraoin, where there is a two-storey house and a boathouse on the shore of the loch. The house was gutted by fire in 1970 and a woman died in the blaze. A gravel path heads east from the house, following the loch shore to a wooden-slat footbridge spanning the outlet. Cross the bridge, turn right (west) and follow the loch's southern shore past dead trees to an isolated tree at gr NH149747. From there, slant gradually uphill south-westwards on pathless, somewhat boggy, grassy ground, aiming for the lowest trees to the right and below Leitir Fhearna's steep slopes, with great views westwards along the loch to Mullach Coire Mhic Fhearchair. About 250m before the burn (Allt na Goibhre), go straight uphill then slant left (east-south-east) and upwards below steeper slopes to reach a flat area above Sron na Leitir Fhearna at 625m. There are good views eastwards from here to Sgurr nan Clach Geala and the other Fannich peaks.

An Teallach from A' Chailleach

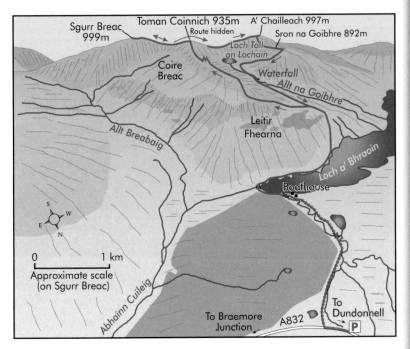

Sgurr Breac 999m
Toman Coinnich 935m
Route hidden
A' Chailleach 997m
Sron na Goibhre 892m
Loch Toll an Lochain
Coire Breac
Waterfall
Allt na Goibhre
Allt Breabaig
Leitir Fhearna
Loch a' Bhraoin
Boathouse
0   1 km
Approximate scale (on Sgurr Breac)
Abhainn Cuileig
To Braemore Junction
A832
To Dundonnell
P

An earthen path between rocks rises fairly steeply to a near-level grassy ridge with occasional outcrops and rather intermittent path. Above 760m, slant up to the right on an easy path that avoids steeper ground with solifluction terraces and gravel areas but provides pleasant views of Loch Toll an Lochain and A' Chailleach. At gr NH150722, zigzag up short grass to the left to regain the ridge; there is another path on steeper, stonier ground above 840m. Easier gradients with a faint path rising through scattered rocks leads to the half-metre-high cairn on Toman Coinnich's summit (935m), with great views of Loch Fannich, Beinn Eighe and the two Munros on either hand, A' Chailleach and Sgurr Breac.

Descend easily south-eastwards on grass and scattered rocks to reach Bealach a' Choire Bhric (869m) then ascend the fairly steep western flank of Sgurr Breac, stony at first then grassy, with a gravel or stony path all the way. Beyond the small cairn on the 995m-high western top, descend 6m on grass and moss then ascend the higher eastern summit (999m), with two small cairns 15m apart. Views eastwards from Sgurr Breac are magnificent.

Return to Bealach a' Choire Bhric, then rise around 30m and traverse the southern side of Toman Coinnich (easy grass and moss with scattered rocks). Steeply descend the western ridge to Bealach Toll an Lochain (815m), where an earthen or gravel path ascends steeply westwards past occasional iron fence posts. Steep, grassy flanks become a well-defined ridge with lovely views of Loch Toll an Lochain below broken mica-schist crags on the right. Above 950m, a strange 'slot' runs parallel with the ridge, to the left. A steep, stony path eases off at 965m (tiny cairn); bear left (south-west) on an earthen path to A' Chailleach's half-metre-high summit cairn (997m), in an area of grass with scattered rocks. Views are outstanding all around, with the Fannichs, Fionn Bheinn, Slioch and An Teallach dominating the scene.

Return north-east to the tiny cairn at 965m then turn left (north) and follow a line of old fence posts (faint path) steeply down grass and scattered rocks. Follow the Sron na Goibhre ridge easily northwards over a little top then turn right at gr NH139725 and descend steeply over bouldery, but straightforward, ground, aiming for the northern end of Loch Toll an Lochain. Before reaching the lochan, bear left on boggy ground, cross the burn easily then descend past the waterfall onto easy, grass slopes and return by the outward route.

151

70

SLIOCH

Towering Slioch overlooks beautiful Loch Maree

Parking: Incheril, Kinlochewe, gr NH038624

Distance: 18km

Height Gain: 1120m

Time: 7–8 hours

Terrain: Easy low-level paths, rough hill path, steep grassy or stony hillsides, narrow ridge

Standard: Moderate to difficult

OS Maps: Gairloch & Ullapool (1:50,000 Landranger sheet 19), Torridon – Beinn Eighe & Liathach (1:25,000 Explorer sheet 433)

The impressive Torridonian sandstone giant Slioch dominates the eastern side of Loch Maree and gives tremendous walking of varied character. Deer stalking takes place, mainly on weekdays, from mid-September to mid-November.

Turn off the A832 700m east of the Kinlochewe junction and follow the road sign 'Incheril' for 600m, then turn left into a large car park. From the information sign, follow wooden steps through young trees and pass through a deer fence (swing gate). Take the direction indicated 'Poolewe by Letterewe' (left), alongside the deer fence, initially on a four-wheel-drive track, then a grassy footpath. The path disappears opposite a small graveyard; keep alongside the deer fence to another fence (gate), cross a small burn then a distinct earth, mud or gravel path follows the deer fence below a steep bracken-covered bank. Descend 8m, continue along the base of a steep bank, cross several small burns and pass through bracken. Go through a gate, descend to the Allt Chnaimhean and cross the wooden bridge, then continue through bracken while traversing a steep, tree-lined bank above the burn, with fine views of Beinn Eighe and its northern outliers on the left. The variable muddy, grassy or gravel path crosses several small burns, passes through patches of native woodland (including oaks and birch) and follows a wide shelf above

Slioch and Loch Maree

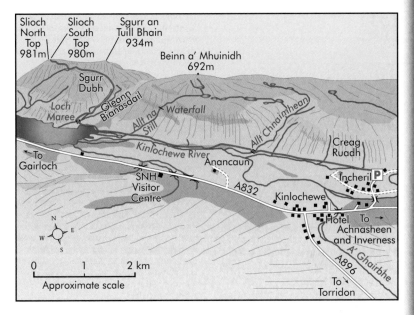

the Kinlochewe River on the left. The path descends to the river bank then rises (with views of Slioch ahead) onto more open grassland, with heather, bog myrtle and rock outcrops, before returning to the river bank. Keep right at the path junction (gr NH021642), follow grass between thick bracken then a gravel path through patchy trees. Beyond a slow-moving water channel, cross the wide, rocky Allt na Still (possibly difficult in wet weather) and pick up a narrow path through bracken, passing a sheep fank to the left then entering birch woods as Loch Maree appears ahead. A gravel path through bracken, grass and occasional trees leads to the loch shore and gravel beaches. Cross the small burn from the Dubh Chlais then rise through bracken, grassy and heather areas to the wooden footbridge over Abhainn an Fhasaigh, a river of lively waterfalls and deep pools, its banks scattered with Scots pines.

Continue towards Letterewe for around 30m beyond the bridge (the path on the right immediately after the bridge is not recommended), then turn right onto the Gleann Bianasdail path for about 0.5km uphill, to gr NH016661, where a cairn marks the Slioch path on the left. This path rises across the moor then ascends steep, rough and unpleasant ground along the line of a small burn and over some minor rock steps to a boggy 505m col, west of Meall Each. The path continues up rough slopes

then crosses boggy ground in Coire na Sleaghaich. Look out for a good path slanting up steep slopes south-westwards from gr NH014683 towards the lochan at gr NH011682; from the eastern end of this lochan, a steep eroded path ascends loose slopes to the north. The gradient gradually eases and the path becomes indistinct on the stony 933m top (small cairn). An easy descent northwards to a col with a tiny lochan at 912m is followed by fairly steep, grass slopes rising to a stone-built triangulation pillar with a partial stone ring shelter (980m). Continue northwards to a dip (964m) and a rise to Slioch's rock-girt northern top (1m-high cairn, 981m), which gives the best views over Loch Maree, the main Torridon hills, A' Mhaighdean and the Fannichs.

Either return the same way or continue eastwards on grassy slopes to pick up a path on a pleasant, mixed-grass-and-rock ridge (around 2m wide for 500m) leading to Sgurr an Tuill Bhain (1m-high cairn, 934m). Steep but straightforward grassy slopes with scattered rocks lead southwards, back to Coire na Sleaghaich; cross the burn easily, and pick up the path back to Kinlochewe.

71

BEINN LAIR

Amazing views across colossal buttresses and cliffs

Parking: Poolewe, gr NG858808
Distance: 37km (from Poolewe, return)
Height Gain: 1100m
Time: 10–12 hours (best split over two days)
Terrain: Tracks, good stalkers paths, grassy and rocky hillsides
Standard: Moderate
OS Maps: Gairloch & Ullapool, Loch Maree (1:50,000 Landranger sheet 19), Gairloch & Loch Ewe and Torridon – Beinn Eighe & Liathach (1:25,000 Explorer sheets 434 and 433)

Although it is one of the finest mountains in Scotland, Beinn Lair is visited relatively rarely compared to its more popular neighbours to the north and south. Unfortunately, the long walk to the foot of the mountain, from either Poolewe or Kinlochewe, puts many people off. However, the area is well suited to a backpacking trip and there are some good campsites near the south-eastern end of Fionn Loch. An ascent of A' Mhaighdean can also be made from Fionn Loch.

Leave cars in the hikers parking area in Poolewe (gr NG858808). Follow the private tarmac road southwards on the eastern bank of the River Ewe, initially with few trees but there is pleasant, natural woodland further on. You will pass the remains of the Red Smiddy ironworks, which lie between the road and the river about 900m from the parking area. Keeping left at Inveran, rise through the woods on a gravel-surfaced road. Beyond the bridge over the Inveran River (which drains Loch Kernsary), the road climbs fairly steeply, then levels out and passes a plantation and the southern tip of Loch Kernsary. Around a corner Kernsary farm comes into view.

Go through the gate just beyond the farm-house and continue into a small glen that ends at another plantation. Turn right, pass through a gate in a deer fence and follow a rough, four-wheel-drive track into the forest. The track

Fionn Loch and Dubh Loch from Beinn Lair

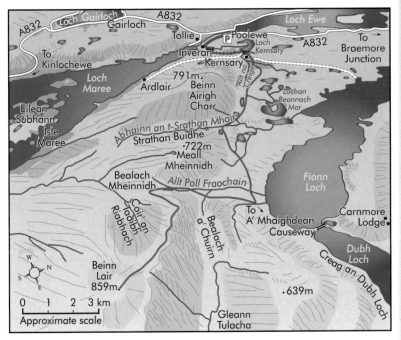

gradually becomes steeper; about 1km from the gate, avoid the former Carnmore footpath heading south-east along Allt na Creige by keeping left and continuing to the track's end at gr NG910790. The 'new' stalkers path (a well-constructed footpath and much drier than the former route) heads south-east and rejoins the 'old' path at the head of Allt na Creige. Further on, a 30m descent leads to the outflow from Loch an Doire Crionaich, a fairly minor stream. The cliffs and boulder fields of Beinn Airigh Charr rise steeply on the right and are an impressive sight.

The river in the narrow defile called Strathan Buidhe can be a serious matter because the ford at gr NG944761 becomes impassable after heavy rain (there is a bridge upstream, at gr NG943756). Once across the river, continue eastwards on the Carnmore path across wide-open moor below the cliffs of Meall Mheinnidh. The path descends around 30m and crosses the Allt Poll Fraochain before approaching the extreme south-eastern end of Fionn Loch, where there are some good camping spots near the Creag an Dubh Loch cliffs and a stream at gr NG975757. If heading directly for Beinn Lair, turn right (before reaching the loch) onto a path that climbs steeply up to the Bealach Mheinnidh pass at 490m, crossing Allt Poll Fraochain easily

en route. At a path junction just before the pass, keep right and continue past rocky outcrops to the pass itself.

From the pass, climb straightforward, but steep, grassy slopes with scattered rocks and occasional rock outcrops towards the end of Beinn Lair's north-west ridge. There is no path but most people stay well away from the lower cliffs, reaching the narrowest section of the north-west ridge at 700m, where there are magnificent spurs, buttresses and tremendous north-facing precipices. The views here are ranked amongst the best in Scotland; Fionn Loch, Dubh Loch and the causeway between them all look a long way down. A steep 100m ascent, stony in places, leads to a shoulder at 830m then it is a steady walk of 0.9km in a south-easterly direction across the summit plateau to the large summit cairn (859m). There are good views of the Torridon peaks, A' Mhaighdean and Mullach Coire Mhic Fhearchair; head north-east towards the cliff edge for the best viewpoints.

Most hikers return the same way but an interesting alternative is to complete the traverse, descending from Bealach Mheinnidh to Letterewe and following the path above the shore of Loch Maree all the way to Incheril, near Kinlochewe.

72

BEINN AIRIGH CHARR

Exquisite scenery including innumerable lochs and mountains

Parking: Poolewe, gr NG858808
Distance: 21km
Height Gain: 890m
Time: 7–9 hours
Terrain: Surfaced roads, gravel tracks and rough, boggy paths, grassy and stony hillsides
Standard: Moderate
OS Maps: Gairloch & Ullapool (1:50,000 Landranger sheet 19), Gairloch & Loch Ewe (1:25,000 Explorer sheet 434)

Although remote from the nearest public road, prominent Beinn Airigh Charr exceeds expectations by providing wonderful views of both Loch Maree's islands and the Dubh Loch's wild hinterland. Gaining the summit is well worth the effort but the outing can be made significantly easier by using a mountain bike on estate tracks.

From Poolewe, walk or cycle 4km along the Kernsary track as described for Beinn Lair. Beyond Loch an Doire Ghairbh, the track curves northwards around a partly quarried hillock. At gr NG883788, look out for a tiny cairn on grass just below a passing place on the right; bicycles can be left near here.

Beyond a 20m-wide flat area of grass and bog myrtle, a reasonably clear path heads southeastwards, slanting uphill and gaining 70m. This path is variably gravelly, stony, boggy, grassy or rough, but it is not particularly hard going. The route becomes increasingly boggy and indistinct in the rather wet flat area before reaching the Kernsary–Ardlair track (gr NG891778), where there is a tiny cairn by the roadside. (This track's direct ascent from Kernsary is steep and is not recommended for cycling.)

Follow the good, gravel-surfaced Ardlair track uphill then down to a col, with great views of Loch Maree's islands. Just before the descent to Ardlair (gr NG893768) a cairn on the left-hand

Beinn Airigh Charr

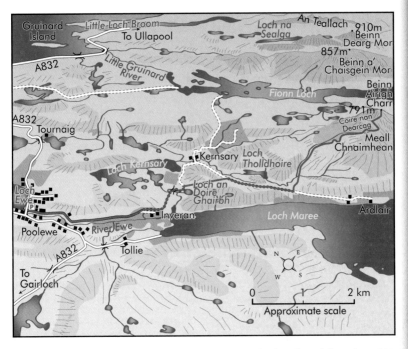

bank marks the path to Beinn Airigh Charr. Follow this path across gently rising moorland to an old sheep fank then descend through thick bracken alternating with muddy sections in grass and heather, past some silver birch, to an interesting craggy gorge where two burns meet. Ford the burn coming from the right then leave the gorge by ascending a boggy path through thick grass and bog myrtle. Continue uphill past some outcrops then descend slightly and follow a rougher section of path near the burn. Continue through grass and heather up a shallow glen past crags and outcrops to the base of Beinn Airigh Charr. Keep right at a junction onto a variable quality path ascending the steeper Coire nan Dearcag; it is often muddy, bouldery and quite hard going. Zigzag steeply on a drier path beneath a craggy area with a large boulder field, then the gradient eases into a grassy corrie at 450m. The path becomes indistinct and boggy so cross the burn on the left and find a stony path that heads towards then slants up the steep corrie headwall. Above the steep section, with impressive crags on both sides, the path nears the burn then rises gradually just left of the col to the east of Meall Chnaimhean, where it peters out.

Continue eastwards for about 150m into a grassy corrie then bear left and straight upwards on pleasant short grass and heather, with a few scattered boulders. On reaching the grassy col between Spidean nan Clach and Beinn Airigh Charr, there are wonderful views across Fionn Loch to the north-east. Spidean nan Clach (left) may be easily ascended on grass with scattered rocks (around 40m ascent). For Beinn Airigh Charr, turn right at the grassy col; a poor path is worn into scree on the right, otherwise, it is a hard slog straight up the flank's centre with very steep grass, loose rocks and outcrops for about 80m. Higher up, trend left on mixed mossy grass, stones and gravel to reach some outcrops at the summit, where there is a 1m-high cairn near the remains of a triangulation pillar (791m).

Views all around are equally fine, with A' Mhaighdean and Beinn Tarsuinn Chaol overlooking Dubh Loch to the east, Beinn Lair and Slioch to the south-east, the Torridon mountains and Loch Maree's islands to the south, and An Teallach peeping over Beinn a' Chaisgein Mor to the north-east. Return to Poolewe by the same route.

73

A' MHAIGHDEAN

Unbeatable views of lochs, cliffs and peaks

Parking: Poolewe, gr NG858808

Distance: 48km

Height Gain: 1350m

Time: 15–17 hours (best spread over several days)

Terrain: Surfaced road, tracks, good stalkers paths, grassy and rocky hillsides

Standard: Moderate to difficult

OS Maps: Gairloch & Ullapool, Loch Maree (1:50,000 Landranger sheet 19), Gairloch & Loch Ewe and Torridon – Beinn Eighe & Liathach (1:25,000 Explorer sheets 434 and 433)

Often regarded as the remotest Munro, A' Mhaighdean (The Maiden), overlooks wild Wester Ross scenery, including the beautiful Dubh Loch, the extraordinary ridge of Beinn Tharsuinn Chaol and the immense rock faces of Beinn Lair. The easiest approach is from Poolewe, via Kernsary, where bicycles can be taken, saving 10km return. However, many people backpack to the Dubh Loch with tents so they can savour the Great Wilderness for several days.

For details of the track and path from Poolewe to Fionn Loch, see the Beinn Lair walk. Where the Beinn Lair path diverges from the main path (gr NG969753), cross the burn and follow the path to Carnmore and Shenavall north-eastwards; descend slightly to a gravel beach on Fionn Loch then continue onto the spit leading to a causeway. Sometimes the 100m-long, concrete-surfaced causeway between Fionn Loch and Dubh Loch is flooded; if so, do not attempt the crossing. Once across the causeway, the path heads north-east across a level grassy area then it ascends steeply, with stony sections, across the flanks of the hillock Carn na Paite. Beyond the point where Carnmore Lodge comes into view, the path descends through thick grass to an old fence line just south of the lodge, with exceptional views of A' Mhaighdean and the Dubh Loch.

At the junction 100m south of the lodge,

A' Mhaighdean and Dubh Loch from Carnmore

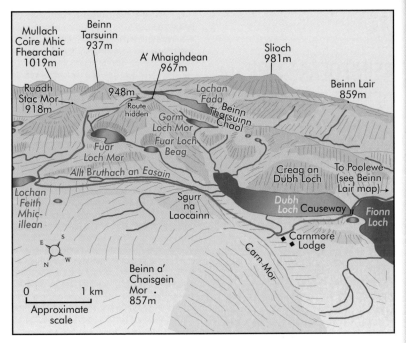

Mullach Coire Mhic Fhearchair 1019m

Beinn Tarsuinn 937m

A' Mhaighdean 967m

Slioch 981m

Ruadh Stac Mor 918m

948m

Route hidden

Lochan Fada

Beinn Lair 859m

Gorm Loch Mor

Beinn Tharsuinn Chaol

Fuar Loch Beag

Fuar Loch Mor

Allt Bruthach an Easain

Creag an Dubh Loch

To Poolewe (see Beinn Lair map)→

Lochan Feith Mhic-illean

Sgurr na Laocainn

Dubh Loch Causeway

Fionn Loch

Carnmore Lodge

Carn Mor

S
E
W
N

0   1 km

Approximate scale

Beinn a' Chaisgein Mor 857m

keep right, cross the burn Allt a' Chairn Mhoir easily then continue on the path towards Shenavall. This path begins a gradual rising traverse across boulder slopes below Sgurr na Laocainn, becoming very steep and stony above 280m. Beyond a small-burn crossing, the gradient eases for a little as the path trends left and upwards, to the north-east. The respite is short-lived with the path making a rising traverse across steep slopes between the burn (Allt Bruthach an Easain) on the right and crags high on the left. Easier gradients lead the path as much as 150m left (west) of the burn then a steep stony rise leads to a small, flat area just west of Lochan Feith Mhic-illean at 510m.

A small cairn marks a junction where a rough path bears right and descends steeply to the loch's outlet. Cross the burn easily then traverse left, rising steeply for 10m to less steep ground with grass and scattered rocks. The path meanders southwards across a level area then rises steeply to the left for about 50m, keeping left of a craggy area to reach another fairly level area at around 640m, with small outcrops, scattered boulders and some tiny lochans. In places, the path is hard to follow, but continue south-east onto a gradually rising, narrow, bouldery shelf perched at 650m, high above the

brilliant blue waters of cliff-girt Fuar Loch Mor and just below the reddish-brown sandstone screes of Ruadh Stac Mor. The path becomes clearer on the ledge then there is a dip of around 15m followed by a steeper rise through outcrops to the Poll Eadhar dha Stac col (750m). A large boulder with an overhang and a small section of dry stone wall provides some shelter on the col's eastern side.

At this point Munro baggers may want to include Ruadh Stac Mor (918m); to access it, a relatively easy route, unseen from below, passes through the precipitous lower crag, then a steep boulder field leads to the natural-stone triangulation pillar and stone-ring shelter on the summit.

To reach A' Mhaighdean from the col, ascend west-south-west on broken pathless slopes with crags, outcrops and grassy areas. The slope becomes steadily steeper making it hard work to the north top's small, grassy plateau (948m, cairn), a fine viewpoint for Fuar Loch Mor and the sandstone north-west ridge. Continue southwards to a dip (c945m) then rise to the odd summit's gneiss blocks (967m, small cairn) for fantastic views of Gorm Loch Mor, Beinn Tharsuinn Chaol, the Dubh Loch and Beinn Lair, particularly enjoyable on a clear day. Return by the outward route.

BEINN DEARG MOR and BEINN DEARG BHEAG

Two fine, isolated peaks in the heart of the great wilderness

Parking: Corrie Hallie, gr NH114851

Distance: 14/26km from Shenavall/Corrie Hallie

Height Gain: 1075/1730m from Shenavall/Corrie Hallie

Time: 9/14 hours from Shenavall/Corrie Hallie

Terrain: Track, rough paths; grass, heather and boulder-strewn hillsides

Standard: Very difficult

OS Maps: Gairloch & Ullapool (1:50,000 Landranger sheet 19), An Teallach & Slioch (1:25,000 Explorer sheet 435)

These fine but remote Corbetts, guarded by un-bridged rivers and steep flanks, are no easy propositions. Most people backpack to Srath na Sealga (an area noted for wild goats and deer) from the Corrie Hallie lay-by on the A832 Braemore Junction–Gairloch road and camp or stay in Shenavall bothy.

Across the road from the Corrie Hallie lay-by, a four-wheel-drive track leads uphill past gorse to a locked gate. Continue on the track, through pleasant, natural-birch woodland, into Gleann Chaorachain. After 2km, the track fords Allt Gleann Chaorachain (footbridge 80m upstream), then ascends more steeply. About 100m beyond the track's highest point (380m), two small cairns on the right mark the footpath to Shenavall, initially gravel but, after about 1km, becoming more bouldery with boggy sections; it is dire in wet weather. Beyond the highest point on the shoulder of Sail Liath, there is a gradual descent on gravel path between sections of purple-coloured, sandstone slabs, with great views of Beinn Dearg Mor ahead. The path becomes rough with boulders and peat then descends steeply beside a small burn to Shenavall. The bothy has seven rooms but only one fireplace; two rooms have concrete floors.

Continue on an easy path heading towards Loch na Sealga for about 400m beyond the bothy; turn left and head across a boggy flood

Shenavall and Beinn Dearg Mor

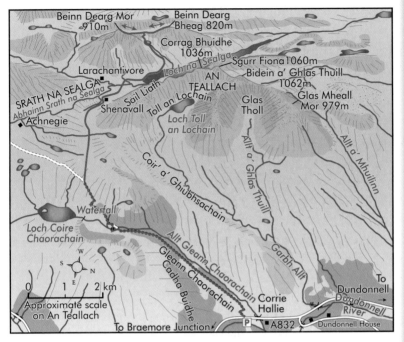

Beinn Dearg Mor 910m

Beinn Dearg Bheag 820m

Corrag Bhuidhe 1036m

Larachantivore

Loch na Sealga

Sgurr Fiona 1060m

AN TEALLACH

Bidein a' Ghlas Thuill 1062m

SRATH NA SEALGA

Abhainn Srath na Sealga

Sail Liath

Shenavall

Toll an Lochain

Glas Tholl

Glas Mheall Mor 979m

Achnegie

Loch Toll an Lochain

Coir' a' Ghiubhsachain

Allt a' Ghlas Thuill

Allt a' Mhuilinn

Waterfall

Loch Coire Chaorachain

Allt Gleann Chaorachain

Gleann Chaorachain

Cadha Buidhe

Garbh Allt

Corrie Hallie

To Dundonnell

Dundonnell River

0 1 2 km

Approximate scale on An Teallach

To Braemore Junction

A832

Dundonnell House

plain with some ditches, which can all be jumped. Aim for the river at gr NH055812, where there is a gravel-based crossing spot about 100m upstream from a right-angled bend at a dead tree. The crossing is potentially very serious and should not be attempted in spate conditions. Do not cross during heavy rain as, later, the river may become impassable. In case of emergency, rough shelter can be obtained on the far side of the river at Larachantivore, 1km south.

From the river, cross more boggy ground to the south-west, then turn right on the gravel track for Loch na Sealga. Just before the track ends at the loch, turn left onto a partly boggy gravel path that follows the shoreline. On reaching the sandy beach at gr NH042816, leave the path and slant westwards across an easy, grass-covered hillside. The route meets the burn from Coire Toll an Lochain at gr NH035816. Keep left of this burn on grass and heather; it suddenly becomes steep, tussocky and eroded due to deer. Above this, the entrance to the corrie is mainly flat and grassy with some bog. Keep left (east) of the beautiful Toll an Lochain, with some red sand beaches on both sides, then head for the col between the two Corbetts, keeping left of the large central buttress and a small area of slabs. Slant to the

right above these rocks (steep, mainly dry, grass), gain the fairly stony col (600m) then turn right (north-west) for Beinn Dearg Bheag. Short grass and heather with scattered rocks leads to a steep cone above 670m, with a patchy path weaving between lots of boulders and outcrops. Easier grass and sandstone outcrops continues to a lovely narrow ridge and a small summit cairn (820m) with fantastic views along the difficult north ridge of the mountain, towards the west coast, and in the other direction to the Fisherfield 'Big Six'.

Return carefully to the 600m col, then tackle Beinn Dearg Mor. Easy grass and scattered rocks leads to a flat area (around 700m), then a loose path goes very steeply up a 150m-high boulder slope. A gradual ridge with vertical drops on the left rises a further 30m to the summit (910m), a fantastic 6m-wide, vertical-sided, grass-covered prow with a 2m-high cairn perched near the edge. The views in every direction are magnificent and dominated by An Teallach, Beinn Dearg, the Fannichs and the Big Six.

Return by way of the col since alternative routes off the mountain are potentially dangerous and may involve serious rock climbing.

AN TEALLACH

A magnificent and exciting ridge traverse

Parking: Corrie Hallie, gr NH114851

Distance: 15km

Height Gain: 1560m

Time: 8–9 hours

Terrain: Track, path, rough bouldery hillsides, grassy or stony ridges, scrambling

Standard: Difficult; mountaineering skills required in winter conditions (grade II/III)

OS Maps: Gairloch & Ullapool (1:50,000 Landranger sheet 19), An Teallach & Slioch (1:25,000 Explorer sheet 435)

An Teallach, often described as the finest mountain in Scotland, is a small massif of spectacular Torridonian sandstone peaks with a pinnacle ridge perched above a deep corrie. Although a direct traverse involves low-grade rock climbing, a competent walker with a good head for heights can easily reach all the tops, while the fearsome Corrag Bhuidhe and Lord Berkeley's Seat can be bypassed entirely on an easy path. In winter conditions, the ridge is a serious mountaineering expedition (grade II/III), but ordinary walkers may enjoy the route in summer, particularly on a reasonably calm sunny day.

Park in the lay-by beside the southbound A832 at Corrie Hallie and follow the track into Gleann Chaorachain as described for Beinn Dearg Mor. Take the boggy Shenavall path as far as the highest point (410m, gr NH085815), then turn right (north-west) and scale the rough flank of Sail Liath (954m). This is not unpleasant, except in wet and slippery conditions. There is no obvious path; just pick a way upward through grass, heather and scattered boulders. The boulders are predominant on the steep ground above about 750m and the dome-like top is capped with angular blocks of Cambrian quartzite scree.

From Sail Liath, continue westwards and descend fairly steeply for 55m to a dip on the ridge. A steep ascent beyond leads to Stob

Corrag Bhuidhe and Sail Liath of An Teallach

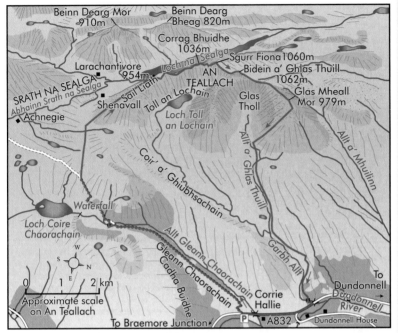

Cadha Gobhlach (960m), where a broad, grassy ridge leads northwards to a stony downhill section and the lowest point on the main ridge, Cadha Gobhlach, at 833m. Steep slopes of loose rock on the 945m-high Corrag Bhuidhe Buttress lie ahead, presenting no great difficulty, but keep left near the top. A narrow ridge then swings westwards and, after a small dip, the sandstone ramparts of Corrag Bhuidhe loom directly above.

Most people avoid Corrag Bhuidhe and Lord Berkeley's Seat by following the obvious traverse path on the western (left) side of the ridge; the direct ascent of the three main pinnacles of Corrag Bhuidhe requires moderate rock climbing skills. However, beyond an intimidating, 10m-high slab with rounded hand and footholds, most of the route is just an airy scramble, with impressive views across the gloomy waters of Loch Toll an Lochain over 500m below. Where the traverse path returns to the ridge (at the low point north of Lord Berkeley's Seat), it is an easy scramble up to the amazing 1036m top of the 'seat', which apparently overhangs the gully below. From Lord Berkeley's Seat, Corrag Bhuidhe's northernmost and highest pinnacle at 1047m is also an easy scramble.

Returning to the low point north of Lord Berkeley's Seat, a fine easy ridge – in places like a sandstone staircase – leads to the beautiful, pyramid-like summit of the 1060m-high Sgurr Fiona. Beyond this peak, zigzag down a steep 140m boulder slope, with impressive buttresses to the right. An easy, uphill gradient leads from the foot of this slope to the highest top, Bidein a' Ghlas Thuill, with a triangulation pillar at 1062m (gr NH069844). For the best view of the day, look southwards across the main ridge and its pinnacles.

To return to Corrie Hallie, continue northwards and descend to a pass at 880m (gr NH070849, where descent to the Glas Tholl corrie is possible via a loose gully), pass over a small 919m-high top then continue easily north-eastwards along a well-defined ridge to the 979m summit of Glas Mheall Mor. About 300m beyond and 40m below the aforementioned summit, the ridge flattens out. From there, descend the steep, south-eastern flank of the hill, characterised with angular quartzite blocks. At around 500m, the gradient eases; follow the Allt a' Ghlas Thuill down heathery slopes with sections of sandstone slab. Beyond the confluence of this stream and the larger water-course, the Garbh Allt (which flows from Loch Toll an Lochain), keep to the northern bank and pick up a path through the woods and rhodo-dendrons down to the A832, about 1km north of Corrie Hallie.

76

CONA' MHEALL

An impressive peak in rugged surroundings

Parking: Inverlael, gr NH182852
Distance: 21km
Height Gain: 1120m
Time: 6–8 hours
Terrain: Forest track, gravel footpath, grassy or stony slopes
Standard: Moderate
OS Maps: Beinn Dearg & Loch Broom (1:50,000 Landranger sheet 20), Beinn Dearg & Loch Fannich (1:25,000 Explorer sheet 436)

The hidden gems of the wild Beinn Dearg range north of the A835 Inverness–Ullapool road include beautiful mountain lochs, cliff-lined corries and the fine, centrally-located peak, Cona' Mheall. Cona' Mheall requires a long walk in but the recommended approach from Inverlael follows a good easy track and footpath. Look out for deer in the high corries north of Beinn Dearg.

Leave cars near the telephone kiosk by the A835 at Inverlael, where there is space for around six vehicles. Pass through the gate and follow a gravel track eastwards, across a grassy field, towards the forestry in Gleann na Sguaib. At the edge of the forest there is a locked gate in a deer fence; pass through the adjacent pedestrian swing gate. The track enters a belt of mature forest that changes to a young plantation with patches of older trees beyond a water-company building and a large forestry shed. Keep right at a junction and rise steadily uphill with young trees on the right, followed by a level track with clear-fell devastation on both sides (this is liable to be replanted). Mixed-age plantation and a short uphill section leads to a four-way junction; keep left, passing water-company tanks and crossing a burn, Allt na Moine. Pass through a section of mature forest, with the River Lael flowing over slabs down on the left, then bear left across a concrete bridge, with a dam and

Cona' Mheall and Loch Coire Lair

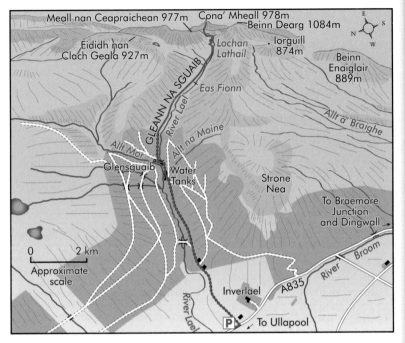

water intake for Ullapool's water supply just upstream. Continue on the main track through an area of bracken and scattered trees, rise uphill alongside a stone wall around the environs of the derelict Glensguaib hut, then keep right and proceed gradually uphill through belts of trees of mixed age. Beyond the track's end, at a turning area, a new deer fence and gate marks the forest's edge.

A good, well-drained, mainly gravel, stalkers path continues south-east into upper Gleann na Sguaib, following a heathery shelf above the Lael. It is a lovely walk, with broken cliffs and natural woodland on Creag na h-Iolaire to the right. Just beyond the waterfall Eas Fionn, there is a junction – keep straight ahead up the glen, getting gradually closer to the river, with some minor burn crossings. The floor of Coire Mathair Lathail levels out above 520m, with the path passing a tiny lochan in a grassy area beneath the impressive cliffs and screes of Beinn Dearg. Steeper slopes lead up to Lochan Lathail at 670m, with steep cliffs on both sides of the corrie (the main burn disappears underground). The path then zigzags up fairly steep, bouldery slopes and passes a strange narrow lochan with lots of bright-green weed at 790m.

Continue to Lochan Uaine, in the pass between Meall nan Ceapraichean and Beinn Dearg (850m); leave the path here and continue eastwards over the rather rough and slabby 884m top. Bypassing this top to the south is not a great option due to steep ground and crags. From the 884m top, there is a fine view southwards into the dramatic Coire Granda. Descend south-eastwards on rough ground to reach another col (813m) then head east-south-east on mainly grassy slopes leading upwards to Cona' Mheall's boulder fields. There are some grassy patches at first but the upper 100m of the slope has a continuous cover of quartz-feldspar-granulite boulders, many of them quite large. Although the majority of these rocks are stable, take great care. The summit (978m) is marked by a 1m-high cairn surrounded by rocks and large boulders. Steep, broken cliffs to the east and north make the summit an excellent viewpoint, with great views of Beinn Dearg, Loch Coire Lair, the crags of Am Faochagach and, to the north, the impressive conical summit of Seana Bhraigh's Creag an Duine.

Return to Inverlael by the outward route. Munro baggers may wish to include Beinn Dearg and Meall nan Ceapraichean but this adds 460m of ascent to an already long day.

77

SEANA BHRAIGH

An exceptionally fine mountain with a deep and formidable corrie

Parking: Corriemulzie Lodge, gr NH327953

Distance: 23km

Height Gain: 850m

Time: 7–9 hours

Terrain: Track, grassy and stony slopes

Standard: Moderate

OS Maps: Beinn Dearg & Loch Broom (1:50,000 Landranger sheet 20), Beinn Dearg & Loch Fannich (1:25,000 Explorer sheet 436)

One of Scotland's remotest and most spectacular mountains, Seana Bhraigh commands wonderful views of both the Beinn Dearg group and the wild moorlands to the north. Cycling on the estate track from Corriemulzie Lodge to Loch a' Choire Mhoir shortens the walk by 16km, but it is quite rough in places.

Turn off the A837 Bonar Bridge–Ledmore Junction road 100m east of Oykell Bridge Hotel and follow the surfaced road on River Oykell's south-western bank for 600m. Beyond some houses, continue on a gravel track for 300m then turn left, cross the River Einig (bridge), then turn right and enter the forestry. Drive a further 2½km to Allt nan Caisean then keep right, cross the bridge and keep right again, following the track nearest the Einig (this track is usually in good condition and is no problem for two-wheel-drive cars). On leaving the forest, keep right, pass the old Duag Bridge schoolhouse and cross the Abhainn Dubhag River (bridge). A small sign just beyond an estate house 2½km from the bridge indicates parking for hill walkers, on the left.

Continue on foot or bicycle steeply uphill through a pine plantation to Corriemulzie Lodge and its outbuildings. Beyond a gate, the track passes through gorse, with great views of Seana Bhraigh and its spectacular neighbour Creag an Duine. The track follows the river bank gradually

The Strath Mulzie approach to Seana Bhraigh

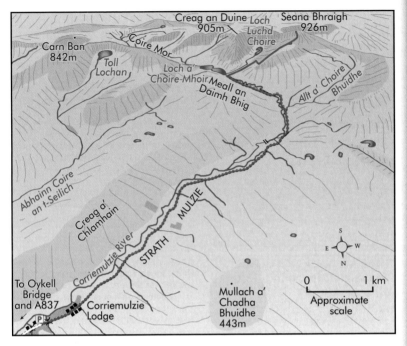

uphill, with fords across several side-streams of varied size. The track crosses the main river at gr NH293907, normally an easy ford with stepping stones (there is a wooden bridge 2km downstream at gr NH299923, but note that the trackless eastern side of the river is quite boggy and it is wise to stay on the western bank in wet weather since Seana Bhraigh is on that side). From the main ford, continue fairly steeply uphill then slightly downhill to the northern end (and outlet) of Loch a' Choire Mhoir; cross fairly easily on stepping stones to the western bank, about 40m downstream from the loch.

Head west-south-west across a grassy area and ascend steep grass slopes well known for wild flowers, keeping the burn from Luchd Choire on the left. The burn cuts through glacial moraine at the corrie's mouth; continue uphill beyond this for 100m then bear right (west) up steep grass slopes. Keep right below bouldery areas and rise steeply upwards on a grassy ramp with blueberry bushes to gain a broad shoulder of blueberries and short grass. Follow this shoulder south-westwards; although it becomes more stony, there is pleasant walking on grassy sections. A short descent on stony turf leads to a small lochan then there is a steep 160m-high rise through scattered boulders and

outcrops, with a reasonable path in the turf higher up. Look out for alpine flowers on the approach to the summit and observe the fine views of the curiously-shaped Loch Luchd Choire, Seana Bhraigh's summit cliffs, and the hills of Coigach and Assynt. The ascent eases off with a level, grassy area at 910m; keep right of the sheer summit cliffs and ascend a further 6m over scattered blocks. The summit (926m) has a stone wall shelter perched on the edge of the abyss. The magnificent views include Beinn Dearg but eyes are always drawn to Loch Luchd Choire.

Most walkers return to Corriemulzie Lodge by the same route. Otherwise, the traverse to Creag an Duine is easy on mossy grass and patches of solifluction terraces at first but the 905m summit cone involves some steep scrambling and the direct descent beyond the top, to Loch a' Choire Mhoir, is not recommended. The circuit from Seana Bhraigh to Carn Ban includes some tedious rough ground near the low point at the head of Coire Mor; although the mixed grassy/stony Carn Ban and its grassy western ridge are easily traversed, the descent to Loch a' Choire Mhoir is extremely steep and slippery, with boulder fields and some crags that should be avoided.

78

CUL BEAG

Superb vistas from solitary Cul Beag

Parking: Head of Loch Lurgainn, gr NC138068
Distance: 6km
Height Gain: 710m
Time: 4–5 hours
Terrain: Rough grassy and heathery hillsides, steep in places
Standard: Moderate
OS Maps: Loch Assynt, Lochinver & Kylesku (1:50,000 Landranger sheet 15), Coigach & Summer Isles (1:25,000 Explorer sheet 439)

Amongst the most impressive of the Assynt and Coigach mountains, Cul Beag is a steep-sided Torridonian sandstone peak with a rocky western face that is best viewed when looking east across Loch Lurgainn. However, the relatively easy southern flank gives hill walkers straightforward access to the top, with great views of Ben More Coigach, particularly during the descent.

Park at any suitable spot near the eastern end of Loch Lurgainn (gr NC138068) and ascend steeply north-east to reach a wide shelf with thick grass and a line of power poles. Cross the shelf and continue up steep grass with some boulders, heather and bog myrtle, keeping between two burns that are around 200m apart. Move closer to the burn on the right, which flows down steep slabs. Where the burn changes direction and the gradient eases, above 220m, there is a section of path but it soon fades out. Keep close to the burn for a short way but, above 270m, bear left (north-east) away from the burn on a fairly steep grass and heather slope with scattered boulders and small outcrops. Above 310m, head northwards up an easier slope with some wet areas. Continue upwards towards high ground left of a small burn, with some broken rock bands and outcrops (one of the rock bands is quite steep); above these, keep a bit more to the right to gain

Loch Lurgainn and Cul Beag

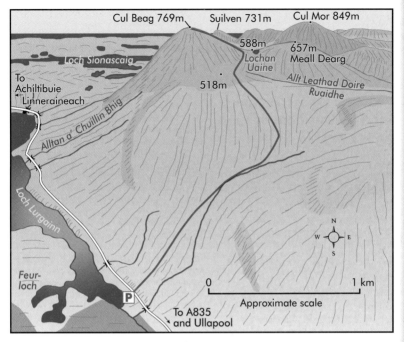

an ill-defined shoulder with fair amounts of easy slab and a view of Cul Beag's stony eastern top, Meall Dearg. A little further on, the steep-sided summit comes into view. Cross the 518m top on its eastern flank, where there are some lovely pink sandstone slabs, scattered boulders and gravelly areas. Descend more rocky ground for about 6m to a dip then keep right and traverse easily on a line following the 510m contour north-eastwards (towards the 588m col between Cul Beag and Meall Dearg), mainly on grass but with some wet areas. Ascend towards the left-hand-side of the col on fairly steep but straight-forward grass with scattered rocks.

Keep left of the col and its pond (Lochan Uaine), rising diagonally northwards up a grassy slope with scattered rocks to reach the northern side of Cul Beag's east-facing flank. This rising traverse gets steadily steeper as height is gained. Easier and drier slopes with grass, juniper, gravel and patches of stony ground lead upwards on the left (west) to even steeper slopes with stony shelves between grassy sections. Occasional sections of path assist upwards progress. There are great views over the crags to the lochan and sandy beach south of Cul Mor but north-westwards the eye is drawn over more lochs with beaches, islands

and woods, towards the impressive profiles of Suilven and Stac Pollaidh. The slope eases above 670m, with scattered outcrops, purple sandstone slabs, grass and moss. Look out for impressive pieces of conglomerate (pebbles in a sandstone matrix) that may be found lying on the ground.

The summit cone rises straight ahead and although it is fairly steep for 30m, a reasonable path leads easily to the spacious and slightly sloping top, which is fairly grassy with relatively few outcrops. A 1m-high cairn marks the summit (769m), at the edge of the steep northern slope. Views include the village of Elphin, the bulky mountain Cul Mor, the isolated bristly ridge of Stac Pollaidh, the Ben More Coigach complex of ridges, peaks and corries, Suilven, the Summer Isles, An Teallach and Beinn Dearg.

Although it is possible to descend the northern slope using a path that starts 25m east of the summit cairn, the mossy grass and scattered rocks with bucket steps may not appeal, especially in wet conditions, so it is best to return by the ascent route.

STAC POLLAIDH

Exhilarating scrambling on an exposed sandstone ridge

Parking: Stac Pollaidh car park, Loch Lurgainn, gr NC107095

Distance: 4½km

Height Gain: 530m

Time: 3½–4½ hours

Terrain: Gravel footpaths, stone stairs, some scrambling

Standard: Difficult

OS Maps: Loch Assynt, Lochinver & Kylesku (1:50,000 Landranger sheet 15), Coigach & Summer Isles (1:25,000 Explorer sheet 439)

Delightful Stac Pollaidh's serrated spine of sandstone towers rises like a bizarre prehistoric creature from the surrounding moors. The ridge traverse includes some exposed scrambling but the extraordinary summit can only be reached by rock climbing. Most people only go as far as a subsidiary top that is 2m lower than the highest point.

Turn off the A835 Ullapool–Ledmore Junction road at Drumrunie and follow the single track road towards Achiltibuie. Leave cars in the parking area at gr NC107095, cross the road and use the gate through the deer fence. A stone-flagged path rises steeply through bracken, gorse, heather and silver birch, becoming less steep once on the open hill. At a junction, keep right, use a gate in the upper deer fence and rise fairly steeply on a mainly gravel path across the grassy moor south-east of Stac Pollaidh. Just beyond a short flat area at 240m, the path heads up to the left, with steep gravel, flag-stones and stone stairs, then it heads right on easier ground. An easy-angled, grassy ramp leads to a level area below the hill's eastern tower, followed by steeper sections of stone stairs and flagstones. At a junction, the right-hand branch continues a northwards traverse below the cliffs, with great views of Cul Beag, Cul Mor and Suilven. To reach Stac Pollaidh's ridge just west of the eastern tower, keep left on

Stac Pollaidh from the south-east

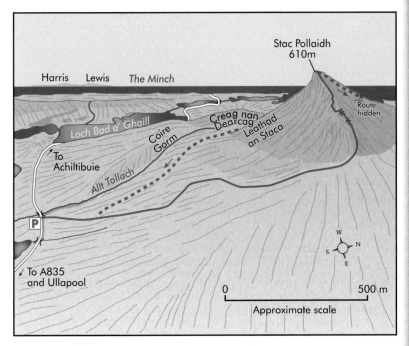

a steep traverse path, with stone stairs and tight zigzags passing a fenced-off area. Around 30m of very steep zigzags and stone stairs leads to the col at 540m. Turn left (east) for an easy 12m ascent to the first of the eastern towers (1m-high cairn on top).

From the col, turn right (west); keep left where the path forks and rise to a 1m-high cairn. The rock tower above this cairn should be bypassed using a traverse path that follows ledges on the left to reach a wide, steep and loose gully. Ascend the gully using hands for balance then exit left about 5m below the ridge. Follow a ledge then scramble awkwardly up a block onto another ledge; scramble easily to a loose area below the ridge crest. Keep left and just below the crest, cross an easy slab (or pass just below it) then a loose and steep ascent to the right leads up to and across the ridge. Follow a path with loose sections and a little easy scrambling then slant upwards to gain the crest, a fairly level section of ridge with lots of 2m–3m-high rock towers on the northern side and some spectacular 15m-high towers on the southern side. Traverse an obvious ledge just below the crest on the northern side; there is an exposed step but the handholds are good. Continue along the narrow ridge then scramble upwards to the right; the cairn (610m) is not the highest point but most people stop here. A 4m-high rock tower requiring moderate rock climbing blocks the ridge to the impressive summit (612m), which has three vertical sides. Superb views include Ben More Coigach, Suilven, Cul Beag and Cul Mor.

Most people return to the car park by the outward route but, in dry conditions, it is possible to descend the gully due north of the 610m cairn. A steep, loose path with occasional easy scrambling leads to loose boulders below the cliffs and ultimately connects with the path traversing the northern flanks of the hill, near a small lochan. Turn left onto stone stairs with easier gravel beyond, then pass below the impressive western prow and its huge boulder field on occasional stone stairs and flagstones. The path trends left, slanting downhill on a mix of stone stairs, gravel and flagstones. Following a short 20m descent (with Allt Tollach below), the path descends steadily leftwards (south-east) towards the deer fence. Go through the swing gate and, at the junction, keep right and downhill to the car park.

80

SUILVEN

Scotland's own spectacular Sugar Loaf

Parking: Near Glencanisp Lodge, gr NC108220

Distance: 19km

Height Gain: 910m

Time: 7–9 hours

Terrain: Road, track, gravel footpath, boggy or steep and loose hill-walkers paths

Standard: Moderate to difficult

OS Maps: Loch Assynt, Lochinver & Kylesku (1:50,000 Landranger sheet 15), Assynt & Lochinver (1:25,000 Explorer sheet 442)

Although neither Munro nor Corbett, Suilven is one of Scotland's most spectacular mountains, a sandstone monolith soaring above the surrounding Lewisian gneiss. Suilven is instantly recognisable, its bizarre profile from Lochinver reminiscent of Rio de Janeiro's Sugar Loaf mountain. Despite its impregnable appearance, there are routes which walkers can use to gain the summit (Caisteal Liath).

In Lochinver, at gr NC094223, turn onto the minor road heading east through lovely silver-birch woodland towards Glencanisp Lodge and park in the area provided at gr NC108220. Continue eastwards on a surfaced road past patches of silver birch, rowans, gorse and bracken, reaching Loch Druim Suardalain just before the lodge. Islets in this attractive loch are protected from grazing animals so they are well covered with Scots pine trees. Pass a quay, cross a cattle grid then enter mixed woodland with rhododendrons. Take the left fork to avoid the fine, stone-built lodge (sign reading 'footpath'), passing behind the main building.

Keep left on a four-wheel-drive track as far as a gate; ignore the 'River Inver (Loop)' sign near the grey-painted corrugated-iron hut and keep right on a muddy, four-wheel-drive track firstly past pines then natural woodland. A good grassy or gravel four-wheel-drive descends to the loch shore, but keep left on a path that rises

Meall Mheadhonach of Suilven

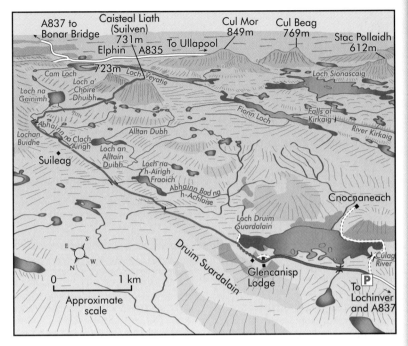

Map labels:
A837 to Bonar Bridge · Caisteal Liath (Suilven) 731m · Elphin · A835 · To Ullapool · Cul Mor 849m · Cul Beag 769m · Stac Pollaidh 612m · 723m · Loch Veyatie · Cam Loch · Loch a' Choire Dhuibh · Loch na Gainimh · Loch Sionascaig · Abhainn na Clach Airigh · Lochan Buidhe · Alltan Dubh · Fionn Loch · Falls of Kirkaig · River Kirkaig · Suileag · Loch an Alltain Duibh · Loch na h-Airigh Fraoich · Abhainn Bad na h-Achlaise · Cnocnaneach · Loch Druim Suardalain · Druim Suardalain · Glencanisp Lodge · Cúlag River · To Lochinver and A837 · P · 0 — 1 km Approximate scale

through bracken to a fence with a swing gate. A grassy then gravel or earthen path follows an old deer fence, gradually rising through heather and gorse, with great views of Suilven across foothills. Beyond a little burn (bridge), rise on slabs or broken rock, steeply in places, pass a reedy lochan then contour along the hillside to another bridge. Ascend steeply, zigzag and cross a broken outcrop to reach easier ground then go gradually downhill between hillocks with slabs. Descend steeply (stony), then a level section leads to more downhill. Another level section of path leads to a bridge then there is a gradual rise to a col with fine views of the river ahead. The path undulates then divides, the left fork heading for Suileag and Little Assynt. Keep right between a stone wall and the river and cross the small burn from Suileag (stepping stones). The gravel path undulates near the river, passing a reedy lochan; further on, the river flows through a curious slot. The path continues fairly level, with some stone bridges, to a wooden bridge for four-wheel-drive vehicles over the main river. Cross this, rise to a level section then a short, steep rise leads to curves to right then left. Descend slightly to a small burn (gr NC168197) where a cairn on the right marks the rough and very boggy hill-walkers path to Suilven.

Turn right and follow this path steeply, rising around 30m through thick, eroded, peat banks with knee-deep mud in places (the route improves further on). Beyond this section, the path is generally level; it passes east of a little lochan, followed by a gradual rise then it is steep, rough and stony for 80m. The path passes between two lochs then ascends directly to Coire Dubh, rising to the left on grass then becoming very steep and loose. Take care on eroded earthen patches, which are slippery in wet conditions.

On reaching Bealach Mor (590m), turn right and ascend gradually on a path across grass and scattered boulders to a strange stone wall that crosses the ridge at 610m. Pass through a gap; keep left then ascend steeply up to the right through two rock bands, using hands for balance. Above the rock bands, steep slopes lead to a level section with a little pond on the right. A short fairly steep descent to a narrow col is followed by a steady 60m rise through outcrops, grass and scattered rocks, leading to Caisteal Liath's 1m-high summit cairn (731m). Views from this lofty perch are magnificent, especially eastwards to the fang of Meall Meadhonach. Return by the outward route.

81

QUINAG

An outstanding ridge traverse with wonderful vistas

Parking: By A894, Quinag car park, gr NC233274

Distance: 9km

Height Gain: 850m

Time: 5–6 hours

Terrain: Rough grassy or stony hillsides, narrow ridges, steep in places, paths

Standard: Moderate to difficult

OS Maps: Loch Assynt, Lochinver & Kylesku (1:50,000 Landranger sheet 15), Assynt & Lochinver (1:25,000 Explorer sheet 442)

Beautifully shaped Quinag, which consists of three Corbetts linked by fine ridges and flanked by steep cliffs, looks great from all directions. However, the best views are from the Kylesku Bridge car park or from Ardvreck Castle by Loch Assynt, where the Duke of Montrose was cruelly betrayed by Christine Macleod in 1650.

The finest approach begins by ascending Spidean Coinich. Park by the A894 Skiag Bridge–Kylesku road (gr NC233274), where there is a disconcerting collection box for the Assynt mountain-rescue team. Walk 50m south along the road then turn right onto a gravel path. Cross a wooden bridge and continue on a boggy path for 60m to a junction; keep left on a muddy path that becomes very boggy across grass and heather. Rise to a burn crossing then continue across boggy moorland with a steady incline towards patchy quartzite slab on Spidean Coinich's eastern flank. The path improves along the upper edge of the escarpment, with some gravelly sections and pleasant slab. Steeper ground is encountered, but it is still easy, with curious, long, narrow sections of slab leading to easier gradients, gently tilted slabs and excellent walking above 420m. Beyond a flat area at 490m, a slope with boulders and grass becomes steeper and more boulder-strewn as far as a stone-ring shelter. The gradient eases a little, with occasional broken slab and lots of boulders

Evening light on Quinag

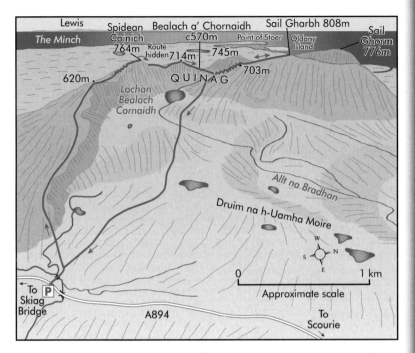

creating a pleasant stone-staircase effect. Enjoy great views across Lochan Bealach Cornaidh to Sail Gharbh, Quinag's highest Corbett.

A gradual, bouldery rise leads to a 620m top with lots of quartzite slab and a 1m-high cairn. Descend on a path between slabs and outcrops to a dip (591m), passing either side of a small pond on broken slab. An intermittent path rises across broken ground that becomes steeper, with gravel or stony zigzags ascending a very steep flank of mixed boulders and grass. The gradient eases off towards the top, where there are two large cairns; a 1m-high cairn marks the summit (764m), a superb viewpoint perched above the northern cliffs. The impressive vista includes Foinaven, Ben Hee, Ben Hope, Ben More Assynt and Suilven.

From Spidean Coinich, head southwards towards Suilven for 50m (horizontally); descend a steep zigzag path on the right (west) for about 15m, then bear right to gain a well-defined, fairly level ridge with purple sandstone boulders and slabs. A steep, bouldery descent leads down to Lochan Ruadh (655m) then a steep rise on a grassy ridge with a mainly earthen path leads to a cairn-less grassy top (714m). Continue on a narrow, steep-sided ridge northwards, gradually descending at first, then steeper down

a ridge with a gravel path on the left (use hands for balance on occasion). Easier zigzags lead to Bealach a' Chornaidh (570m), with mixed grass and rocks. From the bealach, bear right onto an earthen path heading across grass towards Sail Gharbh. A very steep flank with eroded zigzags ascends to the 703m col west of Sail Gharbh, where there is a half-metre-high cairn. (To include Sail Ghorm, turn left here, ascend 20m then traverse the 745m top on its north-eastern side; traverse the steep eastern side of the 687m top then pick up the broad ridge for the summit.)

From the 703m col, continue eastwards on a broad ridge, slabby at first then with sandstone outcrops suddenly changing to quartzite stones and boulders. A steeper rise eases off towards Sail Gharbh's summit, where there is a stone-ring shelter and a concrete triangulation pillar (808m). Views southwards across Assynt and Coigach are particularly good.

Return to 250m north-east of Bealach a' Chornaidh (gr NC203286), then bear left to pick up a rough boggy, sandy and stony path that levels out and becomes drier and sandy near Lochan Bealach Cornaidh. The path then becomes very rough; cross the burn and follow a heathery path leading to a gravel stalkers path that returns to the car park.

82

ARKLE

Fabulous ridge-walking on a remarkable mountain

Parking: Near Achfary, gr NC297402
Distance: 7km
Height Gain: 990m
Time: 6–7 hours
Terrain: Track, paths, grassy or stony hillsides, rough stony ridges, some scrambling
Standard: Moderate to difficult
OS Maps: Cape Wrath (1:50,000 Landranger sheet 9), Foinaven, Arkle, Kylesku & Scourie (1:25,000 Explorer sheet 445)

Of the many steep-sided mountains in Scotland's far north-west, the finest is Arkle, with a wonderful curving ridge and a crown of quartzite boulders and slabs. The Duchess of Westminster's racehorse, Arkle, regarded as the greatest-ever National Hunt horse, has featured on an Irish postage stamp. Deer-stalking information should be checked in season.

Park beside the A838 Lairg–Laxford Bridge road at gr NC297402 then follow the private road on foot to Airdachuillin and Lone. Cross the bridge then continue northwards, passing an attractive, reedy lagoon at Loch Stack's southern end. Pass through silver birch and rhododendrons to reach the stalker's house and outbuildings (Airdachuillin). Beyond the house, the partly surfaced track rises slightly then continues eastwards, with impressive views of Arkle's Moine Thrust escarpment ahead. Cross a grassy plain, with a bridge over a deep burn, to reach the wooden bridge at Lone (the cottage is used by the estate and is kept securely locked).

From Lone, follow a gravel-surfaced track for 100m eastwards then keep left at a junction; cross Allt Horn's wooden bridge onto a rougher, four-wheel-drive track across a grassy moor, leading to a small plantation with some rowans. Enter the woods between three 4m-high rocks; the former gate between the largest boulders is now off its hinges. Continue on a gravelly, four-

Walking on Arkle's summit ridge

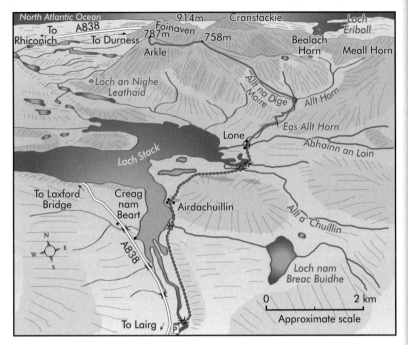

On the map:
North Atlantic Ocean
914m Cranstackie
To Loch Eriboll
To Rhiconich A838
Foinaven 787m
To Durness 758m
Arkle
Bealach Horn Meall Horn
Loch an Nighe Leathaid
Allt na Dige Moire
Allt Horn
Eas Allt Horn
Lone
Abhainn an Loin
Loch Stack
To Laxford Bridge
Creag nam Beart
Airdachuillin
Allt a' Chuillin
N W E S
A838
Loch nam Breac Buidhe
0 2 km
Approximate scale
To Lairg P

wheel-drive track that gets steadily steeper through the pines. On leaving the woods, follow a steep argocat track zigzagging up a grass slope, with great views across Loch Stack to Ben Stack. The gradient eases above 150m, with bridges over two burns.

Immediately beyond the second burn (Allt na Dige Moire, gr NC320432) leave the track and ascend through steep heather on a rough path, the gradient soon easing on a grass-and-heather slope (intermittent faint path). The burn cascades attractively over slabs on the left at around 250m. The path eventually disappears amongst mossy grass, occasional dwarf juniper, heather, broken outcrops and quartzite boulders, this rough terrain changing to tilted broken slabs with grassy and stony areas. Continue north-north-west on short grass and heather, directly towards Arkle's 758m top. On reaching the burn, follow the right-hand (east) bank, pass a small waterfall and ascend grass and gravel with some bouldery areas. Cross a dry water-course on the left at 520m (gr NC317445), then ascend grass, heather and occasional boulders to the right (north-east) of a dry, stony burn bed. Above 650m, compacted gravel and rocks leads to the bouldery 758m top, where there is a 1m-high cairn and good views of both Foinaven and Arkle's summit ridge.

Turn left (west), pass a small cairn and follow a stony or gravel path steeply down a well-defined ridge with zigzags. From a col at 680m, ascend a gravel or stony path on a broad, bouldery ridge with lots of pipe rock. Cross a boulder field, descend slightly to a dip, then a gradual bouldery or stony rise leads to the cairn-free 751m top (gr NC304455). Follow a path down a stony ridge to the north-west, descending about 15m to a dip then rise, with some level areas, on a ridge with a steep drop to the right. The ridge narrows to a bouldery crest that becomes slabby with grassy patches. Pass through an interesting crack in slabs that tilt steeply to the right (east) then scramble easily for 2m using large platforms for footholds. Next, there is a horizontal knife-edge with huge drops on both sides, followed by an extraordinary 40m-long cracked rock slab pavement that is about 6m wide. Ascend through boulders to pick up a path across mixed grass, moss and boulders to reach the 2m-high summit cairn (787m). The summit is a wild spot, a quartzite boulder field with virtually no grass. The magnificent views across the lochs to the north, west and south include Foinaven, Ben Hope and the Reay Forest. Return to the road by the upward route.

83

BEN HOPE

Magnificent panoramas from the northernmost Munro

Parking: Muiseal, gr NC462477
Distance: 7km
Height Gain: 915m
Time: 3–4 hours
Terrain: Paths, grassy hillsides
Standard: Moderate
OS Maps: Cape Wrath, Durness & Scourie (1:50,000 Landranger sheet 9), Ben Hope, Ben Loyal & Kyle of Tongue (1:25,000 Explorer sheet 447)

The northernmost Munro is one of Scotland's most spectacular peaks, with the finest view of

the hill obtained by looking from the north along Loch Hope, a narrow strip of fresh water with pleasant, naturally wooded shores. The name Ben Hope, meaning 'hill of the bay', was coined by Viking seafarers over one thousand years ago. Other local place names with Norse roots indicate that, perhaps in preference to the Faroe Islands or Iceland, some hardy Viking farmers settled in parts of Scotland's northern coastal strip.

Today's explorers will find precipitous cliffs west of the summit providing serious rock climbing on a former sill metamorphosed into biotite-garnet-schist, and the hill's exciting northern ridge soaring from hidden lochans at its foot. Lochans near Ben Hope led many twentieth century geologists astray, however. In a posthumous supplement to his book *The Mineralogy of Scotland* (1901), the Scottish mineralogist and chemist Matthew Forster Heddle stated that he had found either colourless garnets or diamonds in a rock specimen near a lochan 'three miles north east of Ben Hope'. Unfortunately, the specimen vanished for nearly one hundred years and attempts to locate the lochan and the diamonds, in an area of many small lochans, proved fruitless. When the specimen turned up at Glasgow University, it was investigated and found to consist of nothing less than colourless garnets!

To reach Ben Hope, follow the single-track

The north ridge of Ben Hope

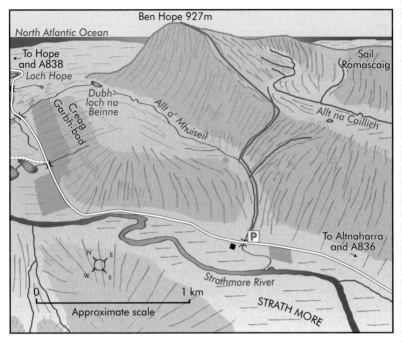

Ben Hope 927m

North Atlantic Ocean

To Hope
and A838

Loch Hope

Dubh
loch na
Beinne

Creag
Garbh-bad

Allt a' Mhuiseil

Sail
Romascaig

Allt na Caillich

P

To Altnaharra
and A836

N E
W S

Strathmore River

STRATH MORE

0   1 km

Approximate scale

road between Hope, on the A838 Tongue–Durness road, and Altnaharra, on the A836 Lairg–Tongue road. The road may become flooded during heavy rain, weather conditions not uncommon in the area. If travelling to or from Altnaharra (one of the coldest places in Scotland in winter), take a look at the Dun Dornaigil broch in Strath More, about 3km south of the Ben Hope parking area and right next to the road. It is a substantial ruin up to 6.7m high, with an extraordinary triangular lintel. The broch is an Iron Age fortified tower, built as a refuge in days when piracy and looting were obviously serious problems.

The easiest way up Ben Hope starts from the roadside parking area at Muiseal (gr NC462477), near a large sheep shed and just south of the Allt a' Mhuiseil, which descends from a wide terrace on the western flanks of the hill. A sign by the car park reads 'Path to Ben Hope'. A path (boggy in places) follows the right-hand side of the burn, ascending steeply to a fork in the burn at the 180m level (not to be confused with the other tributary lower down). Take the right-hand branch upwards and pass through a wide, mainly grassy, gap in the Leitir Mhuiseil crags. The gap becomes narrower near the top, at 400m, where the ground is steepest;

there is a fairly obvious path. Once on less-steep ground above Leitir Mhuiseil, turn left (north-north-east) onto the south-facing flank of Ben Hope and ascend a further 100m on mainly short-turf grassy slopes with scattered rocks. The slope becomes steeper for about 100m then the gradient gradually decreases on the long approach, with grass and scattered rocks, to the 927m-high summit. A concrete triangulation pillar sits on a rock plinth, with a stone shelter on the north side offering some protection from prevailing winds.

Views from the summit range far and wide on a clear day. The northern and eastern ridges cradle several wild corries dotted with substantial lochans. Further away, the screes of Foinaven lie to the west, the peaks and tors of Ben Loyal lie to the east, southwards there are the hills of the Reay Forest and Ben More Assynt beyond, while to the south-east there is the bulk of Ben Klibreck. Looking north beyond Loch Hope, the North Atlantic Ocean stretches beyond the horizon to the Faroe Islands and the North Pole.

Return to the road by retracing steps, taking care on the steep sections, especially during or after wet weather.

84

BEN LOYAL

A fascinating, multi-topped mountain of outstanding character

Parking: Inchkinloch, gr NC599442

Distance: 11km

Height Gain: 820m

Time: 4½–5½ hours

Terrain: Mainly grassy slopes and ridges, summit rock tor, occasional paths

Standard: Moderate

OS Maps: Strath Naver (1:50,000 Landranger sheet 10), Ben Hope, Ben Loyal & Kyle of Tongue (1:25,000 Explorer sheet 447)

Ben Loyal, a queen amongst Scotland's mountains and composed of syenite, a hard igneous rock, presents her most majestic profile to the north. Approaching the hill from the north is certainly scenic but routes from the Kyle of Tongue are not recommended due to very steep and potentially slippery slopes. The easiest approach is from the south, starting at the estate cottage Inchkinloch (gr NC599442), near the head of Loch Loyal and on the A836 Lairg–Tongue road. It is not a busy route and mainly firm ground allows for pleasant walking. Deer stalking takes place between mid-August and mid-October.

Leave cars by the Inchkinloch cottage or by the stalking information sign just north of the bridge over the river there. Follow an argocat trail for 20m west of the sign, cross a small burn then turn right (north-north-west) on an initially faint argocat trail through grass and heather; it becomes clearer on steeper grassy ground after a few minutes walking. Above 170m, the gradient decreases but the trail becomes faint as it crosses a gradually sloping, and reasonably dry, moor composed of grass and bog myrtle. Keep straight ahead (north-north-west) when the trail heads off to the left. Slant up and leftwards for around 60m on a steep, but easy, dry mossy-grass slope above 250m then stop to enjoy the extensive views including Morven (Caithness), the Ben Griams, Ben Klibreck and the Reay Forest.

Loch Hakel and Ben Loyal

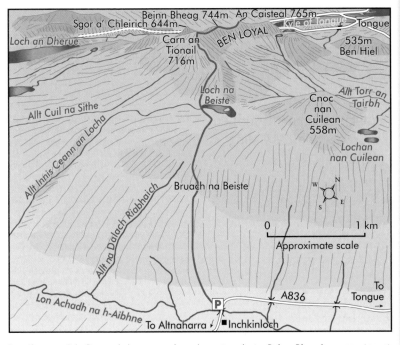

A uniform, mainly firm and dry, grass slope continues towards Ben Loyal, the summit rock tower visible ahead. Just before Loch na Beiste, an argocat trail passes through an area of small peat hags. Continue westwards across alternating boggy and drier areas to the loch's outflow and step across the burn.

From the loch, head directly for the slabby outcrop at the foot of Ben Loyal's south top, Carn an Tionail (outcrop at 550m, gr NC579473), zigzagging across an area of wet, peaty channels at first then rising steadily on mainly firm grass. On gaining Carn an Tionail's south-eastern shoulder, there are good views of Loch Loyal and Beinn Stumanadh. Beyond a flat area with ponds (440m), steep but easy mossy grass and heather leads to the slabby outcrop; keep right but bear left above the rocks. Steep, rough ground leads to easier short mossy turf. Keep left on good, dry turf then ascend directly (north-west) on steep, longer grass, past some outcrops, to reach Carn an Tionail's summit (716m), a flat area of stony moss and grass with a small cairn and great views westwards towards Ben Hope.

Continue northwards on golf-course-like turf to a col (680m), then ascend steep grass to a shoulder on Beinn Bheag at 700m. Steep short grass with occasional rocks leads north-westwards to Beinn Bheag's grassy top at 744m; there is a steep drop just beyond the tiny cairn. To reach Ben Loyal's summit, bear right (north-east) on mossy grass and descend to a level area at 700m. Keep left of the large boulder sitting on a hillock. A well-defined ridge with some stony areas and a clear path leads to the vertical southern end of the summit tower (An Caisteal). Keep left and ascend short grass, traverse the western side of the tower (passing a curious stone with a circular hole in it) and gain a high-level path that rises to the right, onto the tower's steep northern side. Zigzag through the syenite boulders and outcrops (sometimes on steep grass) and scramble easily up a 1½m-high rock step; bear left on rock slab with patchy turf to reach the summit's triangulation pillar, which is made of local stone. Beware of 15m-high cliffs immediately to the south! Allow time to enjoy the exceptional views, including the north coast and the wild moors of Sutherland and Caithness. The steep northern flanks of the mountain can be well appreciated from the summit.

Return to the road by following the same route in reverse.

85

GOATFELL

A tourist route with excellent views of Arran's peaks and ridges

Parking: Walk from Brodick ferry terminal or park at Arran Brewery, gr NS013376
Distance: 10km
Height Gain: 870m
Time: 4½–5½ hours
Terrain: Forest tracks, gravel/stony footpath with some stone stairs
Standard: Moderate
OS Maps: Isle of Arran (1:50,000 Landranger sheet 69), Isle of Arran (1:25,000 Explorer sheet 361)

Beautiful Arran is often referred to as 'Scotland in miniature' and the rugged northern half is mountainous on an almost alpine scale. The highest peak on the island is the shapely Corbett, Goatfell, easily reached from Brodick and a great introduction to the Arran hills.

From the Brodick ferry terminal, follow the A841 road 3km northwards, towards Lochranza. Leave cars in the large parking area opposite the Wineport restaurant and the Arran Brewery (gr NS013376). A sign on the north side of the main road directs walkers towards Goatfell: follow the gravel track between the buildings, pass another sign and ascend through mixed forest. Keep right at a junction, continue alongside a field, cross a surfaced road then follow another gravel track (signed). There are also two information signs near this junction. Pass through rhododendron and coniferous forest then mixed woodland. Keep right then straight on and take the signed left fork at the next junction. The gravel four-wheel-drive track bears right with the Goatfell path signed straight on. A good gravel path follows the plantation's edge, with the summit now visible ahead. At 120m, pass through a gap in an old wall with a fence then ascend pleasantly through bracken, silver birch, rowans and heather. The path enters open ground and becomes steeper with stone stairs, rising past a waterfall on the left and crossing

Goatfell from Consolation Tor

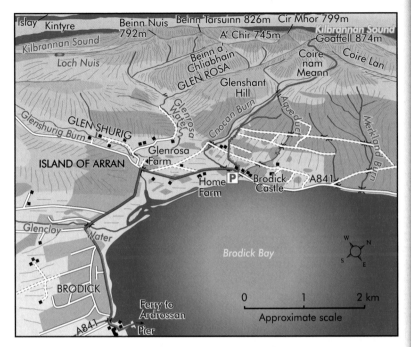

the aqueduct (footbridge) taking water to Brodick Castle at 295m. Look left for fine views of Beinn Nuis, Beinn Tarsuinn and A' Chir.

Beyond the gate in the deer fence (315m), the excellent mostly gravel path ascends gradually across a grass-and-heather moor, with long, flat sections, but it becomes steeper above 380m, rising steadily to Goatfell's eastern shoulder. The path becomes stony or bouldery, with some slabs and paved sections, getting rougher on approaching the Meall Breac ridge at 610m.

The path bears left (west) once on the gradual ridge and joins the path from Corrie at 630m. Steep stone stairs among boulders and some huge blocks lead upwards just left (south) of the ridge line then a rough path rises steadily to steeper, boulder-strewn ground with stone stairs. Hands may be required for balance when passing between boulders. To avoid precipitous rock bands, the path slants uphill with stone stairs, to the left (south) – not as shown on the OS maps. Beyond a bend, the path rises steeply to the right to gain the summit (874m), with outcrops, boulders and some grass. A concrete triangulation pillar and a viewpoint indicator sit next to each other on a granite slab. On a clear day, fantastic views include the islands of the Firth of Clyde (Ailsa Craig, the Cumbraes, Bute

and Holy Island), the spectacular but vicious-looking fangs of Cir Mhor and the Witch's Step (Ceum na Caillich), the far Paps of Jura, parts of the southern Highlands and even Slieve Snaght in Donegal.

Most people return to Brodick by the upward route. A much longer alternative heads north from the summit, ascends the Corbett Cir Mhor and returns via Glen Rosa. Count on an additional 430m of ascent plus an extra 7km (allow eight to nine hours in total). Descend northwards from Goatfell towards the Stacach ridge, where an easy, sandy path traverses the bases of several rock towers on the left (west). From the 760m col beyond Stacach, a path ascends easily to the large summit outcrop on North Goatfell (818m); pass this on the left (south-west) then gain the north-west ridge and descend to the Saddle (432m). A steep, loose path ascends Cir Mhor, keeping left high up, with some minor scrambling up on the right for the last 50m. The summit (799m) is another magnificent and rather airy viewpoint. Easily descend Cir Mhor's south-west ridge (steep, but no scrambling) then follow the good gravel path down Glen Rosa from the 591m col and return to Brodick.

86

BEINN TARSUINN

Wonderful ridge-walking through incomparable scenery

Parking: Walk from Brodick ferry terminal or park at Glen Rosa campsite, gr NS001377

Distance: 14km

Height Gain: 940m

Time: 6–7 hours

Terrain: Gravel track, gravel/stony or boggy footpaths, some stone stairs, grassy hillsides

Standard: Moderate to difficult

OS Maps: Isle of Arran (1:50,000 Landranger sheet 69), Isle of Arran (1:25,000 Explorer sheet 361)

Although less-frequented than some of the north Arran hills, Beinn Tarsuinn and its neighbour Beinn Nuis are good for hill walking, with superb views all around.

There is only limited parking for non-campers at the Glen Rosa campsite (gr NS001377). Follow the good Glen Rosa track alongside woods as far as a gate and stile. Continue on a rougher four-wheel-drive track to a sheep fank, where there is a swing gate. The track narrows to become a sandy river-bank path, with great views up Glen Rosa to Cir Mhor and the Witch's Step.

Cross Garbh Allt on a wooden footbridge then ascend the steep bank behind the NTS sign to pick up the path on the northern side of the gully. It is a steep ascent through bracken and long grass, bog myrtle and bog asphodel. Enter the Garbh Allt native-tree regeneration enclosure via a swing gate then continue very steeply with sections of stone stairs. Once the gradient eases, another swing gate leads out of the enclosure. A boggy footpath gradually rises across the moor, keeping close to the burn and waterfall on the left.

Use a swing gate in a deer fence to enter the Coire a' Bhradain enclosure (heather sprigs on the nearby fence warn low-flying birds). About 200m horizontally beyond the gate (at gr NR970388), a path descends steeply into the

Beinn Nuis and Beinn Tarsuinn from Glen Rosa

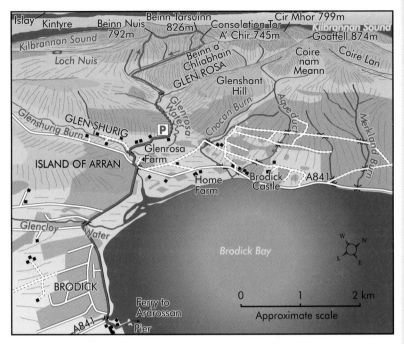

gully on the left (the main Coire a' Bhradain path continues straight on). Cross the burn using stepping stones then ascend steeply and follow a boggy path across the moor towards a gate in the deer fence. Beyond the gate, rise gradually to steeper slopes above 400m, where the now rough and partly eroded path ascends steeply through heather, granite slabs and outcrops (use hands for balance). There are fine views of the Beinn Nuis cliffs and A' Chir to the right of Beinn Tarsuinn. A good new path ascends short grass and heather steeply above 600m, then traverses a steep slope northwards to gain the south ridge of Beinn Nuis at 670m. The bouldery or gravel path ascends steep grass past impressive granite outcrops, with some easy slab. On the summit, there is a curious small cairn on gravel about 1m below the highest point. Enjoy magnificent views of the Arran hills and westwards to Kintyre.

Continue northwards towards Beinn Tarsuinn on a good stony/gravel path that descends past the amazing Flat Iron Tower to reach a col at 709m. The ridge northwards features lots of outcrops, with impressive gullies and steep cliffs to the right. The path ascends gradually then, after a leftwards traverse, an easy scramble on the right leads back to the ridge. A gradual rise leads to a wide grassy area with excellent views. The ridge narrows with some outcrops then a steep rise past some outcrops and large boulders leads to another flat area, a dip, then uphill to the summit (826m), where there is a 4m-long outcrop but no cairn. Views are great all around.

Descend very steeply north-eastwards between outcrops, with easy scrambling in places and an interesting 'window' to pass through. Less steep, but still craggy, lower ground leads to a steep 4m-high slab, level with the 10m-high Consolation Tor. Avoid the slab using an easy path, initially on the left then traversing underneath. Take the path to the right of the tor, descend and pass through an extraordinary 2m-high rock arch. Cross boulders and traverse northwards to meet the path to Beinn a' Chliabhain, turn right and descend to a level ridge and col (595m), with near-vertical drops on the left and superb views of A' Chir's precipitous slabs and chasms. Turn right at the col and descend easy grass and heather between outcrops to the grassy and occasionally boggy floor of Coire a' Bhradain. Easy ground leads to a fence and stile then a boggy path continues to the gate at gr NR970388. Follow the path to Glen Rosa and back to the campsite.

87

BEN MORE (MULL)

Glorious island views and seascapes from Mull's highest point

Parking: Dhiseig, Loch na keal, gr NM494359

Distance: 10km (13km with A' Chioch)

Height Gain: 970m (1070m with A' Chioch)

Time: 4½–5½ hours (6–7 hours with A' Chioch)

Terrain: Gravel track; boggy/gravel/stony paths, scree-covered or rocky ridges

Standard: Moderate (difficult by A' Chioch route)

OS Maps: Iona & West Mull (1:50,000 Landranger sheet 48), Isle of Mull East (1:25,000 Explorer sheet 375)

There are several ways up Ben More, the Isle of Mull's highest point, the most popular being the straightforward tourist route from Dhiseig, by Loch na Keal. The more exciting ridge traverse from A' Chioch appears intimidating but it is not as drastic as it looks. Deer stalking takes place from August to 20 October.

The tourist route begins by the southern Loch na Keal road (B8075), at gr NM494359. Park on the grass (on the road's shore side) and follow the fairly steep gravel track uphill towards Dhiseig, the pleasant Abhainn Dhiseig burn on the right, with silver birch and rowans on its banks. Just before Dhiseig, a pithy sign on the right curiously points in the direction labelled 'up'.

Keep right of the stunted trees protecting the houses (on grass) as far as a gate; then bear right on an easy, mainly grassy path, following the burn's pleasant little gorge. At 130m, there is a 3m-high waterfall with rowan trees; step over the fence there. Beyond the fence, the path continues with flat-slab, gravel or boggy sections across a grass-and-bog-myrtle moor. The gradient eases above 170m but boggy underfoot conditions continue to 300m.

Before reaching a steep-sided gorge that is difficult to cross above 320m, the path crosses the burn (easy in normal conditions) then a normally wet and muddy path ascends the

Mull's Ben More overlooks Loch na Keal

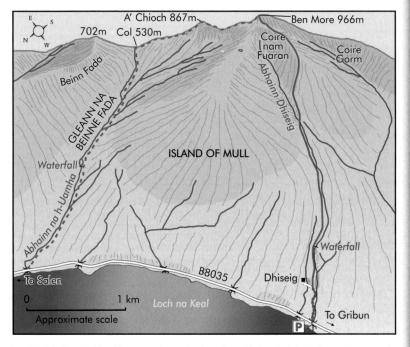

burn's right-hand side. The route is easily followed but may be unpleasant in wet weather. Becoming steeper, the path keeps well to the right of the burn above 450m, rising over broken, slippery ground with patchy rock outcrops and gravel, as well as stony and muddy sections. Above 550m, the path becomes less steep and ascends the grassy hillside directly for Ben More's west-pointing ridge, its flanks covered in patches of grey, basalt scree above 650m. This broad, poorly-defined ridge then becomes steeper, with scree predominant; beyond a fairly level shoulder above 790m, an easily followed scree path rises steadily to the almost level stone-covered summit area. The summit is marked with a 1½m-high cairn and a stone ring shelter, but the triangulation pillar marked on old maps has long-since disappeared. On a clear day, views extend from Ben Nevis to Ireland, but the most amazing scene is the dramatic eastern ridge to A' Chioch. The summit rocks and cairn are magnetic and may cause compass deflections up to 180 degrees.

It is advisable to return the same way. If a traverse of A' Chioch is desired, it is recommended to ascend A' Chioch first. Start where the B8035 crosses the Abhainn na h-Uamha (gr NM507368). Follow a poor and often indistinct path on this burn's right bank, south-eastwards into Gleann na Beinne Fada, which is a boggy place at the best of times. There are frequent waterfalls where the burn leaps basalt steps that delineate old lava flows, the finest fall (at 150m) being around 10m high. Continue easily to the 530m col at gr NN538345 then turn right (south) and ascend the A' Chioch ridge, initially easy on grass then mainly on scree, but with loose rock and frequent, narrow, rock bands above 620m. There is a gravel or scree path in places. The route is not difficult but it is very steep for 80m just below the cairned summit (867m), where there is a fine view of Ben More. A gradual descent on mixed grass and rocks leads to a steeper 50m drop directly down the crest to a col at 765m (don't attempt to descend northwards from the col since it is dangerous). Beyond the col, a narrow, notched, mixed grassy-and-rocky ridge rises steadily for around 100m; keep left of the crest on a path, if required. The final 100m section to Ben More's summit is very steep with slippery scree paths and some easy scrambling with a sense of exposure. From the summit, descend to Dhiseig via the tourist route.

88

SGURR OF EIGG (AN SGURR)

An astonishing, primeval-looking peak

Parking: Arisaig harbour, gr NM658864, then ferry required

Distance: 9km

Height Gain: 410m

Time: 3–4 hours

Terrain: Tracks, rough boggy paths, rough hillsides

Standard: Moderate

OS Maps: Rum, Eigg & Muck (1:50,000 Landranger sheet 39), Rum, Eigg, Muck, Canna & Sanday (1:25,000 Explorer sheet 397)

A jewel in the Hebridean sea, the island of Eigg draws attention from every direction. The Sgurr of Eigg (An Sgurr, or simply the Sgurr), an inselberg created by a viscous pitchstone lava flow, is only 393m high but its outrageous profile more than makes up for its height. The peak has vertical cliffs on three sides and it reminds many people of primeval times and lost worlds.

Of the ferries between Eigg and the mainland, only the MV *Sheerwater* from Arisaig allows enough time to complete the walking route and return to the mainland the same day. From the Sheerwater pier, follow the road for 50m past the Eigg tearoom and craft shop. Keep left on a surfaced road and walk uphill, past the 1997 memorial. Enter a mixed forest with bracken and brambles; the trees give way to a field on the left, with an incongruous, pink-painted house on the right. An un-surfaced track continues beyond the house, between the trees and the field. At a junction, keep left for 20m (with a wooden building on the right) then keep right at a second junction, where there is a post with coloured markers. Continue uphill into a mixed forest with lots of beech. Go through a gate at the edge of the woods, where there are interesting wind-blasted trees and rhododendrons, then enter a rough field and head towards the buildings directly in line with the Sgurr.

Pass the wind turbine just right of the

The Sgurr of Eigg

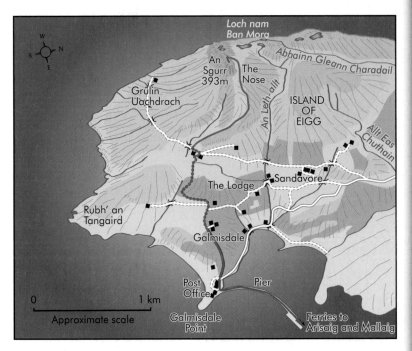

An Sgurr
393m
The Nose
Loch nam Ban Mora
Abhainn Gleann Charadail
An Leth-allt
Grulin Uachdrach
ISLAND OF EIGG
Allt Eas Chuthain
The Lodge
Sandavore
Rubh' an Tangaird
Galmisdale
Post Office
Pier
Galmisdale Point
Ferries to Arisaig and Mallaig

0 .... 1 km
Approximate scale

buildings, go through a gate then turn left on a good gravel track beside the wall guarding the house. Around 50m beyond the house, a cairn on the right with a red marker indicates the rough path to the Sgurr. Rise steeply onto easier, heather moorland on a muddy, well-worn and occasionally stony path that may be slippery following wet weather. The view of the Sgurr, with Muck to the left, is quite amazing.

Beyond a horizontal, basalt outcrop with a small cairn on top, bear right (cairn), fairly level at first then rising gradually, with a rough, muddy, eroded path leading to another easy outcrop. Cross a heathery moor, levelling out but with steep upward slopes and scree on the left. The generally muddy path crosses grassy, heathery, peaty and wet areas then a steady rise leads to an indistinct path that disappears into a sphagnum bog.

A path slants up a dry but boulder-strewn slope on the left, below a cliff; follow this uphill to a bouldery notch, with columnar basalt on the right. Beyond a cairn at 335m, bear left to find an easy, 2m-high rock wall that is even easier on its right. Above the wall, keep slanting up to the right, firstly over broken rock then on a path that levels out. Look for red-spot marks showing the way. Pass a pond, keeping left on rock slab.

A rough, boggy and peaty path keeps right of various rises on the ridge, one of them crowned with the remains of an ancient fort. Continue past or across areas of columnar pitchstone, the column tops creating curious lumps on the rock slab. Beyond several boggy dips, cross more columnar slab into another boggy dip then ascend past red-spot marks to an extraordinary sloping rock pavement on the left. Cross the pavement then ascend a heathery slope leading to the summit (393m), where a cylindrical, concrete-and-stone-chip triangulation pillar is perched only 5m away from the abyss. The intriguing and relatively flat summit area includes bare rock, columnar pitchstone and grassy areas. However, it is the view that commands attention, with silvery seas, islands, little houses nestling in shelter from the wind, the majestic Cuillin of Skye and Rum, and mainland peaks in profusion.

Although it is possible to descend southwards to Grulin from the flat area near the 335m cairn and return to Galmisdale on a gravel track, most people return by the outward route.

89

RUM CUILLIN

Traverse Rum's amazing rocky ridge

Parking: Mallaig, gr NM674969, then ferry required

Distance: 18km

Height Gain: 1700m, 1440m if bypassing Hallival and Trallval

Time: 9–11 hours

Terrain: Rough boggy paths, steep pathless hillsides; grassy, stony and rock ridges

Standard: Difficult; some scrambling may be bypassed

OS Maps: Rum, Eigg & Muck (1:50,000 Landranger sheet 39), Rum, Eigg, Muck, Canna & Sanday (1:25,000 Explorer sheet 397)

The mysterious isle of Rum's main attraction for walkers is a magnificent ridge formed from the core of an early Tertiary volcano, with two Corbetts, Askival and Ainshval. Access to the island is no longer restricted and ferries now dock at a new quay. In winter conditions, mountaineering skills are required (grade I/II).

From the north end of the road bridge 50m south of Kinloch Castle, cross the stile (sign: 'Rum Coolin') and follow a muddy path on the river bank. Ignore the wooden bridge; keep straight and pass through an overgrown wall (gate). Beyond two buildings, follow the Coire Dubh pony track past an SNH sign, through a gate and onto a heather-covered moor with scattered pines. The mainly gravel, but poorly-drained, track has flooded and boggy sections, with stepping stones across side streams. At 190m, there is a small concrete dam below a narrow ravine. Proceed steeply uphill to a deer fence with a gate bolted top and bottom (keep closed). Several boggy paths lead uphill into the corrie, the best being nearest the main burn. The mainly grassy, flat-floored Coire Dubh contains huge rocks up to 3m high and a broken stone-built dam (cross the burn here). Keep to the corrie's centre (avoiding paths left and right); a path just left of the main burn rises through grass, heather, wild flowers and scattered rocks.

Hallival from Askival

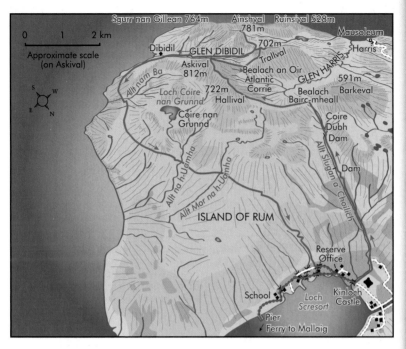

It gets steeper with rock outcrops then easier, stony ground leads to the col Bealach Bairc-mheall (466m), with great views of the main ridge south and east.

Turn left (south-east) for the intimidating-looking Hallival (722m). A broad, featureless, stony ridge leads upwards, with some flat areas, to the base of the summit cone, which features bands of hard allivalite crags between softer, peridotite terraces. Keep left on grass then right on boulders and scree, slanting steeply upwards, to break through the upper crags for the summit; easy scrambling and not as difficult as it looks. To descend to the 599m col with Askival, head south on turf past the curious burrows of the Manx shearwater (an oceanic bird) then keep right of centre, with very steep continuous easy scrambling on blocks; use hands for balance. Keep right (west) and pass through a gap in the crag just above the col. (Otherwise, avoid Hallival easily on its western flank by a boulder-strewn, horizontal ledge at 550m.)

Beyond the col, a faint path leads up and down through scattered rock and outcrops then rises via a fine, bright-green, grass-covered ridge to the monolith known as the Askival Pinnacle; direct ascent is a 'difficult' rock climb. Keep left on steep grass slopes with some rock outcrops. There are a few easy scrambling moves on reconnecting with the ridge above the pinnacle then easier ground leads to Askival's triangulation pillar on a rock platform (812m). Now descend the west ridge; avoid initial steep rock by bearing left down rocks and grass, then trend right and follow a broad, rough ridge to the grassy Bealach an Oir (455m). From the bealach, ascend steep grass and scattered stones to reach an easier-angled shoulder. About 100m of steeper ground leads to Trallval's double summit, with some excellent scrambling on gabbro and peridotite and an airy approach to the higher (western) top at 702m. The steep rocky descent to Bealach an Fhuarain (c510m) creates difficulties, even in clear weather; for the easiest route, go directly south from Trallval's eastern top. (Trallval can be avoided by easily traversing grass slopes between the bealachs.)

For Ainshval (781m), keep right of the buttress above Bealach an Fhuarain on small scree, gain a flat grassy area above, then a short scramble and steep scree in the Grey Corrie (keeping a fearsome-looking rock ridge to the right) leads to the 1m-high summit cairn and more magnificent views. The best way off Ainshval is to return to Bealach an Fhuarain, descend grassy Glen Dibidil then follow the rough, boggy coastal path back to Kinloch.

90

SOUTHERN CUILLIN

Exposed and thrilling scrambling on rock peaks and ridges

Parking: Glen Brittle beach car park, gr NG409206
Distance: 13km
Height Gain: 1240m
Time: 10–12 hours
Terrain: Gravel and rough boulder paths; considerable and often difficult scrambling on boulder fields, ridges and steep rock faces
Standard: Strenuous; very difficult
OS Maps: South Skye & Cuillin Hills (1:50,000 Landranger sheet 32), Skye: Cuillin Hills (1:25,000 Explorer sheet 411)

The fearsome-looking mountains around the Cuillin's spectacular Coir' a' Ghrunnda (on the island of Skye) include sections of very serious rock climbing, but this route to three fine summits only involves scrambling (in winter, mountaineering skills are required, grade II/III). Well-constructed access paths offer a pleasant approach.

From the Glen Brittle beach car park, walk through the campsite, turn right and cross the fence behind the toilets. A well-drained gravelly, stony or paved path rises steeply up grass slopes, crossing a four-wheel-drive track. The gradient eases near a burn at 120m; at a path junction (no cairn), keep right and cross the burn easily on broken slab. Another fine, well-drained, gravel path rises gradually across grass and heather moor, with excellent views of Coire Lagan and its peaks. Beyond a small loch the path crosses Allt Coire Lagan on boulders or slab (normally easy).

Continue uphill on a good path that twists through an area of large boulders. At a junction (no cairn, gr NG435197), keep left and ascend steadily. Traverse below Sron na Ciche's south-facing crags on a rougher section of path, with boulders and some slab. Keeping close under the lowest crags, at gr NG445193 the path bears left between the last two crags and rises steeply, with boulders, some loose rock and stone stairs.

Sgurr nan Eag and Loch Coir' a' Ghrunnda

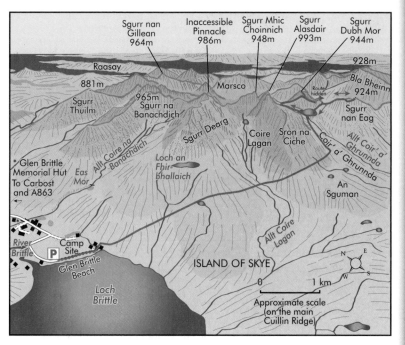

The view backwards includes Soay and an arc of boulder moraine. Ahead lie the amazing Coir' a' Ghrunnda slabs, the broken cliffs of Sgurr nan Eag, and the main Cuillin ridge peeking over the lip of the corrie.

A rough, unimproved path with lots of boulders rises gradually on a wide, sloping shelf about 70m above the corrie floor, crossing scree then keeping left of a large crag to gain another cairned route on a boulder-strewn shelf above. The gradient eases on approaching an area of slabs and steep rock faces at 600m; keep far left with hard scrambling up a particularly steep corner, then continue upwards, keeping right. Boulder-strewn ground leads easily to Loch Coir' a' Ghrunnda, with sandy beaches, impressive slabs and a surreal peridotite mountain backdrop.

From the loch, an indistinct path rises fairly easily north-north-west through mixed outcrops, loose rock and boulders towards Sgurr Alasdair's cliffs; at 790m (gr NG450205), trend right with some steep moderate scrambling to gain the main ridge just north-west of Bealach Coir' an Lochain (855m). Continue south-east on a rough easy-angled ridge of peridotite boulders for Sgurr Dubh na Da Bheinn (938m, cairn). Fairly loose, straightforward paths on the northern side of an east-pointing ridge-spur lead towards the 886m col below Sgurr Dubh Mor. Traverse three pinnacles in turn: on the right (south), left,

then right. To ascend Sgurr Dubh Mor's steep face, follow a broad ledge horizontally right, then go left up a gully, traverse right then left again to pass under a difficult corner. Ascend right above the corner, with some hard moves; a loose ascent leads up to the left, then a path to the right leads to a short wall below the airy summit (944m, small cairn on a knife-edge slab).

Return to Sgurr Dubh na Da Bheinn then descend its southern ridge, steepest near the 805m col below Caisteal a' Gharbh-choire's overhang (moderate scrambling on very rough perdotite). At the col, there is an interesting slab with a gap underneath. Keep left (east) of Caisteal a' Gharbh-choire on an easy traverse path to reach Bealach a' Gharbh-choire (797m). Next, scramble up the northern ridge of Sgurr nan Eag until it becomes difficult, then keep right of the crest. The tedious 400m-long summit ridge has three bumps; on finding the second bump's 3m-high, vertical, south-eastern face, backtrack and scramble down to easier but boulder-covered ground to the south-west. The summit (924m, 1½m-high cairn) overlooks the beautiful curving ridges of Sgurr a' Choire Bhig and Gars-bheinn. Return to Bealach a' Gharbh-choire, descend large rough peridotite blocks to Coir' a' Ghrunnda (left) and follow the outward route back to Glen Brittle.

91

SGURR ALASDAIR

Fantastic views of Scotland's finest alpine ridge

Parking: Glen Brittle beach car park, gr NG409206

Distance: 8km

Height Gain: 990m

Time: 4½–5½ hours

Terrain: Gravel paths, scree slopes, loose scree gully, exposed easy scrambling

Standard: Difficult; in winter, mountaineering skills are required

OS Maps: South Skye & Cuillin Hills (1:50,000 Landranger sheet 32), Skye: Cuillin Hills (1:25,000 Explorer sheet 411)

The highest peak in Skye's Cuillin Hills, Sgurr Alasdair (993m), is named after Sheriff Alexander Nicholson, who made the first ascent of the Great Stone Chute in 1873. The stone chute is hard work and there is a danger of falling rocks.

From the car park at Glen Brittle beach, walk through the campsite, turn right and cross the fence behind the toilets. A well-drained, gravelly, stony or paved path rises steeply up grass slopes, crossing a four-wheel-drive track. The gradient eases near a burn (gr NG420203); at a cairn-less path junction keep left on the Coire Lagan path and cross the burn after 200m (stepping stones). Continue across fairly level ground then rise steadily uphill on a good path, with a steep, paved section. The moor becomes increasingly bouldery and the path becomes rough in places while steeper sections alternate with easier ground. The path passes some gigantic gabbro boulders abandoned by a melting glacier at the end of the last glaciation.

Above 350m, past Loch an Fhir-bhallaich, there are good views of the dark-brown, glacier-scoured Coire Lagan slabs ahead, with Sron na Ciche's impressive cliffs to the right. Two 1m-high cairns at 380m mark where the paths from Glen Brittle House and the beach meet and continue as a stony path rising steadily towards the corrie's slabs, with several easy burn crossings. At the slabs, ascend steeply on a

Evening light on Sgurr Alasdair

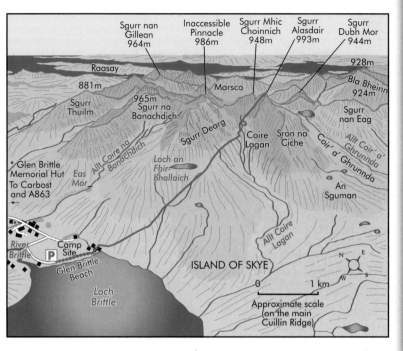

Sgurr nan Gillean 964m
Inaccessible Pinnacle 986m
Sgurr Mhic Choinnich 948m
Sgurr Alasdair 993m
Sgurr Dubh Mor 944m
Raasay
881m
Marsco
928m
Sgurr Thuilm
965m Sgurr na Banachdich
Bla Bheinn 924m
Sgurr Dearg
Coire Lagan
Sron na Ciche
Sgurr nan Eag
Allt Coire na Banachdich
Loch an Fhir-bhallaich
Allt Coir' a' Ghrunnda
Coir' a' Ghrunnda
Glen Brittle Memorial Hut To Carbost and A863
Eas Mor
An Sguman
Allt Coire Lagan
Camp Site
River Brittle
Glen Brittle Beach
ISLAND OF SKYE
Loch Brittle
0 1 km
Approximate scale (on the main Cuillin Ridge)

bouldery path then, keeping left of a steep slab, go straight up onto the rock and scramble easily up broken slab with loose stones on shelves, trending right higher up (it is easier than it looks). Alternatively, a marginally easier gap in the slabs about 25m to the right involves some steep steps, joining the other route after gaining 20m. A bouldery and stony path then slants up to the right, towards the waterfalls and water slides on the Allt Coire Lagan. Keep near the waterslide above the main waterfall on steep and somewhat loose slopes to reach easier ground, with mixed slab and gravel. Continue easily near the burn to reach the heart-shaped, greenish-coloured Loch Coire Lagan (565m). The weed-filled loch is not very impressive but its setting is extraordinary, with slabs guarding the outlet and a backdrop of immense crags and extensive grey scree fans.

Cross slabs and stony areas to pass the loch on its northern side (left). To ascend Sgurr Alasdair, turn right, pass the stone rings then rise past boulders, keeping left of a large outcrop to gain the right-hand side of the Great Stone Chute scree fan above and toil up the scree for around 70m. Where the scree merges with crags below Sgurr Sgumain, slant up to the left towards the top of the fan then continue up

the right-hand-side of the broad screes at the base of the stone chute, with the cliffs of Sgurr Alasdair rising immediately on the right. Beyond an overhang, the stone chute (following a line of weakness caused by a felsite intrusion) narrows to around 20m, bends to the left and becomes extremely steep and loose with precariously perched large boulders and unpleasant baldy areas. Paths appear and disappear due to rock fall, but there is usually a loose path near the top of the stone chute.

On gaining the top (960m), where there is usually a stone-ring shelter, wonderful views of Loch Coir' a' Ghrunnda and Sgurr nan Eag lie ahead. Look in the other direction for equally fantastic views of Sgurr Mhic Choinnich and the Inaccessible Pinnacle. To reach Sgurr Alasdair's summit, turn right and scramble easily up a narrow ridge of broken basalt slabs. An airy ledge above the stone chute leads to easier ground and the small summit with its cairn (992m). Views include Rum, Eigg, the Western Isles, the mainland and Ben Nevis; closer to hand, the Cuillin's peaks rise in jagged profusion.

Return to Glen Brittle by the same route – there is no other easy way down.

92

SGURR DEARG and SGURR MHIC CHOINNICH

Sensational ridges and rock climbing on Scotland's hardest Munro

Parking: Glen Brittle Memorial Hut, gr NG412216
Distance: 9km
Height Gain: 1140/1180m without/with Inaccessible Pinnacle
Time: 7–9 hours
Terrain: Gravel paths, scree and boulder slopes, knife-edge rock ridges, exposed scrambling with moderate rock climbing optional
Standard: Very difficult
OS Maps: South Skye & Cuillin Hills (1:50,000 Landranger sheet 32), Skye: Cuillin Hills (1:25,000 Explorer sheet 411)

Arguably the hardest mountains in Scotland to climb, Skye's Sgurr Mhic Choinnich and the Inaccessible Pinnacle of Sgurr Dearg offer sensational scrambling and moderate-grade rock climbing, with serious exposure of truly alpine standards (in winter, mountaineering skills are required, grade II/III).

Park opposite the Glen Brittle Memorial Hut (gr NG412216), follow the road southwards for 50m then turn left on a good gravel path. Cross Allt Coire na Banachdich (bridge) and continue steadily uphill across grassy moorland, past the attractive 25m-high waterfall Eas Mor and its tree-lined gorge. Keep right at a junction near the top of the gorge, continue for 300m to another junction then keep left for the western ridge of Sgurr Dearg, rising steeply up grassy slopes with scattered boulders and outcrops. The grass ends abruptly at 450m then a worn path on steep scree rises to broken rock and a crumbly geological dyke on Sron Dearg (600m). Continue on an easier path, with cairns across boulders above 730m. Beyond the flat top of Window Buttress (800m), cairns lead easily upwards then keep slightly right of centre and scramble on steeper blocks and outcrops for around 80m to reach Sgurr Dearg Beag (929m), with wonderful views all around.

The ridge descends to a 915m col and narrows, with a difficult-looking rock tower

Inaccessible Pinnacle, Sgurr na Banachdich and Sgurr a' Ghreadaidh from Sgurr Mhic Choinnich

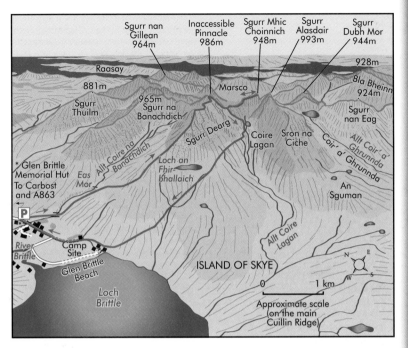

Sgurr nan Gillean 964m
Inaccessible Pinnacle 986m
Sgurr Mhic Choinnich 948m
Sgurr Alasdair 993m
Sgurr Dubh Mor 944m
Raasay
881m
928m
Marsco
Bla Bheinn 924m
Sgurr Thuilm
965m Sgurr na Banachdich
Sgurr Dearg
Coire Lagan
Sron na Ciche
Sgurr nan Eag
Allt Coir' a' Ghrunnda
Coir' a' Ghrunnda
*Glen Brittle Memorial Hut To Carbost and A863
Eas Mor
Allt Coire na Banachdich
Loch an Fhir-bhallaich
An Sguman
River Brittle
Camp Site
Glen Brittle Beach
Allt Coire Lagan
ISLAND OF SKYE
Loch Brittle
0   1 km
Approximate scale (on the main Cuillin Ridge)

ahead (it is only a moderate scramble). To avoid the tower, follow paths on ledges, with short scrambles between them, rising on the Coire Lagan (right-hand) side of the ridge. There is a little exposure before the ridge crest is regained, with fine views of the Inaccessible Pinnacle ahead, and an easy path just on the left. From the 978m cairn opposite the pinnacle there are wonderful views north to Sgurr na Banachdich and Sgurr a' Ghreadaidh, and south to Sgurr Mhic Choinnich and Sgurr Alasdair. It is even possible to see St Kilda on a clear day.

The vertical western face of the Inaccessible Pinnacle is graded a very difficult rock climb. The optional 'easier' eastern ridge is a moderate rock climb, only to be attempted with appropriate equipment and both climbing and abseil experience. Carefully descend to the pinnacle's base by keeping right on broken slabs with loose rock. The eastern ridge begins with a steep ramp and good holds, but moves onto an airy 30cm-wide crest with vertical drops on both sides. Just below the halfway belay point, there is a distinct lack of holds but, above halfway, it is considerably easier to the top (986m). An in-situ plastic-sheathed steel sling may be used to abseil down the western face.

From the stone rings below the pinnacle,

descend to the right of the loose An Stac ridge, keeping close to the rock wall, mainly on small scree. Look for a small cairn (not always present) marking a bend to the left and descent of a geological dyke that is broken up into steps and possibly scree covered. Keep close to the An Stac cliff on the left. A scree path then leads under a buttress and up 15m to Bealach Coire Lagan (820m). Continue on a level ridge then descend to the right to pass a notch at 804m.

Ahead, the blunt north-western end of Sgurr Mhic Choinnich looks difficult but a hard scramble with some exposure leads up corners amongst large blocks with signs of wear, 20m to the right. Scramble up to the right then keep just left of a narrow rooftop ridge that leads to a gap; beyond this, rise on ledges just right of the airy, basalt-slab ridge to reach the small summit cairn (948m) and intrusive memorial plaque.

Return to Bealach Coire Lagan then descend a steep scree path below An Stac to pick up a gravel path leading to Loch Coire Lagan. Follow the path to the campsite as described for the Sgurr Alasdair route (the branch path leading directly to the Glen Brittle Memorial Hut via Loch an Fhir-bhallaich is currently very boggy). From the campsite, a track leads northwards towards the hut.

93

ROUND OF COIR' A' GHREADAIDH

Stupendous knife-edge ridges with fearsome drop-offs

Parking: Glen Brittle SYHA hostel, gr
NG409225
Distance: 10km
Height Gain: 1220m
Time: 6–8 hours
Terrain: Gravel approach paths, steep
gradients, narrow loose and shattered
ridges, hard scrambling in places
Standard: Strenuous, very difficult; in
winter, mountaineering skills are
required, grade II/III
OS Maps: South Skye & Cuillin Hills
(1:50,000 Landranger sheet 32), Skye:
Cuillin Hills (1:25,000 Explorer sheet 411)

The fantastic round of Coir' a' Ghreadaidh on
Skye's Black Cuillin ridge includes sections of
hard scrambling and complex route finding. It is
no place for novices.

A gravel footpath ascends steadily eastwards into Coir' a' Ghreadaidh from Glen Brittle's
SYHA hostel, with lovely pools and waterfalls.
At Allt Coir' an Eich, turn right and follow this
burn's right-hand side into Coir' an Eich. At
around 370m, the path becomes intermittent;
cross the grassy corrie floor then ascend steep
basalt scree slopes, hard work to 640m. Easier
walking then leads through the upper corrie to
boulder and scree slopes with occasional paths.
Keep just right of An Diallaid's saddle to gain
Sgurr na Banachdich's flank above the ridge to
Sgurr nan Gobhar. Continue on various paths,
with loose rock and patchy slab, to Sgurr na
Banachdich's cairn (965m), about 100m south
on the main ridge. Look out for golden eagles
soaring in updrafts above the Cuillin's pinnacles
and precipices.

Descend steeply northwards with ledges
and crevices just left of the main ridge then bear
right to reach the Banachdich-Thormaid col
(888m). The difficult-looking basalt peak Sgurr
Thormaid (926m) is named after Norman Collie,
a nineteenth-century climber and pioneer of
Cuillin routes. Go horizontally left (north-east),
ascend a wide gully, keep left again on a dead-

The knife-edge crest of Sgurr a' Ghreadaidh's south top

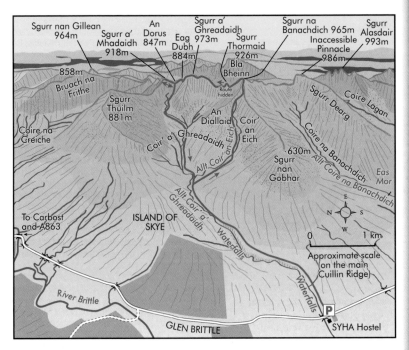

Sgurr nan Gillean 964m
Sgurr a' Mhadaidh 918m
An Dorus 847m
Eag Dubh 884m
Sgurr a' Ghreadaidh 973m
Sgurr Thormaid 926m
Bla Bheinn
Sgurr na Banachdich 965m
Inaccessible Pinnacle 986m
Sgurr Alasdair 993m
858m
Bruach na Frithe
Sgurr Thuilm 881m
Coire na Creiche
Route hidden
An Diallaid
Coir' a' Ghreadaidh
Coir' an Eich
Coire Lagan
Sgurr Dearg
Allt Coir' an-Eich
630m
Sgurr nan Gobhar
Coire na Banachdich
Allt Coire na Banachdich
Eas Mor
To Carbost and A863
Allt Coir' a' Ghreadaidh
ISLAND OF SKYE
Waterfalls
N E S W
0   1 km
Approximate scale on the main Cuillin Ridge
River Brittle
Waterfalls
GLEN BRITTLE
P
SYHA Hostel

end ledge then ascend steeply to the right (moderate scrambling) to gain the ridge just below the summit. Beyond the summit, continue easily downwards (a little scrambling) on slab to reach the Three Teeth, rotten gabbro fangs up to 12m high. Keep right (south of the teeth) on an easy ledge, pass bivouac sites then descend to a dip (850m) with stone-ring shelters.

Paths link ledges just left of the ridge to Sgurr a' Ghreadaidh, with easy scrambling as far as a 2m-high rock step (moderate scrambling). Just beyond this, Sgurr a' Ghreadaidh's south top (970m) is a sensational, shattered, gabbro crest with a tiny cairn, but there is a traverse path low on the left (west side). The knife-edge is amazingly exposed, with one section requiring sitting astride, *a cheval*. More prolonged hard scrambling descends airily to a dip (955m), where the traverse path regains the main ridge. Rise to a vertical rock step then avoid it using a traverse path on the left (west). Go around a corner then scramble easily (right) up to the north top's cairn (973m).

Continuing northwards, walk past the Wart (a large rock excrescence) on easy broken slab (one short scramble). At the chasm Eag Dubh, avoid a steep rock step (with poor holds) by keeping far right and descending to a broad sloping ledge running left (north) beneath the difficulty. From Eag Dubh, continue northwards and down the ridge towards An Dorus, with some scrambling. At An Dorus, keep left and face inwards to down-climb an intimidating 6m-high wall using good holds (there is a hidden hold halfway down that can't be seen from above). Then keep right to gain the col (847m) and keep right again into a loose slot to avoid a 2m-high wall on the north (Mhadaidh) side. The ridge to Sgurr a' Mhadaidh is steep but easy scrambling; ledges on the left (west) facilitate progress. The summit cairn (918m) lies at the far end of an impressive tilted slab with a large crack for footholds. The views of Loch Coruisk from here are amongst the finest in the Cuillin.

The safest descent returns to An Dorus, turns right (west) and descends a steep bald gully towards Glen Brittle, with an unstable fan of large boulders below. Keep left-of-centre while descending and follow a small ravine down to the burn and the flats of upper Coir' a' Ghreadaidh (680m), then thread a way through slabs to another level section at around 520m. A gravel path on the burn's right bank descends steeply to the main grassy floor of the corrie then continues (left of the burn) downwards to the hostel.

199

94

BRUACH NA FRITHE

Easy scrambling and stunning mountain vistas

Parking: Head of Glen Brittle, gr NG424259
Distance: 11km
Height Gain: 915m
Time: 5½–6½ hours
Terrain: Gravel paths; scree, boulder and broken rock slopes; narrow ridges; easy grassy and gravelly corrie
Standard: Moderate to difficult; in winter, mountaineering skills are required, grade I/II
OS Maps: South Skye & Cuillin Hills (1:50,000 Landranger sheet 32), Skye: Cuillin Hills (1:25,000 Explorer sheet 411)

Bruach na Frithe is the Skye Cuillin's easiest ascent but route finding in Fionn Choire requires good navigation in mist. The hill may also be ascended from Sligachan, with the option of ascending via Coir' a' Bhasteir.

Leave cars in the parking area at the top of Glen Brittle (gr NG424259), cross the road and follow the gravel footpath signposted 'Sligachan', with great views into Coire na Creiche on the right. Keep left (junction at 50m), cross the Allt an Fhamhair below a waterfall (difficult in spate) then rise gradually uphill, parallel to the forest's edge. It is mostly pleasant gravel underfoot, becoming wetter and occasionally rough beyond the forestry, with several minor burn crossings. Slightly steeper ground leads to the pass Bealach a' Mhaim, where there is a large cairn.

Just before the col's largest lochan, turn right at a cairn, cross the lochan's diminutive outflow and follow an indistinct path towards patchy scree on steep slopes below Bruach na Frithe's north-west ridge. A gravel path slants left and upwards then bears right up steep gravel and mossy turf onto a gradually sloping, but featureless, area of mixed grass and gravel. Head south on a path to a broad, flat ridge then follow an intermittent scree path or scuffed turf more steeply uphill to the base of a steep scree slope (610m). A cairned, zigzag path helps the ascent up hard-packed gravel for almost 100m.

Sgurr nan Gillean from Sgurr a' Bhasteir

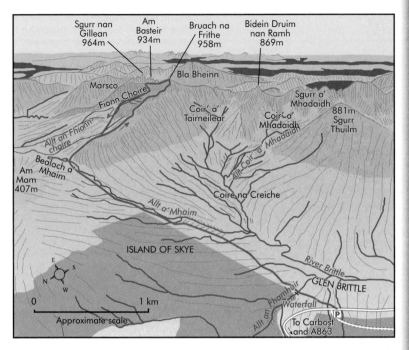

Great views include MacLeod's Maidens and MacLeod's Tables to the north-west.

The ridge narrows to 3m-wide and changes from grassy with outcrops to steep and stony; use hands occasionally for balance. A path on the right leads to a dyke; return to the fairly level narrow crest (at 750m) then take a horizontal path to the right, soon slanting upwards along a dyke and scree shelves (with a little easy scrambling). Regain the ridge but use paths on the right to avoid any difficulties. At 800m, an obvious scree path leaves the ridge on the right, with some easy scrambling on a dyke cut into the gabbro, followed by a scree path, ledges and more dykes (all easy but steep). A well-jointed dyke running parallel to the ridge provides an easy scramble to the summit (958m), where there is a cylindrical triangulation pillar and an adjacent stone-ring shelter.

Bruach na Frithe is a magnificent view-point: east to the jagged spires of Sgurr nan Gillean and Am Basteir; south-east towards Bla Bheinn and Clach Glas; south across the triple peaks of Bidein Druim nan Ramh to the central and southern Cuillin.

To descend Fionn Choire, follow the craggy and stony ridge east. To avoid difficult rock steps, descend 4m (north) on slippery but easy shelves, then follow a scree path leading steeply down to the 903m col with Sgurr a' Fionn Choire; bypass this peak on its northern side. Descend an easy scree path to the left, pass underneath a crag then ascend on a gravel or boulder path to the next col, Bealach nan Lice (c895m). Descend a disintegrating dyke just right of the main ridge crest, then keep left (north) for the craggy ridge towards Sgurr a' Bhasteir and the finest views of Am Basteir and the Bhasteir Tooth. Just before the col below Sgurr a' Bhasteir (c860m), descend left into Fionn Choire on an intermittent path through scree and outcrops that leads down to a boulder-strewn shelf with some grass and little ponds. This easy route meets the direct path from Bealach nan Lice, then follows the left side of the burn (flowing underground in places) down to 600m; at 600m, head north-west, cross another burn, then continue on gently sloping grass and stones to the 575m col at gr NG456262. Continue north-west on featureless grass and gravel towards Bruach na Frithe's north-west ridge just above Bealach a' Mhaim, and return to Glen Brittle by the outward route.

95

BLA BHEINN

Spectacular alpine scenery on an exceptional mountain

Parking: Head of Loch Slapin (Allt na Dunaiche), gr NG561217

Distance: 8km

Height Gain: 1030m

Time: 5–6 hours

Terrain: Gravel paths; scree, boulder and broken rock slopes; knife-edged ridge, bypassed by a gully with some easy scrambling

Standard: Moderate to difficult; in winter, mountaineering skills are required, grade I/II

OS Maps: South Skye & Cuillin Hills (1:50,000 Landranger sheet 32), Skye: Cuillin Hills (1:25,000 Explorer sheet 411)

Majestic Bla Bheinn (Blaven) stands alone from the main part of Skye's Cuillin ridge but it is considered by many to be the finest peak on the island. The route described here is better than the so-called 'tourist route' from Coire Uaigneich, which is not particularly pleasant and requires careful navigation in mist.

Leave cars in the large parking area 100m south of the road bridge over Allt na Dunaiche (gr NG561217). From the northern end of the car park, descend stone stairs and follow a path downhill through a swing gate to the road bridge, cross this then turn immediately left onto a well-drained gravel and stony path (deer fence with swing gate). A gradual ascent near the attractive tree-lined burn leads across grass and heather moorland to another swing gate. The slope becomes steeper, with a waterfall on the left and the path becoming more stony and bouldery underfoot. The immense gabbro cliffs of Bla Bheinn and its satellites dominate the scene ahead.

The gradient eases on approaching the Allt na Dunaiche ford, normally easy but knee-deep or worse when in spate. Across the burn, the path rises across the moor to ford the Coire Uaigneich burn, with large boulders and possibly difficult to cross in spate. The path continues onto a flank about 30m above this burn, steep and loose in places, with some broken slab.

Bla Bheinn and Clach Glas from Torrin

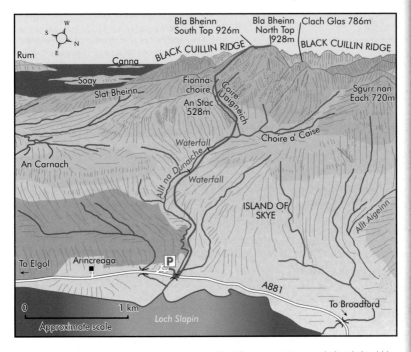

Above 410m, the path enters the grassy Fionna-choire and crosses two burns to reach a 4m-high boulder (gr NG53562117). Loch Fionna-choire is a curious body of water perched in a col to the east. The path disappears near the boulder; keep left of the second burn and follow it through boulders onto the formidable-looking scree slope beyond. A fairly obvious path makes easy work of most of the slope; ascend the final 100m of loose boulders to reach the western end of the col at the head of Fionna-choire (gr NG532211, 610m), where there is a large, flat boulder. Turn right (north-west) to ascend Bla Bheinn's south top; various paths weave between patchy broken outcrops and loose rock, steeply at first but not particularly difficult. The route leads to Bla Bheinn's south ridge about 80m south of the south top; turn right to reach the 1m-high cairn (926m), on stony ground at the north-western end of a surprisingly grassy area.

Although the view of islands, peaks, lochs and glens is exceptional, continue to the main summit for even more spectacular vistas. About 50m of easy, stony ground leads north and gradually downwards, descending 15m to reach a narrow rock rib plunging precipitously to the 895m notch between Bla Bheinn's two tops.

This ridge is not recommended and should be bypassed on the right (east); descend 20m to the right, into a steep, loose gully leading to another gully that splits the eastern face of Bla Bheinn below the notch between the two tops. On reaching a large trapped block below a steep wall near the bottom of the first gully, use the top of the block for handholds and take some airy steps to the north-west to enter the steep and loose main gully between the two tops. A short ascent in this gully leads to the notch. Turn right (north-east), rising steeply for 15m to an easy-angled shoulder. A path over mixed grass and stones leads to the broad, stony, north top (928m), with a cylindrical triangulation pillar and an adjacent broad-based 1½m-high cairn.

The views include the rock climber's Clach Glas ridge, the granite screes of the Red Cuillin, the main Cuillin ridge with Sgurr nan Gillean prominent, and the islands of Rum and Eigg. Spend at least an hour on the top if it is a clear day. It is best to return the same way; traversing the block in the gully is slightly more difficult when heading south but it is still preferable to the tourist route's loose scree path.

96

MARSCO

Precipitous Marsco provides great views of the Cuillin

Parking: Eas a' Bhradain waterfall, gr NG534267
Distance: 8km
Height Gain: 720m
Time: 4–5 hours
Terrain: Boggy paths, grassy and rocky slopes; narrow, grassy, summit ridge
Standard: Moderate to difficult; in winter, mountaineering skills are required, grade I
OS Maps: South Skye and Cuillin Hills (1:50,000 Landranger sheet 32), Skye: Cuillin Hills (1:25,000 Explorer sheet 411)

Most of Skye's Red Cuillin peaks are guarded by formidable and often mobile scree slopes but beautifully shaped Marsco is an exception. Geologists find Marsco particularly interesting and a type of intrusive igneous rock (Marscoite) has been named after the hill.

If starting from Loch Ainort, park in the large lay-by near the 10m-high Eas a' Bhradain waterfall (gr NG534267). From the southern end of the lay-by, cross the road and descend from the embankment to pick up a boggy path passing to the right of the waterfall. This path, following Allt Coire nam Bruadaran, is in very poor condition after prolonged wet weather. Beyond the waterfall, a grass-and-bog path follows the burn, which tumbles attractively over slabs and rock steps. Across the burn, beyond the boulder-strewn ridge Druim Eadar Da Choire, rise the Black Cuillin peaks Belig and Garbh-bheinn. The corrie flattens out with thick grass and heather and numerous small and easy burn crossings. Keep close to the main burn on a river-bank path. Beyond a steep slope on the right, cross Allt Mam a' Phobuill and continue across a flat area (by the main burn) to the base of steeper slopes leading to the Marsco–Garbh-bheinn col. The path disappears but the ground improves, with firm short grass and heather, but it is quite steep in places. Keep right of the steep waterslide near the head of

Marsco from Garbh-bheinn

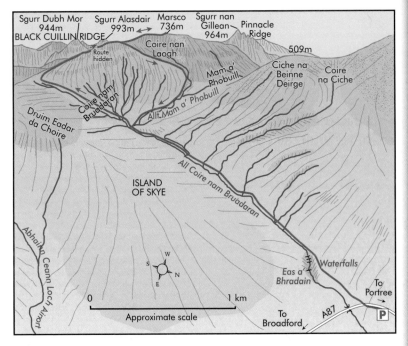

the corrie. Drier ground with short grass and granite boulders leads to the right of the col and the base of Marsco's south-east ridge at gr NG518243. The spectacular view includes Beinn Dearg to the north and Bla Bheinn to the south-east.

Turn right and follow the line of rusty fence posts steeply up Marsco's south-east ridge, generally keeping left on slightly easier ground. Good, dry grass with scree patches and broken outcrops leads to a very steep section with boulders predominant. An indistinct path through boulders and scree may be found in places. Above 550m, views include almost the whole Black Cuillin main ridge, Rum, Eigg, and Mull's Ben More. Follow the fence line up boulders with some easy scrambling, then bear left to avoid 10m of steep, broken rock (580m). A short scramble leads to a quite grassy and less steep ridge that flattens out and narrows at the base of a precipitous, broken, gabbro crag at 620m. A path leads out horizontally to the left; follow this for around 20m then ascend steep broken ground, without a path, to the right (use hands for balance) and regain the well-defined ridge above the crag. Pass over a minor top (643m) and descend gradually, mainly on grass, to a col (630m) where the fence posts go down into

Coire nan Laogh, to the right (north). From the col, a path leads up a broad ridge with short grass, some scattered rocks and occasional outcrops. Look back for a fine view of Bla Bheinn, Clach Glas and Garbh-bheinn beyond Marsco's south-east ridge. The broad, grassy ridge to Marsco's summit flattens out then a short rise leads to the surprising, beautiful, narrow grass ridge, only half-a-metre wide with precipitous drops on both sides. The small summit cairn (736m) at the northern end of this ridge is a great place to enjoy wonderful views including Harris, Torridon, Kintail, Loch Hourn, and the main Black Cuillin ridge beyond Glen Sligachan.

The easiest way down is to return to the 630m col on the south-east ridge and follow the fence posts north into Coire nan Laogh, down steep grass slopes (steps in turf), with some scree and scattered rocks. The path becomes a bit boggy lower down. Don't cross the burn but keep right, descending reasonably dry grass slopes into Coire nam Bruadaran (no path). Fairly extensive tussocks low down may be avoided by keeping close to the Allt Mam a' Phobuill. Pick up the main path and return to the road.

97

BEN TIANAVAIG

Sublime views from a beautiful peak

Parking: Camastianavaig, gr NG509389
Distance: 5km
Height Gain: 413m
Time: 4–5 hours
Terrain: Path, grassy slopes
Standard: Easy
OS Maps: North Skye (1:50,000 Landranger sheet 23), Portree and Bracadale (1:25,000 Explorer sheet 410)

The wonderful Ben Tianavaig includes some of the finest easy walking on Skye, with cliffs on the eastern side of the hill featuring pinnacles reminiscent of the Trotternish Ridge further north. Immediately south of the hill an astonishing crofter's rebellion, known as the Battle of the Braes, took place in 1882.

When crofters were refused continued rental of grazing land, some withheld rent and Angus Martin, a sheriff officer from Portree, was sent to evict these recalcitrant Highlanders. However, a party of women and children accosted the officials on the roadway and the eviction papers were burned! On hearing this, the sheriff of Inverness-shire contacted the chief constable of Glasgow and requested that fifty policemen be sent to Skye to restore order. The Braes folk set up sentries but after the summons for eviction expired they relaxed their guard. On 17 April, they were taken unawares when a force of sheriff officers and fifty-seven policemen arrived early in the morning. Around one hundred sleepy locals (mainly women, children and older men, since most young men were away fishing) turned out to confront the police. Following the arrest of five crofters, the police were attacked with sticks and boulders hurled down slopes. People on both sides were injured, some seriously. During vicious hand-to-hand fighting, rancid urine was thrown over some policemen,

Ben Tianavaig from Sconser

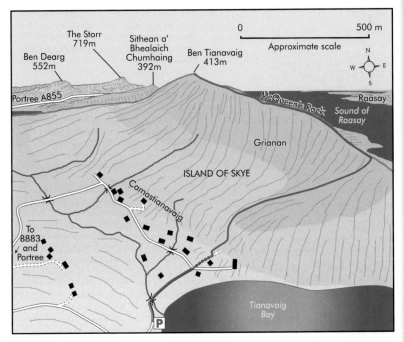

but they escaped with their prisoners. The five crofters were later convicted but sympathisers paid their fines. The government sent warships to cruise the lochs around Skye and armed troops patrolled crofting villages. Following a public outcry, in 1883 Gladstone's government set up a Royal Commission of Inquiry, which reported tyrannical behaviour by estate factors. Consequently, the Crofter's Holdings Act, which required fair setting of rents, was passed by parliament in 1886. Some Braes rents were reduced by as much as 70 per cent. Just north of Gedintailor, a roadside cairn commemorates the events.

The B883 Braes road turns off the A87 Kyle of Lochalsh–Portree road about 3km south of Portree. Follow this road for 3km, then turn left on the minor road through Camastianavaig. Keep left at the junction, then right and descend to the stony beach at the head of Tianavaig Bay. Just across a bridge over a fair-sized burn, there is a parking area with a picnic table on the left. From the picnic area, walk back across the bridge and up the hill to the post box. Keep left of the house there and go 10m up a track to a gate, turn left (a tiny wooden sign says 'Hill Path') and follow a muddy lane into a field. Keep straight on but right of the fence, follow the clear path uphill and leftwards when the fence

turns left, then continue fairly steeply uphill. The path, quite wet and muddy after rain, passes a ruined shieling below a small crag. Higher up, the path crosses grassy terrain then passes through an area of heather-and-rock outcrops until it fades out in a flat ground at around 120m. Fine walking on short grass and heather leads to a rock knobble on the skyline. Pass some rock outcrops and rise past the boulders under the knobble to reach a little col just to its north. There is a very steep cliff to the east! Wonderful views include Dun Caan across the Sound of Raasay and the Cuillin to the south.

Sections of sheep path lead easily across short grass and heather, northwards along the ridge. It is a steady ascent, with a flat area at 240m. A broken cliff of friable basalt, McQueen's Rock, forms the eastern side of the ridge all the way to the top. The upper section of golf-course-like grass has no path. On the summit there is a small cairn 2m below the cylindrical triangulation pillar (413m), a good place to admire the impressive views of the crumbly pinnacles to the east, the south ridge and Portree. Return by the outward route.

98

QUIRAING

Hike through a remarkable landscape of peaks, pinnacles and mesas

Parking: By the Staffin–Uig hill road, gr NG440679

Distance: 4km

Height Gain: 250m

Time: 2–3 hours

Terrain: Path, some scrambling and very steep, potentially dangerous slopes

Standard: Moderate

OS Maps: North Skye (1:50,000 Landranger sheet 23), Trotternish & The Storr (1:25,000 Explorer sheet 408)

The Quiraing, a spectacular area of peculiar crumbly basaltic rock formations near the northern tip of Skye, is unique in Britain. Some people baulk at the precipitous slopes leading to the Table but, in dry conditions, the route is safe if due care is taken.

From the A855 road in Staffin, take the narrow single-track road towards Uig for about 3km. Just past a sharp double bend through cliffs, there is a large parking area on the left, but it fills up quickly on sunny days.

At the car park, cross the road to the sign 'Flodigarry via Quiraing 2.8m' and follow the cliff-edge earthen or gravel path, high above the double bend. Ascend around 5m to a long, fairly level, section of mostly gravel path, with great views southwards. Beyond an extremely steep traverse of grass-and-heather slopes, an easy rock step descends towards a gully with a small burn. A fairly easy albeit slippery slab (2m) leads directly into the gully then an easy scramble ascends a ledge. The path continues easily, with alternating rocky and earthen sections, ascending slightly across a rock fall of interesting vesicular basalt. Traverse further steep grass slopes then cross two small burns descending via wispy waterfalls from the Creag Loisgte cliffs above. Traverse the steep slope above the second burn, head right and around a corner, then rise to a muddy section (keep away from the exposed

The Table at the Quiraing

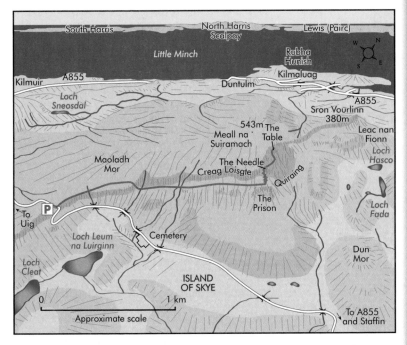

right-hand edge; a slip here could be fatal). The path passes beautiful, grassy hollows to reach a 10m dip then rises over gravel to the large blocks below the north wall of the Prison, a curious castle-like feature on the right. High up on the left amongst the cliffs towers a 36m-high pinnacle known as the Needle.

At the eastern end of the col between the Prison and the Needle, a 1m-high cairn marks the ascent to the Table. Turn to the left (north) then ascend precipitous slopes below the Needle. There are several paths at an angle of 45 degrees to the horizontal, mostly badly eroded, muddy if wet, and covered in loose gravel, but there are good footholds in the turf in places. Currently it is easiest to keep left when looking up then cut back to the right to reach the base of the Needle. Ascend or descend with great care and beware of people above or below in case of rock fall. Pass easily behind the base of the Needle, then an easy gravel path curves to the right and rises to a narrow slot, with a 10m ascent that is a trifle loose but relatively easy. From the top of the slot (where there is a curious hole), go down slightly (northwards) between the cliffs and pinnacles on either side, then a steep stony path goes upwards. Keep left at a junction, pass a large

hollow to the left, then keep left again on a rocky or gravel path that enters a miniature grassy and mossy glen with scattered rocks. This path ascends to the northern end of the Table (500m), which is an extraordinary, slightly sloping, grass-covered area surrounded by near-vertical drops and soaring pinnacles or cliffs. Locals have reputedly used the Table for shinty matches! There is no access to the main hill (Meall na Suiramach, 543m), due to crumbly vertical cliffs. The best viewpoint is the 'mini Table', 20m above the northern end of the Table.

There are several dead-end paths and steep dangerous gullies below the Table; return to the car park by following the outward route. On the way, it is possible to follow an exposed path around the Prison, where there is a superb basalt dyke up to 5m high on the south side. With due care, the west peak of the Prison can be ascended from the south side. Descend the north-west flank on a steep path to reach the main path and return to the car park by the outward route.

209

99

BEINN MHOR

Exceptional landscapes with loch and seascapes predominant

Parking: Abhainn Roag, Mill Croft, gr NF768346

Distance: 12km

Height Gain: 640m

Time: 4–5 hours

Terrain: Gravel track, boggy moorland, grassy hillside, narrow grassy ridge

Standard: Moderate

OS Maps: Benbecula & South Uist (1:50,000 Landranger sheet 22), Benbecula & South Uist (1:25,000 Explorer sheet 453)

South Uist is an island of contrasts, with a serene western coast separated from a wilder eastern side by a rough mountainous spine that includes Beinn Mhor, the highest point on the island. This effective barrier allowed Bonnie Prince Charlie and his followers successfully to hide in a tiny cave, secure from the eyes of government troops, for several weeks following the Jacobite defeat at Culloden in 1746. The loyal people of Gleann Coradail, 2½km east of Beinn Mhor, were cruelly evicted following the escape of the Prince and the now deserted coastline echoes only to the plaintive wailing of seabirds.

Beinn Mhor is one of Scotland's finest small mountains and its summit provides wonderful views not only of the Uists and Barra, but also Skye and other parts of the Hebrides. Clear days are not common but they are well worth waiting for. The best place to park, unfortunately with very limited space, is by the A865 Lochmaddy–Lochboisdale (Loch nam Madadh–Loch Baghasdail) road, just south of the Abhainn Roag (gr NF768346). From there, follow a surfaced track across a cattle grid and head east, between an old derelict house and a modern cottage with a garden including young trees and (disconcertingly) pampas grass. The track, with a good, dry, gravel surface, rises onto a grassy and heathery moor and ends abruptly

The north-facing cliffs of Beinn Mhor, South Uist

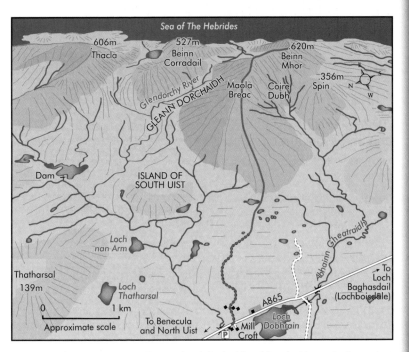

in an area of extensive peat cuttings. A dry, grassy path continues for around 200m south-east, past more peat cuttings and swampy pools; beyond the end of this path, keep left towards the base of a hillock, avoiding very boggy ground near a small lochan on the right. Keep just to the right (west) of the larger lochan (gr NF778338) on drier, heathery ground, then continue south-east from this lochan's southern end onto a level and rather rough boggy moor with swampy pools. A section of short grass and heather gives way to thicker vegetation near the base of Beinn Mhor; continue eastwards onto soft, dry grass and heather that rises steadily to a level area with scattered rocks at 290m (Maola Breac). Pleasant views of the flat-topped Thacla and the more rounded Beinn Corradail improve on gaining height beyond Maola Breac.

Rise steadily upwards on the broad ridge south-east of Maola Breac, mainly on short, dry grass with scattered rocks. Above a flat area at 540m, the ridge bends southwards and ascends fairly steeply to 600m. The following 0.75km to the south-east is a delightful, almost level, roof-top ridge consisting mainly of short grass, with some rock outcrops and grassy humps; broken ground falling precipitously to Gleann Sheileasdail on the left leads eastwards to a sheer cliff hacked by vicious-looking rock chasms just below the summit. The easily traversed ridge narrows to only 2m wide in places; keep right to avoid any exposure. At the southern end of the ridge, a final steep rise of around 20m includes a rock step (keep right for the easiest route). At the summit (620m) there is a stone-built triangulation pillar within a 3m-wide stone ring shelter. Views include Loch Aineort to the south and the peaks Beinn Corradail and Thacla to the north, and eastwards to the Inner Hebrides and the mainland, but the finest scene is westwards, over the machair-backed beaches and further westwards to the Atlantic.

Most people return to the public road by the same route. Although it is possible to continue over Beinn Corradail to Thacla from the flat area at 540m on Beinn Mhor's ridge, the route is long, with rough ground and some seriously rocky sections that are best avoided. Route finding may be difficult even on a clear day, so the traverse is advised for experienced walkers only.

100

AN CLISEAM (CLISHAM)

The ancient, but beautiful, stony hills of north Harris

Parking: Abhainn Mharaig (Maaruig River), gr NB174058
Distance: 5km
Height Gain: 650m
Time: 3–4 hours
Terrain: Boggy or stony paths, grassy hillsides, stony ridge
Standard: Moderate
OS Maps: Tarbert & Loch Seaforth (1:50,000 Landranger sheet 14), North Harris & Loch Seaforth (1:25,000 Explorer sheet 456)

The highest point and the only Corbett in the Western Isles is the rocky peak An Cliseam on Harris, with magnificent views that deserve a clear day. Leave cars in the substantial parking area by the A859 Tarbert–Stornoway road, at the bridge over the Abhainn Mharaig (Maaruig River on older maps, gr NB174058). An Cliseam is the spectacular hill north-west of the car park, a cone-shaped chunk of ancient Lewisian gneiss. Keep right of the Abhainn Mharaig and follow it uphill, past the water-supply sign. There is an indistinct boggy path by the river bank with scattered rocks in the grass and heather. This path crosses easily to the left bank but remains poor and boggy until crossing the burn's left branch above a fork (gr NB170060), becoming a little steeper and drier on shorter grass between the burn's left and right branches.

The path suddenly disappears but the route is obvious; aim directly for the summit cone across scattered rocks, grass, heather and occasional slippery boggy sections. The gradient eases with occasional small sections of slab and increasing amounts of scattered rock. The slope becomes steeper again above 400m, with drier ground and even more scattered rocks. Keep a direct aim on the cone, with small broken crags to the right and mainly steep, firm, dry grass and heather underfoot. There is no path on this section but there are occasional scuffed areas

An Cliseam from Ardhasaig

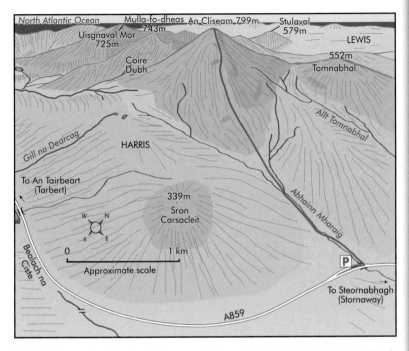

in the turf. There are large boulders below a crag that runs across the slope at 550m; bypass this crag easily on the right, where a stony path appears. This path is steep and dry and soon changes into scuffed turf or turf steps with gravel sections while ascending through grass, scattered rocks and occasional small boulder fields. It is a good, fast route up the mountain (another path that runs parallel to this one, 200m to the north-east, is wet, boggy and slippery and is definitely not recommended). There are occasional cairns as the turf or gravel path gains height; boulders and small outcrops are also passed. Look backwards for great views across Toddun and out across the Minch to the interesting profiles of the Shiant Islands and northern Skye. To the north-east, the odd Seaforth Island almost fills Loch Seaforth, with the wild, remote Pairc district of Lewis lying beyond.

The ridge becomes better defined above 700m, with a clear path slightly on the north-eastern side, ascending past outcrops, boulders and loose stones. The path then follows the ridge crest when the ridge broadens and becomes less steep. On levelling out at 780m, the ridge becomes bouldery and slabby with relatively little grass; look out for a small stone ruin just to

the south. The summit cairn appears ahead, reached by following the broad, level but very rocky summit ridge. Oddly, the cairn is hollow; it is a 1m-high, stone ring around a concrete triangulation pillar (799m) but there is no easy way in. It is possible to pass it on the south side, either above or below a small outcrop. Continue to a 1m-high cairn at the north-western end of the summit ridge for the finest views to the west: Mulla-fo-dheas, Uisgnaval Mor and the distant St Kilda.

Although most walkers descend by the same route, it is possible to include Mulla-fo-dheas (best with two cars since the route finishes 7km from the Abhainn Mharaig). The westwards descent from An Cliseam to the 605m col first crosses a boulder field then mixed grass and boulders. A bouldery then grassy ridge rises westwards to An t-Isean (690m), then a narrow 30m descent is followed by a steep climb through large outcrops, crags and slabs to reach the 1m-high summit cairn (743m). The fine southern shoulder, Mo Buidhe, initially fairly steep but grassy with scattered rocks, becomes easier lower down. Beyond more rocky areas even lower down, pick up the path leading from the Abhainn Thorabraidh to Bun Abhainn Eadarra.

101

CONACHAIR (ST KILDA)

Incredible panoramas of vertical sea cliffs and sheer-sided islands

Parking: Ferry terminal on Harris (usually Leverburgh), gr NG012863
Distance: 7km
Height Gain: 470m
Time: 3 hours
Terrain: Concrete road; mossy, grassy or heathery hillsides; vertical cliffs adjacent
Standard: Easy to moderate
OS Maps: Sound of Harris (1:50,000 Landranger sheet 18), North Lewis (1:25,000 Explorer sheet 460)

The wonderful islands and sea stacks of St Kilda – one of Scotland's four World Heritage sites – are amongst the most amazing places on Earth, with unimaginable scenic beauty, prolific birdlife and a tragic human history, a society lost forever when the remaining islanders were evacuated in 1930. Nowadays the main island, Hirta, is staffed by the National Trust for Scotland in summer but British Army contractors QinetiQ maintain a radar base and are on-site all year. Private vessels can land visitors on Hirta when conditions are favourable. Angus Campbell takes day-trip passengers from Harris to St Kilda three times weekly, May to September, weather permitting.

Hirta has been inhabited from Stone Age times but, for the one thousand years until 1930, the residents were tough, self-sufficient Gaelic-speaking people who lived by harvesting seabirds and their eggs, no mean feat considering the vertical cliffs and dangerous landing platforms constantly washed by surging surf. St Kildan men developed extra-long big toes to cope with climbing the vertical-sided stacks in bare feet or in socks. The islands were frequently cut off from the rest of Scotland for months on end. However, growing dependency on 'luxuries' and population problems (partly due to the often fatal custom of anointing newborn babies' umbilical cords with toxic fulmar oil, but also partly due to young people

Soay from Mullach Mor

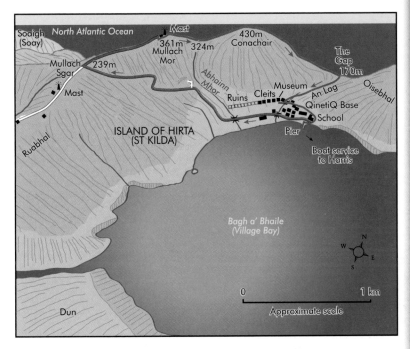

Soaigh (Soay) · North Atlantic Ocean · Mast · 361m Mullach Mor · 324m · 430m Conachair · The Gap 170m · Mullach Sgar 239m · Mast · Abhainn Mhor · Ruins · Cleits · Museum · An Lag · QinetiQ Base · School · Oisebhal · Ruabhal · ISLAND OF HIRTA (ST KILDA) · Pier · Boat service to Harris · Bagh a' Bhaile (Village Bay) · N W E S · Dun · 0 1 km · Approximate scale

packing their bags and leaving) led to the evacuation.

Once ashore on Hirta, turn left and follow the concrete road westwards along the shore, past the QinetiQ base, to the helipad. To the right, Soay sheep wander around on grassy fields backed by ruinous cottages and some of the island's mysterious-looking cleits (store-houses). Leftwards, the imposing towers of Dun (178m) protect the village from the ravages of southerly storms. Turn right just before the helipad and follow the road steeply uphill, with the tiny burn, Abhainn Mhor, on the right. Beyond the weather station, the road zigzags to a col at 239m; if there is time, leave the road and follow the broad, grassy ridge westwards for 700m to the Lover's Stone, a dangerously exposed projecting rock where St Kildan men proved extraordinary abilities of balance.

The road continues from the 239m col to the radar station on Mullach Mor (361m), with great views westwards across Glen Bay and Am Campar (216m) to the cliffs of Soay, soaring 376m directly from the ocean. Now head east on soft, spongy, mossy grass (often very wet) to the col at 324m and ascend the western flank of Conachair, passing some cleits on the way. Great skuas (bonxies) add to the fun by mounting aerial attacks on unwary walkers! There is no path but the steep, mossy grass is fairly dry and pleasant. The summit (430m) has an odd little cairn and a slight depression in the grass; the north-facing cliffs are the highest in Britain. Views are exceptional in all directions but the eye is invariably drawn to the north-east, where the mighty fangs of Boreray (384m), Stac Lee (172m) and Stac an Armin (196m) rise out of the sea. These islands host the world's largest gannet colony and, although 6km distant, clouds of thousands of birds can clearly be seen.

Continue east-south-east on mainly dry, mossy grass then an indistinct path along the cliff edge to the next col, the Gap, at 170m. The sheer granophyre (a variety of granite) cliff north of the Gap is home to thousands of nesting birds, including fulmars and puffins. If short of time, miss out the heathery Oiseval (290m) and descend short, heathery grass into the grassy glen An Lag to the south-west of the Gap, passing well-preserved cleits and keeping left of the sheep enclosures on a grassy path. A gap in the Head Dyke and a steeper slope leads to the main street, where one of the restored houses (No 3), former home of the MacDonalds, now contains a small museum.

Glossary

Commonly-used words and abbreviations (abbr) are explained here. Scottish, anglicised Gaelic and Gaelic words are identified by the letters S, AG and G, respectively.

aber (AG)	confluence or river mouth
allt (G)	burn, stream
abhainn (G)	river
aonach (G)	ridge
arête	knife-edge ridge
argocat	amphibious, all-terrain, eight-wheel-drive vehicle
ban, bhan (G)	fair, white
basalt (geological)	a fine-grained, dark, basic, igneous rock
beag, bheag (G)	small
bealach, bhealach (G)	mountain pass
beg (AG)	small
beinn, bheinn (G)	hill or mountain
belay	a means to attach a climbing rope to a safe anchor point
ben (S)	hill or mountain
bidean, bidein (G)	sharp peak or pinnacle
binnein (G)	sharp peak or pinnacle
blocky	predominantly consisting of blocks of rock
bodach (G)	old man
bothy (S)	mountain hut, cottage, refuge or shelter
bouldery	climbing jargon for boulder-strewn
brae (S)	slope, usually steep
braigh (G)	upland or plateau
broch	a circular, dry-stone tower
buidhe, bhuidhe (G)	yellow or tawny
burn (S)	stream
cailleach (G)	old woman, witch
cairn (S)	pile of stones marking a route or summit
caisteal (G)	castle or rock tower resembling a castle

caorach (G)	sheep
carn, charn, chairn (G)	cairn or rocky hill
ceann (G)	head
cioch, ciche (G)	female breast
clach (G)	stone or boulder
cliff-girt ridge	ridge with cliffs on both sides
coille (G)	woodland
col	mountain pass
coire, coir', choire (G)	cirque; a rounded mountain valley
Corbett	hill top between 2,500 and 3,000 feet above sea level, with at least 500 feet re-ascent on all sides
cornice	dangerous snowdrift overhanging a steep slope or cliff
corrie (S)	cirque; a rounded mountain valley
creag, chreag (G)	cliff
damh, daimh (G)	stag
diorite (geological)	coarse-grained intrusive igneous rock, usually hard and black-coloured
dearg, dheirg (G)	red
dubh, dhubh, duibhe (G)	black
dyke (geological)	intrusive sheet of igneous rock cutting through host rocks
eag (G)	notch
eagach (G)	notched
eas, easan (G)	waterfall
exposed	a scramble or rock climb where a fall would be dangerous
felsite (geological)	fine-grained, intrusive, igneous rock, friable and usually pink-coloured

fionn, fhionn (G)	fair, white	Munro	hill or mountain top over 3,000 feet above sea level
fraoch (G)	heather		
fuar (G)	cold		
fuaran, fhuarain (G)	spring (water)	NTS (abbr)	National Trust for Scotland
gabbro (geological)	coarse-grained, intrusive, igneous rock, usually hard and black or greenish-black-coloured	odhar, odhair (G)	greyish-brown or yellow-pale brown
		OS (abbr)	Ordnance Survey, UK national mapping agency
gabhar, gobhar (G)	goat		
garbh, ghairbh (G)	rough		
glas, ghlais (G)	grey-green	pap (S)	female breast
gleann, glen (G, S)	valley	peat hags	in a peat bog, raised areas of normal ground covered with grass and heather
gr (abbr)	Ordnance Survey map grid reference		
granophyre (geological)	intrusive, granite-like volcanic rock with graphic texture		
		peridotite (geological)	olivine-rich intrusive igneous rock, weathered surface sandy-brown-coloured
inbhir, inver (G, AG)	confluence or river mouth		
inselberg	an isolated, rocky hill	pipe rock (geological)	quartzite with fossilized marine worm burrows
kin (AG)	head	phyllite (geological)	cleaved metamorphic rock of type between slate and schist
lairig, lairige (G)	sloping hillside; deeply incised mountain pass	psammite (geological)	metamorphic rock, usually a former sandstone
laoigh, lui (G, AG)	calf		
liath, leithe (G)	grey		
loch (G, S)	lake or fiord	quartz-feldspar-granulite (geological)	metamorphic rock with coarse interlocking grain and little or no layering, usually grey or greyish-white-coloured
lochan, lochain (G)	small lake		
mac (S)	son		
mam, mhaim (G)	breast-shaped hill or a pass between breast-shaped hills		
Manx shearwater	an oceanic bird	rhyolite (geological)	fine-grained or glassy volcanic rock, formerly lava, often grey or pink-coloured
meadhonach, mheadhonach (G)	in-between, middling		
meall, mheall (G	hill	RSPB (abbr)	Royal Society for the Protection of Birds
mhic (G)	son		
mica-schist (geological)	coarse-grained metamorphic rock usually with marked undulose cleavage and mica crystals, typically grey-coloured	ruadh (G)	reddish
		scree	accumulation of weathered rock fragments at foot of a cliff
mor, mhor (G)	big, large	sgor, sgorr (AG)	peak
more (AG)	big, large	sgurr (G)	peak

sheepfank (S)	sheepfold, pen for temporarily holding sheep	steall (G)	spout, waterfall
		stob (G)	thorn, sharp peak
shieling (S)	hut for agricultural workers	stuc (G)	hill or peak
sill (geological)	intrusive sheet of igneous rock injected parallel to host rocks	toll, tholl, tuill, thuill (G)	deep, dark hole or hollow; similar to a corrie or cirque
slabby	describing an area where rock slab is predominant	top/tops	highest point/points on a hill or mountain, including subsidiary summits
SMC (abbr)	Scottish Mountaineering Club	tor (AG)	small rocky peak on a much larger hill
SNH (abbr)	Scottish Natural Heritage	uaine (G)	green
solifluction (geological)	downhill creep of soil or scree due to freeze-thaw cycles	uisg, uisge (G)	water
srath, strath (G, S)	wide, flat-floored valley	white-out	dangerous combination of lying or falling snow with fog, zero visibility
sron (G)	promontory		
stac (G)	stack, peak		

Translations of Selected Scottish Hill Names

This list should not be taken as definitive since some words are open to further or different interpretation. The Gaelic names are as shown on Ordnance Survey maps.

A' Chailleach – the old woman
A' Chioch – the breast
A' Chralaig – the basket or creel
Ainshval – stronghold mountain
Am Bathach – the cattle shelter
Am Bodach – the old man
Am Fasarinen – the gaps or passes
An Cabar – the antler
An Caisteal – the castle
An Cliseam – meaning obscure
An Garbhanach – the rough one (rough ridge)
An Gearanach – the short one (short ridge)
An Riabhachan – brindled or speckled one
An Sgurr – the peak
An Teallach – the forge
Aonach air Chrith – shaky or trembling ridge
Aonach Beag – short ridge
Aonach Buidhe – yellow ridge
Aonach Eagach – notched ridge
Aonach Meadhoin – middle ridge
Aonach Mor – long ridge
Arkle – shieling mountain or shieling of the back
Askival – ash-tree mountain

Beinn a' Bhuird – hill of the table
Beinn Achaladair – hill of the field by the hard water
Beinn a' Chreachain – clam-shaped hill or hill with bare summit
Beinn a' Chrulaiste – rocky hill
Beinn a' Ghlo – hill of mist
Beinn Airigh Charr – rough shieling hill
Beinn Alligin – jewelled hill
Beinn an Dothaidh – hill of scorching
Beinn an Lochain – hill of the lochan
Beinn Bhan – white hill
Beinn Bheag – little hill
Beinn Bheoil – mouth hill
Beinn Bhuidhe – yellow hill
Beinn Damh – stag hill
Beinn Dearg Bheag – little red hill
Beinn Dearg Mor – big red hill
Beinn Dorain – hill of the streamlet or otter
Beinn Eighe – file hill
Beinn Fhionnlaidh – Findlay's hill
Beinn Ghlas – grey-green hill
Beinn Lair – mare's hill
Beinn MacDuibh – Macduff's hill
Beinn Mheadhoin – middle hill
Beinn Mheadhonach – middle hill

Beinn Mhor – big hill
Beinn na h-Eaglaise – hill of the church
Beinn nan Caorach – hill of the sheep
Beinn nan Eachan – hill of the horses
Beinn na Socaich – hill of the snout
Beinn Nuis – face hill
Beinn Odhar – greyish-brown hill
Beinn Sgritheall – scree hill
Beinn Tarsuinn – transverse hill
Beinn Trilleachan – oyster-catcher's hill
Ben Alder – hill of rock and water
Ben Arthur – Arthur's hill
Ben Avon – hill of the river
Ben Cruachan – hill of heaped rocks
Ben Hope – hill of the bay
Ben Lawers – hoof or claw hill
Ben Ledi – hill of God
Ben Lomond – beacon hill
Ben Loyal – law mountain
Ben Lui – calf's hill
Ben More – big hill
Ben Nevis – venomous hill
Ben Rinnes – promontory hill
Ben Starav – hill of the rustling noise
Ben Tianavaig – hill of the harbour
Ben Wyvis – hill of terror or noble hill
Bidean nam Bian – pinnacle of the mountains or animal hides
Bidein a' Ghlais Thuill – pinnacle of the grey-green hollow
Bidein Toll a' Mhuic – pinnacle of the pig's hollow
Binnein Mor – big pinnacle
Bla Bheinn – blue or warm hill
Braigh Coire Chruinn-bhalgain – upland of the corrie of round lumps
Bruach na Frithe – slope of the heath moor
Buachaille Etive Mor – great shepherd of Etive
Bynack Beg – little height
Bynack More – big height

Cac Carn Beag – little pile of shit
Cac Carn Mor – big pile of shit
Cairn Bannoch – rocky hill of the point
Cairn Gorm – blue rocky hill
Caisteal a' Gharbh-choire – castle of the rough corrie
Caisteal Liath – grey castle
Carn a' Choire Bhoidheach – rocky hill of the beautiful corrie
Carn an Tionail – rocky hill of the gathering

219

Carn Ban – white rocky hill
Carn Liath – grey rocky hill
Carn Mor Dearg – big red rocky hill
Carn nan Gabhar – rocky hill of the goats
Cir Mhor – big comb
Clach Leathad – stony slope
Cnap a' Chleirich – priest's knobble
Cobbler, The – forked hill
Coinneach Mhor – big moss
Conachair – uproar, clamour or fury
Cona' Mheall – enchanted or adjoining hill
Corrag Buidhe – yellow finger
Creag a' Mhaim – cliff of the pass
Creag an Duine – cliff of the man
Creag Coire na Fiar Bhealaich – cliff of the corrie of the oblique pass
Creag Meagaidh – cliff of the boggy place
Creag na Caillich – old woman's cliff
Creise – narrow defile or place of panic or horrors
Cul Beag – little back

Druim nam Bo – ridge of the cow
Druim Shionnach – ridge of the fox

Faochag – periwinkle
Fiacaill a' Choire Chais – tooth of the steep corrie
Fraoch Bheinn – heather hill
Fuar Tholl – cold hollow

Garbh Chioch Bheag – small, rough breast
Garbh Chioch Mhor – big, rough breast
Glas Bheinn Mhor – big, grey-green hill
Glas Mheall Mor – big, grey-green hill
Glas Leathad Mor – big, grey-green slope
Gleouraich – noise of combat (battle)
Goatfell – goat hill

Hallival – slab mountain

Ladhar Bheinn – forked or hoofed hill
Leabaidh an Daimh Bhuidhe – bed of the tawny stag
Liathach – the grey one
Lochnagar – small loch of the laughter-like sound

Maol Chinn-dearg – bald red head
Marsco – seagull
Meall a' Bhuiridh – rounded hill of roaring (of stags)
Meall a' Charra – hill of the rocky projection or shelf
Meall an t-Snaim – rounded hill of the knot
Meall Buidhe – rounded yellow hill
Meall Dearg – rounded red hill
Meall Garbh – rounded rough hill
Meall nan Tarmachan – rounded hill of the ptarmigans

Meall Tri Tighearnan – rounded hill of the three lords
Monamenach – middle hill
Mullach an Rathain – summit of the row of teeth
Mullach Fraoch-choire – summit of the heathery corrie
Mullach Mor – big summit
Mulla-fo-dheas – south summit

Na Gruagaichean – the young girls (maidens)

Puist Coire Ardair – posts (gullies) of the high corrie

Quinag – milk pail
Quiraing – the pillared enclosure

Rois-bheinn – horse or wooded mountain
Ruadh Stac Mor – big red peak

Saileag – little heel
Sail Gharbh – rough heel
Sail Ghorm – blue-green heel
Sail Liath – grey heel
Schiehallion – fairy hill of the Caledonians
Seana Bhraigh – old upland
Sgor an Iubhair – peak of the yew
Sgorr Craobh a' Chaorainn – rowan-tree peak
Sgorr nam Fiannaidh – peak of Fingal's warriors
Sgurr a' Bhealaich Dheirg – peak of the red pass
Sgurr a' Ghreadaidh – peak of the lashing (winds)
Sgurr Alasdair – Alistair's peak
Sgurr a' Mhadaidh – peak of the fox, wolf or mastiff
Sgurr a' Mhaim – peak of the breast (rounded hill)
Sgurr an Airgid – peak of silver
Sgurr an Tuill Bhain – peak of the fair hollow
Sgurr Breac – speckled peak
Sgurr Coire Choinnichean – mossy corrie peak
Sgurr Dearg – red peak
Sgurr Dubh Mor – big black peak
Sgurr Dubh na Da Bheinn – black peak of two hills
Sgurr Eilde Beag – small hind's peak
Sgurr Fhuaran – spring peak
Sgurr Fiona – fair peak
Sgurr Ghiubhsachain – Scots pine forest peak
Sgurr Mhic Choinnich – MacKenzie's peak
Sgurr Mhor – big peak
Sgurr na Ba Glaise – peak of the grey cow
Sgurr na Banachdich – meaning obscure
Sgurr na Carnach – rocky peak
Sgurr na Ciche – peak of the breast
Sgurr na Ciste Duibhe – peak of the black chest or coffin
Sgurr na Lapaich – peak of the bog
Sgurr na Moraich – peak of the shellfish

Sgurr nan Coireachan – peak of the corries
Sgurr nan Eag – peak of the notches
Sgurr nan Saighead – peak of the arrows
Sgurr nan Spainteach – peak of the Spaniards
Sgurr na Sgine – peak of the knife
Sgurr of Eigg – peak of the notched island
Sgurr Thormaid – Norman's peak
Slioch – the spear
Spidean a' Choire Leith – pinnacle of the grey corrie
Spidean Coinich – mossy pinnacle
Spidean Coir' an Laoigh – pinnacle of the calf's corrie
Spidean Coire nan Clach – pinnacle of the stony corrie
Spidean Mialach – lousy pinnacle (regarding ticks)
Spidean Toll nam Biast – pinnacle of the hollow of beasts
Sron a' Choire – nose (projecting peak) of the corrie
Sron an Isean – nose of the young bird
Sron Bealach Beithe – nose of the pass of birches
Sron Coire a' Chriochairean – nose of the corrie of the boundary man
Sron Coire na h-Iolaire – nose of the corrie of the eagle
Sron Gharbh – rough nose
Stac Pollaidh – peak of the peat bog
Stob a' Choire Odhair – peak of the light-brown-coloured corrie
Stob a' Coire Liath Mhor – peak of the big, grey corrie
Stob Cadha Gobhlach – peak of the narrow, forked pass
Stob Choire Claurigh – peak of the corrie of brawling
Stob Coire a' Chairn – peak of the corrie of the cairn
Stob Coire a' Chearcaill – peak of the hooped (circular) corrie
Stob Coire Altruim – peak of the corrie of rearing
Stob Coire a' Mhail – peak of the corrie of the rent
Stob Coire an Laoigh – peak of the calf's corrie
Stob Coire an t-Sneachda – peak of the snowy corrie
Stob Coire Cath na Sine – peak of the corrie of crosswinds
Stob Coire Easain – peak of the corrie of the waterfall
Stob Coire Gaibhre – peak of the goat's corrie
Stob Coire Leith – peak of the grey corrie
Stob Coire na Ceannain – peak of the corrie of the little head
Stob Coire na Cralaig – peak of the corrie of the basket or creel

Stob Coire nam Beith – peak of the corrie of birches
Stob Coire nan Cearc – peak of the corrie of grouse hens
Stob Coire nan Lochan – peak of the corrie of the small lochs
Stob Dearg – red peak
Stob Diamh – stag's peak
Stob Garbh – rough peak
Stob na Broige – peak of the shoe
Stob na Doire – peak of the grove (small woodland)
Stob Poite Coire Ardair – peak of the pot of the high corrie
Streap – climb
Streap Comhlaidh – climb adjoining
Stuc a' Chroin – peak of pain or harm
Stuchd an Lochain – peak of the small loch
Suilven – pillar mountain

Toman Coinnich – mossy hill
Tom na Gruagaich – young girl's hill
Trallval – troll mountain

Index of Mountain Names

(by page number)

First published in 2009 by Fort Publishing Ltd, 12 Robsland Avenue, Ayr, KA7 2RW

Front-cover photograph by Mark Hamblin: the north Cuillin from near Sligachan.

Back-cover photograph by Graeme Cornwallis: Loch Hourn and Beinn Sgritheall from Ladhar Bheinn's Coire Dhorrcail path.

Title-page photograph by Grame Cornwallis: Beinn MacDuibh and the Lairig Ghru from Creag an Leth-choin.

All maps by Linda M. Dawes

Typeset by 3btype.com · 0131 658 1763

Printed by Bell and Bain Ltd

224 ISBN: 978-1-905769-16-2